Edith Wharton

THE RECKONING
and other stories

Selected and edited by JANET BEER

PHŒNIX

A PHOENIX PAPERBACK

This edition first published in Great Britain by
Phoenix Paperbacks in 1999
Selection, Introduction and other critical apparatus
© Phoenix Paperbacks, 1999

Orion Publishing Group
Orion House
5 Upper Saint Martin's Lane
London WC2H 9EA

Typeset at The Spartan Press Ltd, Lymington, Hants
Printed in Great Britain by
The Guernsey Press Co. Ltd, Guernsey, C.I.

British Library Cataloguing-in-Publication
Data is available on request

ISBN: 0 75380 721 1

Contents

Note on the Author and Editor

EDITH WHARTON was born in New York in 1862 into a wealthy and well-connected family. She was educated at home by governesses, spent a significant part of her childhood travelling with her parents in Europe and made her début into New York society in 1879. She married a Bostonian, Edward Wharton, but the marriage was not happy and ended in divorce in 1913 by which time Edith Wharton had established a permanent residence in France.

Although writing was always an important part of Edith Wharton's life and she wrote her first novel, *Fast and Loose*, when she was fourteen, she did not publish a novel until she was forty. Her first, *The Valley of Decision*, a historical romance set in eighteenth-century Italy, came out in 1902, and she then went on to produce more than forty volumes of travel writing, short stories, novels, autobiography and criticism. Wharton was made a fellow of the American Academy of Letters in 1930; amongst her best known works are *The House of Mirth* (1905), *Ethan Frome* (1911), *The Custom of the Country* (1913) and *The Age of Innocence* (1920), for which she received the Pulitzer Prize.

Edith Wharton was born a wealthy woman and her earnings from her fiction, including the sale of film rights, ensured that she remained one. She was successful with the critics as well as with the reading public and her reputation today stands as high as in her lifetime. She died in 1937 in France and is buried at Versailles.

JANET BEER is Professor and Head of the Department of English at the Manchester Metropolitan University. She is the author of *Edith Wharton: Traveller in the Land of Letters* and *Kate Chopin, Edith Wharton and Charlotte Perkins Gilman: Studies in Short Fiction*. She is currently working on a literary life of Edith Wharton.

Introduction

Edith Wharton published her first volume of short stories, *The Greater Inclination*, in 1899 and went on to produce ten more collections in between writing the novels, travel books, criticism and autobiography for which she is best known. The short story genre, however, was one in which she felt entirely comfortable; as she wrote to Robert Grant, the novelist, in 1907: 'As soon as I look at a subject from the novel-angle I see it in its relation to a larger whole, in all its remotest connotations; & I can't help trying to take them in, at the cost of the smaller realism that I arrive at, I think, better in my short stories. This is the reason why I have always obscurely felt that I didn't know how to write a novel. I feel it more clearly after each attempt, because it is in such sharp contrast to the sense of authority with which I take hold of a short story.' Edith Wharton used 'the sense of authority' she brought to the short story to experiment with themes, with language, symbolism and structure; from the elegiac tone of 'Roman Fever', a story of loss and regret, to the brilliantly sustained joke that is 'Xingu', Wharton matches her subject to her style, her social to her rhetorical register. The stories offered here span Wharton's writing life – between 'Souls Belated', which featured in her first collection, to 'All Souls'', published posthumously in *Ghosts* in 1937 – and all display the confidence and clarity of a writer at home with her chosen form whether for the purposes of comedy, tragedy or the ghost story.

The majority of the stories chosen for this volume centre crucially on relations between men and women and, in particular, the question of marriage and its future in a world where women were becoming increasingly intolerant of the limitations imposed upon them. Wharton was not the only prominent woman to be concerned with this question in the decades before and after the turn of the century but she was not interested in involving herself in movements for social reform. Although she had a keen sense of the moral integrity of her work, disavowing the value of any fiction without 'a purpose', she did not seek to proselytize or carry her often iconoclastic ideas about marriage beyond the limits of the text. In her writing she was working through a number of ideas about the nature of the marriage contract, the contradictions between the legal and the romantic ties that bind and the social consequences of the dependence of women upon marriage for their economic as well as emotional well-being. Wharton's women, in general, find that they must marry and, more often than not, that they must stay married, but not necessarily to the right person. Notwithstanding the clear-eyed view – and personal experience – which Wharton had of the misery of an unhappy marriage, she remained an adherent of marriage as the best means of supporting the needs of the individual and the family. She is recorded as having said to her friend Charles du Bos: 'Ah, the poverty, the miserable poverty, of any love that lies outside of marriage, of any love that is not a living together, a sharing of all' – a cry from the heart which would have been echoed by many of her protagonists.

Many of the men in Wharton's stories show intolerance or even contempt for their wives; there is little pity and much scorn for the limitations of the young girl whose sole destiny was to be a wife. Lethbury, in 'The Mission of Jane' sees only his wife's short-comings, and when a woman attempts to escape from the constraints of her pre-ordained role, as in 'The Long Run', the man cannot find the courage to accompany her. Waythorn in the story, 'The Other Two', describes his wife thus: 'She was "as easy as an old shoe" – a shoe that too many feet had worn. Her elasticity was the result of tension in too many different directions. Alice Haskett – Alice Varick – Alice Waythorn – she had been each in turn, and had left hanging to each name a little of her privacy, a little of her personality, a little of the inmost self where the unknown god abides.' He is critical of her for the very thing that drew him to her – her ability to be the perfectly accommodating wife. The semi-professional bride-to-be, Alice, is a barometer of the changing times; she is accepted in society, hostesses are simply grateful that they do not have to adjust their guest lists to avoid inviting husbands two and three to the same event. Alice Waythorn is, however, despite her multiple marriages, no threat to society; she is at heart a conformist like the four-times-married heroine of Wharton's 1913 novel, *The Custom of the Country*, Undine Spragg, who wants nothing more than 'to be respectable without being bored'. Alice has used marriage as the only means at her disposal to improve her social standing and economic situation.

The story which opens this collection, 'Souls Belated', shows a different side to the failure of marriage, where the woman is torn between the prevailing morality and the struggle to locate an alternative way of life. Edith Wharton's European scenes are often peopled with those who are wandering the world in search of a place of refuge from the public gaze only to find that there is no such place; in the absence of the marriage contract there is also an absence of meaning and authenticity as Lydia Tillotson comes to understand: '[. . .] I begin to see what marriage is for. It's to keep people away from each other. Sometimes I think that two people who love each other can be saved from madness only by the things that come between them – children, duties, visits, bores, relations – the things that protect married people from each other.'

Edith Wharton had a sharp eye for human frailty, whether the self-regard of the society matron with too little of substance to occupy her mind, like Mrs Ballinger in 'Xingu', or the suscepti- bility of the poor farmer trapped in a harsh climate and a loveless marriage as in 'Bewitched' – the only story in this volume to be concerned with life outside the leisured classes. Here Wharton exploits the conventions of the supernatural tale to examine what happens when the social organization cannot accommodate 'the handsomest girls anywhere round' especially when they run 'wild'. Edith Wharton saw the potential for 'wild'ness in the most conventional life; she knew that the act of taking one's chance for escape could exact a terrible price, she also knew that inaction could hold worse terrors.

THE RECKONING
and other stories

Souls Belated

1

Their railway-carriage had been full when the train left Bologna; but at the first station beyond Milan their only remaining companion – a courtly person who ate garlic out of a carpet-bag – had left his crumb-strewn seat with a bow.

Lydia's eye regretfully followed the shiny broadcloth of his retreating back till it lost itself in the cloud of touts and cab-drivers hanging about the station; then she glanced across at Gannett and caught the same regret in his look. They were both sorry to be alone.

'*Par-ten-za!*' shouted the guard. The train vibrated to a sudden slamming of doors; a waiter ran along the platform with a tray of fossilized sandwiches; a belated porter flung a bundle of shawls and band-boxes into a third-class carriage; the guard snapped out a brief *Partenza!* which indicated the purely ornamental nature of his first shout; and the train swung out of the station.

The direction of the road had changed, and a shaft of sunlight struck across the dusty red velvet seats into Lydia's corner. Gannett did not notice it. He had returned to his *Revue de Paris*, and she had to rise and lower the shade of the farther window. Against the vast horizon of their leisure such incidents stood out sharply.

Having lowered the shade, Lydia sat down, leaving the length of the carriage between herself and Gannett. At length he missed her and looked up.

'I moved out of the sun,' she hastily explained.

He looked at her curiously: the sun was beating on her through the shade.

'Very well,' he said pleasantly; adding, 'You don't mind?' as he drew a cigarette-case from his pocket.

It was a refreshing touch, relieving the tension of her spirit with the suggestion that, after all, if he could *smoke* – ! The relief was only momentary. Her experience of smokers was limited (her

husband had disapproved of the use of tobacco) but she knew
from hearsay that men sometimes smoked to get away from
things; that a cigar might be the masculine equivalent of
darkened windows and a headache. Gannett, after a puff or two,
returned to his review.

It was just as she had foreseen; he feared to speak as much as
she did. It was one of the misfortunes of their situation that they
were never busy enough to necessitate, or even to justify, the
postponement of unpleasant discussions. If they avoided a question it was obviously, unconcealably because the question was
disagreeable. They had unlimited leisure and an accumulation of
mental energy to devote to any subject that presented itself; new
topics were in fact at a premium. Lydia sometimes had premonitions of a famine-stricken period when there would be nothing left
to talk about, and she had already caught herself doling out
piecemeal what, in the first prodigality of their confidences, she
would have flung to him in a breath. Their silence therefore might
simply mean that they had nothing to say; but it was another
disadvantage of their position that it allowed infinite opportunity
for the classification of minute differences. Lydia had learned to
distinguish between real and factitious silences; and under
Gannett's she now detected a hum of speech to which her own
thoughts made breathless answer.

How could it be otherwise, with that thing between them? She
glanced up at the rack overhead. The *thing* was there, in her
dressing-bag, symbolically suspended over her head and his. He
was thinking of it now, just as she was; they had been thinking of
it in unison ever since they had entered the train. While the
carriage had held other travellers they had screened her from his
thoughts; but now that he and she were alone she knew exactly
what was passing through his mind; she could almost hear him
asking himself what he should say to her. . . .

The thing had come that morning, brought up to her in an
innocent-looking envelope with the rest of their letters, as they
were leaving the hotel at Bologna. As she tore it open, she and
Gannett were laughing over some ineptitude of the local guide-
book – they had been driven, of late, to make the most of such
incidental humors of travel. Even when she had unfolded the
document she took it for some unimportant business paper sent

abroad for her signature, and her eye travelled inattentively over the curly *Whereases* of the preamble until a word arrested her: – Divorce. There it stood, an impassable barrier, between her husband's name and hers.

She had been prepared for it, of course, as healthy people are said to be prepared for death, in the sense of knowing it must come without in the least expecting that it will. She had known from the first that Tillotson meant to divorce her – but what did it matter? Nothing mattered, in those first days of supreme deliverance, but the fact that she was free; and not so much (she had begun to be aware) that freedom had released her from Tillotson as that it had given her to Gannett. This discovery had not been agreeable to her self-esteem. She had preferred to think that Tillotson had himself embodied all her reasons for leaving him; and those he represented had seemed cogent enough to stand in no need of reinforcement. Yet she had not left him till she met Gannett. It was her love for Gannett that had made life with Tillotson so poor and incomplete a business. If she had never, from the first, regarded her marriage as a full cancelling of her claims upon life, she had at least, for a number of years, accepted it as a provisional compensation, – she had made it 'do.' Existence in the commodious Tillotson mansion in Fifth Avenue – with Mrs Tillotson senior commanding the approaches from the second-story front windows – had been reduced to a series of purely automatic acts. The moral atmosphere of the Tillotson interior was as carefully screened and curtained as the house itself: Mrs Tillotson senior dreaded ideas as much as a draught on her back. Prudent people liked an even temperature; and to do anything unexpected was as foolish as going out in the rain. One of the chief advantages of being rich was that one need not be exposed to unforeseen contingencies: by the use of ordinary firmness and common sense one could make sure of doing exactly the same thing every day at the same hour. These doctrines, reverentially imbibed with his mother's milk, Tillotson (a model son who had never given his parents an hour's anxiety) complacently expounded to his wife, testifying to his sense of their importance by the regularity with which he wore galoshes on damp days, his punctuality at meals, and his elaborate precautions against burglars and contagious diseases. Lydia, coming from a smaller town, and entering New York life through the portals of the

Tillotson mansion, had mechanically accepted this point of view as inseparable from having a front pew in church and a parterre box at the opera. All the people who came to the house revolved in the same small circle of prejudices. It was the kind of society in which, after dinner, the ladies compared the exorbitant charges of their children's teachers, and agreed that, even with the new duties on French clothes, it was cheaper in the end to get everything from Worth; while the husbands, over their cigars, lamented municipal corruption, and decided that the men to start a reform were those who had no private interests at stake.

To Lydia this view of life had become a matter of course, just as lumbering about in her mother-in-law's landau had come to seem the only possible means of locomotion, and listening every Sunday to a fashionable Presbyterian divine the inevitable atonement for having thought oneself bored on the other six days of the week. Before she met Gannett her life had seemed merely dull: his coming made it appear like one of those dismal Cruikshank prints in which the people are all ugly and all engaged in occupations that are either vulgar or stupid.

It was natural that Tillotson should be the chief sufferer from this readjustment of focus. Gannett's nearness had made her husband ridiculous, and a part of the ridicule had been reflected on herself. Her tolerance laid her open to a suspicion of obtuseness from which she must, at all costs, clear herself in Gannett's eyes.

She did not understand this until afterwards. At the time she fancied that she had merely reached the limits of endurance. In so large a charter of liberties as the mere act of leaving Tillotson seemed to confer, the small question of divorce or no divorce did not count. It was when she saw that she had left her husband only to be with Gannett that she perceived the significance of anything affecting their relations. Her husband, in casting her off, had virtually flung her at Gannett: it was thus that the world viewed it. The measure of alacrity with which Gannett would receive her would be the subject of curious speculation over afternoon-tea tables and in club corners. She knew what would be said – she had heard it so often of others! The recollection bathed her in misery. The men would probably back Gannett to 'do the decent thing'; but the ladies' eyebrows would emphasize the worthlessness of such enforced fidelity; and after all, they would be right. She had put herself in a position where Gannett 'owed' her something; where, as a gentleman, he was bound to 'stand the damage.' The idea of accepting such compensation had never crossed her mind; the so-called rehabilitation of such a marriage had always seemed to her the only real disgrace. What she dreaded was the necessity of having to explain herself; of having to combat his arguments; of calculating, in spite of herself, the exact measure of insistence with which he pressed them. She knew not whether she most shrank from his insisting too much or too little. In such a case the nicest sense of proportion might be at fault; and how easy to fall into the error of taking her resistance for a test of his sincerity! Whichever way she turned, an ironical implication confronted her: she had the exasperated sense of having walked into the trap of some stupid practical joke.

Beneath all these preoccupations lurked the dread of what he was thinking. Sooner or later, of course, he would have to speak; but that, in the meantime, he should think, even for a moment, that there was any use in speaking, seemed to her simply unendurable. Her sensitiveness on this point was aggravated by another fear, as yet barely on the level of consciousness; the fear of unwillingly involving Gannett in the trammels of her dependence. To look upon him as the instrument of her liberation; to resist in herself the least tendency to a wifely taking possession of his future; had seemed to Lydia the one way of maintaining the dignity of their relation. Her view had not changed, but she was aware of a growing inability to keep her thoughts fixed on the essential point – the point of parting with Gannett. It was easy to face as long as she kept it sufficiently far off: but what was this act of mental postponement but a gradual encroachment on his future? What was needful was the courage to recognize the moment when, by some word or look, their voluntary fellowship should be transformed into a bondage the more wearing that it was based on none of those common obligations which make the most imperfect marriage in some sort a center of gravity.

When the porter, at the next station, threw the door open, Lydia drew back, making way for the hoped-for intruder, but none came, and the train took up its leisurely progress through the spring wheat-fields and budding copses. She now began to hope that Gannett would speak before the next station. She watched him furtively, half-disposed to return to the seat opposite his, but there was an artificiality about his absorption that restrained her. She had never before seen him read with so conspicuous an air of warding off interruption. What could he be thinking of? Why should he be afraid to speak? Or was it her answer that he dreaded?

The train paused for the passing of an express, and he put down his book and leaned out of the window. Presently he turned to her with a smile.

'There's a jolly old villa out here,' he said.

His easy tone relieved her, and she smiled back at him as she crossed over to his corner.

Beyond the embankment, through the opening in a mossy wall, she caught sight of the villa, with its broken balustrades, its stagnant fountains, and the stone satyr closing the perspective of a dusky grass-walk.

'How should you like to live there?' he asked as the train moved on.

'There?'

'In some such place, I mean. One might do worse, don't you think so? There must be at least two centuries of solitude under those yew-trees. Shouldn't you like it?'

'I – I don't know,' she faltered. She knew now that he meant to speak.

He lit another cigarette. 'We shall have to live somewhere, you know,' he said as he bent above the match.

Lydia tried to speak carelessly. '*Je n'en vois pas la nécessité!* Why not live everywhere, as we have been doing?'

'But we can't travel forever, can we?'

'Oh, forever's a long word,' she objected, picking up the review he had thrown aside.

'For the rest of our lives then,' he said, moving nearer.

She made a slight gesture which caused his hand to slip from hers.

'Why should we make plans? I thought you agreed with me that it's pleasanter to drift.'

He looked at her hesitatingly. 'It's been pleasant, certainly; but I suppose I shall have to get at my work again some day. You know I haven't written a line since – all this time,' he hastily emended.

She flamed with sympathy and self-reproach. 'Oh, if you mean *that* – if you want to write – of course we must settle down. How stupid of me not to have thought of it sooner! Where shall we go?

Where do you think you could work best? We oughtn't to lose any more time.'

He hesitated again. 'I had thought of a villa in these parts. It's quiet; we shouldn't be bothered. Should you like it?'

'Of course I should like it.' She paused and looked away. 'But I thought – I remember your telling me once that your best work had been done in a crowd – in big cities. Why should you shut yourself up in a desert?'

Gannett, for a moment, made no reply. At length he said, avoiding her eye as carefully as she avoided his: 'It might be different now; I can't tell, of course, till I try. A writer ought not to be dependent on his *milieu*; it's a mistake to humor oneself in that way; and I thought that just at first you might prefer to be—'

She faced him. 'To be what?'

'Well – quiet. I mean—'

'What do you mean by "at first"?' she interrupted.

He paused again. 'I mean after we are married.'

She thrust up her chin and turned toward the window. 'Thank you!' she tossed back at him.

'Lydia!' he exclaimed blankly; and she felt in every fiber of her averted person that he had made the inconceivable, the unpardonable mistake of anticipating her acquiescence.

The train rattled on and he groped for a third cigarette. Lydia remained silent.

'I haven't offended you?' he ventured at length, in the tone of a man who feels his way.

She shook her head with a sigh. 'I thought you understood,' she moaned. Their eyes met and she moved back to his side.

'Do you want to know how not to offend me? By taking it for granted, once for all, that you've said your say on this odious question and that I've said mine, and that we stand just where we did this morning before that – that hateful paper came to spoil everything between us!'

'To spoil everything between us? What on earth do you mean? Aren't you glad to be free?'

'I was free before.'

'Not to marry me,' he suggested.

'But I don't *want* to marry you!' she cried.

She saw that he turned pale. 'I'm obtuse, I suppose,' he said slowly. 'I confess I don't see what you're driving at. Are you tired of the whole business? Or was I simply a – an excuse for getting away? Perhaps you didn't care to travel alone? Was that it? And now you want to chuck me?' His voice had grown harsh. 'You owe me a straight answer, you know; don't be tenderhearted!'

Her eyes swam as she leaned to him. 'Don't you see it's because I care – because I care so much? Oh, Ralph! Can't you see how it would humiliate me? Try to feel it as a woman would! Don't you see the misery of being made your wife in this way? If I'd known you as a girl – that would have been a real marriage! But now – this vulgar fraud upon society – and upon a society we despised and laughed at – this sneaking back into a position that we've voluntarily forfeited: don't you see what a cheap compromise it is? We neither of us believe in the abstract "sacredness" of marriage; we both know that no ceremony is needed to consecrate our love for each other; what object can we have in marrying, except the secret fear of each that the other may escape, or the secret longing to work our way back gradually – oh, very gradually – into the esteem of the people whose conventional morality we have always ridiculed and hated? And the very fact that, after a decent interval, these same people would come and dine with us – the women who talk about the indissolubility of marriage, and who would let me die in a gutter today because I am "leading a life of sin" – doesn't that disgust you more than their turning their backs on us now? I can stand being cut by them, but I couldn't stand their coming to call and asking what I meant to do about visiting that unfortunate Mrs So-and-so!'

She paused, and Gannett maintained a perplexed silence.

'You judge things too theoretically,' he said at length, slowly. 'Life is made up of compromises.'

'The life we ran away from – yes! If we had been willing to accept them' – she flushed – 'we might have gone on meeting each other at Mrs Tillotson's dinners.'

He smiled slightly. 'I didn't know that we ran away to found a new system of ethics. I supposed it was because we loved each other.'

'Life is complex, of course; isn't it the very recognition of that fact that separates us from the people who see it *tout d'une pièce*? If *they* are right – if marriage is sacred in itself and the individual must always be sacrificed to the family – then there can be no real marriage between us, since our – our being together is a protest

against the sacrifice of the individual to the family.' She interrupted herself with a laugh. 'You'll say now that I'm giving you a
lecture on sociology! Of course one acts as one can – as one must,
perhaps – pulled by all sorts of invisible threads; but at least one
needn't pretend, for social advantages, to subscribe to a creed that
ignores the complexity of human motives – that classifies people
by arbitrary signs, and puts it in everybody's reach to be on Mrs
Tillotson's visiting-list. It may be necessary that the world should
be ruled by conventions – but if we believed in them, why did we
break through them? And if we don't believe in them, is it honest
to take advantage of the protection they afford?'

Gannett hesitated. 'One may believe in them or not; but as long
as they do rule the world it is only by taking advantage of their
protection that one can find a *modus vivendi*.'

'Do outlaws need a *modus vivendi*?'

He looked at her hopelessly. Nothing is more perplexing to man
than the mental process of a woman who reasons her emotions.

She thought she had scored a point and followed it up
passionately. 'You do understand, don't you? You see how the
very thought of the thing humiliates me! We are together today
because we choose to be – don't let us look any farther than that!'
She caught his hands. '*Promise* me you'll never speak of it again;
promise me you'll never *think* of it even,' she implored, with a
tearful prodigality of italics.

Through what followed – his protests, his arguments, his final
unconvinced submission to her wishes – she had a sense of his but
half-discerning all that, for her, had made the moment so
tumultuous. They had reached that memorable point in every
heart-history when, for the first time, the man seems obtuse and
the woman irrational. It was the abundance of his intentions that
consoled her, on reflection, for what they lacked in quality. After
all, it would have been worse, incalculably worse, to have
detected any overreadiness to understand her.

2

When the train at night-fall brought them to their journey's end
at the edge of one of the lakes, Lydia was glad that they were not,
as usual, to pass from one solitude to another. Their wanderings,
during the year, had indeed been like the flight of outlaws:

through Sicily, Dalmatia, Transylvania and Southern Italy they
had persisted in their tacit avoidance of their kind. Isolation, at
first, had deepened the flavor of their happiness, as night
intensifies the scent of certain flowers; but in the new phase on
which they were entering, Lydia's chief wish was that they should
be less abnormally exposed to the action of each other's thoughts.

She shrank, nevertheless, as the brightly-looming bulk of the
fashionable Anglo-American hotel on the water's brink began to
radiate toward their advancing boat its vivid suggestion of social
order, visitors' lists, Church services, and the bland inquisition of
the *table-d'hôte*. The mere fact that in a moment or two she must
take her place on the hotel register as Mrs Gannett seemed to
weaken the springs of her resistance.

They had meant to stay for a night only, on their way to a lofty
village among the glaciers of Monte Rosa; but after the first
plunge into publicity, when they entered the dining-room, Lydia
felt the relief of being lost in a crowd, of ceasing for a moment to
be the center of Gannett's scrutiny; and in his face she caught the
reflection of her feeling. After dinner, when she went upstairs, he
strolled into the smoking-room, and an hour or two later, sitting
in the darkness of her window, she heard his voice below and saw
him walking up and down the terrace with a companion cigar at
his side. When he came up he told her he had been talking to the
hotel chaplain – a very good sort of fellow.

'Queer little microcosms, these hotels! Most of these people live
here all summer and then migrate to Italy or the Riviera. The
English are the only people who can lead that kind of life with
dignity – those soft-voiced old ladies in Shetland shawls somehow
carry the British Empire under their caps. *Civis Romanus sum*. It's
a curious study – there might be some good things to work up
here.'

He stood before her with the vivid preoccupied stare of the
novelist on the trail of a 'subject.' With a relief that was half
painful she noticed that, for the first time since they had been
together, he was hardly aware of her presence.

'Do you think you could write here?'

'Here? I don't know.' His stare dropped. 'After being out of
things so long one's first impressions are bound to be tremen-
dously vivid, you know. I see a dozen threads already that one
might follow—'

He broke off with a touch of embarrassment.

'Then follow them. We'll stay,' she said with sudden decision.

'Stay here?' He glanced at her in surprise, and then, walking to the window, looked out upon the dusky slumber of the garden.

'Why not?' she said at length, in a tone of veiled irritation.

'The place is full of old cats in caps who gossip with the chaplain. Shall you like – I mean, it would be different if—'

She flamed up.

'Do you suppose I care? It's none of their business.'

'Of course not; but you won't get them to think so.'

'They may think what they please.'

He looked at her doubtfully.

'It's for you to decide.'

'We'll stay,' she repeated.

Gannett, before they met, had made himself known as a successful writer of short stories and of a novel which had achieved the distinction of being widely discussed. The reviewers called him 'promising,' and Lydia now accused herself of having too long interfered with the fulfilment of his promise. There was a special irony in the fact, since his passionate assurances that only the stimulus of her companionship could bring out his latent faculty had almost given the dignity of a 'vocation' to her course: there had been moments when she had felt unable to assume, before posterity, the responsibility of thwarting his career. And, after all, he had not written a line since they had been together: his first desire to write had come from renewed contact with the world! Was it all a mistake then? Must the most intelligent choice work more disastrously than the blundering combinations of chance? Or was there a still more humiliating answer to her perplexities? His sudden impulse of activity so exactly coincided with her own wish to withdraw, for a time, from the range of his observation, that she wondered if he too were not seeking sanctuary from intolerable problems.

'You must begin tomorrow!' she cried, hiding a tremor under the laugh with which she added, 'I wonder if there's any ink in the inkstand?'

Whatever else they had at the Hotel Bellosguardo, they had, as Miss Pinsent said, 'a certain tone.' It was to Lady Susan Condit that they owed this inestimable benefit; an advantage ranking in Miss Pinsent's opinion above even the lawn tennis courts and the

resident chaplain. It was the fact of Lady Susan's annual visit that
made the hotel what it was. Miss Pinsent was certainly the last to
underrate such a privilege: – 'It's so important, my dear, forming
as we do a little family, that there should be someone to give *the
tone*; and no one could do it better than Lady Susan – an earl's
daughter and a person of such determination. Dear Mrs Ainger
now – who really *ought*, you know, when Lady Susan's away –
absolutely refuses to assert herself.' Miss Pinsent sniffed derisively.
'A bishop's niece! – my dear, I saw her once actually give in to
some South Americans – and before us all. She gave up her seat at
table to oblige them – such a lack of dignity! Lady Susan spoke to
her very plainly about it afterwards.'

Miss Pinsent glanced across the lake and adjusted her auburn
front.

'But of course I don't deny that the stand Lady Susan takes is
not always easy to live up to – for the rest of us, I mean.
Monsieur Grossart, our good proprietor, finds it trying at times, I
know – he has said as much, privately, to Mrs Ainger and me.
After all, the poor man is not to blame for wanting to fill his
hotel, is he? And Lady Susan is so difficult – so very difficult –
about new people. One might almost say that she disapproves of
them beforehand, on principle. And yet she's had warnings – she
very nearly made a dreadful mistake once with the Duchess of
Levens, who dyed her hair and – well, swore and smoked. One
would have thought that might have been a lesson to Lady
Susan.' Miss Pinsent resumed her knitting with a sigh. 'There are
exceptions, of course. She took at once to you and Mr Gannett –
it was quite remarkable, really. Oh, I don't mean that either – of
course not! It was perfectly natural – we *all* thought you so
charming and interesting from the first day – we knew at once
that Mr Gannett was intellectual, by the magazines you took in;
but you know what I mean. Lady Susan is so very – well, I won't
say prejudiced, as Mrs Ainger does – but so prepared *not* to like
new people, that her taking to you in that way was a surprise to
us all, I confess.'

Miss Pinsent sent a significant glance down the long laurustinus alley from the other end of which two people – a lady and
gentleman – were strolling toward them through the smiling
neglect of the garden.

'In this case, of course, it's very different; that I'm willing to admit. Their looks are against them; but, as Mrs Ainger says, one can't exactly tell them so.'

'She's very handsome,' Lydia ventured, with her eyes on the lady, who showed, under the dome of a vivid sunshade, the hour-glass figure and superlative coloring of a Christmas chromo.

'That's the worst of it. She's too handsome.'

'Well, after all, she can't help that.'

'Other people manage to,' said Miss Pinsent skeptically.

'But isn't it rather unfair of Lady Susan – considering that nothing is known about them?'

'But, my dear, that's the very thing that's against them. It's infinitely worse than any actual knowledge.'

Lydia mentally agreed that, in the case of Mrs Linton, it possibly might be.

'I wonder why they came here?' she mused.

'That's against them too. It's always a bad sign when loud people come to a quiet place. And they've brought van-loads of boxes – her maid told Mrs Ainger's that they meant to stop indefinitely.'

'And Lady Susan actually turned her back on her in the *salon?*'

'My dear, she said it was for our sakes; that makes it so unanswerable! But poor Grossart *is* in a way! The Lintons have taken his most expensive *suite*, you know – the yellow damask drawing-room above the portico – and they have champagne with every meal!'

They were silent as Mr and Mrs Linton sauntered by; the lady with tempestuous brows and challenging chin; the gentleman, a blond stripling, trailing after her, head downward, like a reluctant child dragged by his nurse.

'What does your husband think of them, my dear?' Miss Pinsent whispered as they passed out of earshot.

Lydia stooped to pick a violet in the border.

'He hasn't told me.'

'Of your speaking to them, I mean. Would he approve of that? I know how very particular nice Americans are. I think your action might make a difference; it would certainly carry weight with Lady Susan.'

'Dear Miss Pinsent, you flatter me!'

Lydia rose and gathered up her book and sunshade.

'Well, if you're asked for an opinion – if Lady Susan asks you for

one – I think you ought to be prepared,' Miss Pinsent admonished
her as she moved away.

3

Lady Susan held her own. She ignored the Lintons, and her little
family, as Miss Pinsent phrased it, followed suit. Even Mrs Ainger
agreed that it was obligatory. If Lady Susan owed it to the others
not to speak to the Lintons, the others clearly owed it to Lady
Susan to back her up. It was generally found expedient, at the
Hotel Bellosguardo, to adopt this form of reasoning.

Whatever effect this combined action may have had upon the
Lintons, it did not at least have that of driving them away.
Monsieur Grossart, after a few days of suspense, had the satisfaction of seeing them settle down in his yellow damask *premier*
with what looked like a permanent installation of palm-trees and
silk sofa-cushions, and a gratifying continuance in the consump-
tion of champagne. Mrs Linton trailed her Doucet draperies up
and down the garden with the same challenging air, while her
husband, smoking innumerable cigarettes, dragged himself de-
jectedly in her wake; but neither of them, after the first encounter
with Lady Susan, made any attempt to extend their acquaintance. They simply ignored their ignorers. As Miss Pinsent
resentfully observed, they behaved exactly as though the hotel
were empty.

It was therefore a matter of surprise, as well as of displeasure, to
Lydia, to find, on glancing up one day from her seat in the garden,
that the shadow which had fallen across her book was that of the
enigmatic Mrs Linton.

'I want to speak to you,' that lady said, in a rich hard voice that
seemed the audible expression of her gown and her complexion.

Lydia started. She certainly did not want to speak to Mrs
Linton.

'Shall I sit down here?' the latter continued, fixing her
intensely-shaded eyes on Lydia's face, 'or are you afraid of being
seen with me?'

'Afraid?' Lydia colored. 'Sit down, please. What is it that you
wish to say?'

Mrs Linton, with a smile, drew up a garden-chair and crossed
one open-work ankle above the other.

'I want you to tell me what my husband said to your husband last night.'

Lydia turned pale.

'My husband – to yours?' she faltered, staring at the other.

'Didn't you know they were closeted together for hours in the smoking-room after you went upstairs? My man didn't get to bed until nearly two o'clock and when he did I couldn't get a word out of him. When he wants to be aggravating I'll back him against anybody living!' Her teeth and eyes flashed persuasively upon Lydia. 'But you'll tell me what they were talking about, won't you? I know I can trust you – you look so awfully kind. And it's for his own good. He's such a precious donkey and I'm so afraid he's got into some beastly scrape or other. If he'd only trust his own old woman! But they're always writing to him and setting him against me. And I've got nobody to turn to.' She laid her hand on Lydia's with a rattle of bracelets. 'You'll help me, won't you?'

Lydia drew back from the smiling fierceness of her brows.

'I'm sorry – but I don't think I understand. My husband has said nothing to me of – of yours.'

The great black crescents above Mrs Linton's eyes met angrily.

'I say – is that true?' she demanded.

Lydia rose from her seat.

'Oh, look here, I didn't mean that, you know – you mustn't take one up so! Can't you see how rattled I am?'

Lydia saw that, in fact, her beautiful mouth was quivering beneath softened eyes.

'I'm beside myself!' the splendid creature wailed, dropping into her seat.

'I'm so sorry,' Lydia repeated, forcing herself to speak kindly; 'but how can I help you?'

Mrs Linton raised her head sharply.

'By finding out – there's a darling!'

'Finding what out?'

'What Trevenna told him.'

'Trevenna – ?' Lydia echoed in bewilderment.

Mrs Linton clapped her hand to her mouth.

'Oh, Lord – there, it's out! What a fool I am! But I supposed of course you knew; I supposed everybody knew.' She dried her eyes and bridled. 'Didn't you know that he's Lord Trevenna? I'm Mrs Cope.'

Lydia recognized the names. They had figured in a flamboyant elopement which had thrilled fashionable London some six months earlier.

'Now you see how it is – you understand, don't you?' Mrs Cope continued on a note of appeal. 'I knew you would – that's the reason I came to you. I suppose *he* felt the same thing about your husband; he's not spoken to another soul in the place.' Her face grew anxious again. 'He's awfully sensitive, generally – he feels our position, he says – as if it wasn't *my* place to feel that! But when he does get talking there's no knowing what he'll say. I know he's been brooding over something lately, and I *must* find out what it is – it's to his interest that I should. I always tell him that I think only of his interest; if he'd only trust me! But he's been so odd lately – I can't think what he's plotting. You will help me, dear?'

Lydia, who had remained standing, looked away uncomfortably.

'If you mean by finding out what Lord Trevenna has told my husband, I'm afraid it's impossible.'

'Why impossible?'

'Because I infer that it was told in confidence.'

Mrs Cope stared incredulously.

'Well, what of that? Your husband looks such a dear – any one can see he's awfully gone on you. What's to prevent your getting it out of him?'

Lydia flushed.

'I'm not a spy!' she exclaimed.

'A spy – a spy? How dare you?' Mrs Cope flamed out. 'Oh, I don't mean that either! Don't be angry with me – I'm so miserable.' She essayed a softer note. 'Do you call that spying – for one woman to help out another? I do need help so dreadfully! I'm at my wits' end with Trevenna, I am indeed. He's such a boy – a mere baby, you know; he's only two-and-twenty.' She dropped her orbed lids. 'He's younger than me – only fancy! a few months younger. I tell him he ought to listen to me as if I was his mother; oughtn't he now? But he won't, he won't! All his people are at him, you see – oh, I know *their* little game! Trying to get him away from me before I can get my divorce – that's what they're up to. At first he wouldn't listen to them; he used to toss their letters over to me to read; but now he reads them himself, and answers 'em too, I fancy; he's always shut up in his room, writing. If I only knew what his plan is I could stop him fast enough – he's such a simpleton. But he's dreadfully deep too – at times I can't make him out. But I know he's told your husband everything – I knew that last night the minute I laid eyes on him. And I *must* find out – you must help me – I've got no one else to turn to!'

She caught Lydia's fingers in a stormy pressure.

'Say you'll help me – you and your husband.'

Lydia tried to free herself.

'What you ask is impossible; you must see that it is. No one could interfere in – in the way you ask.'

Mrs Cope's clutch tightened.

'You won't, then? You won't?'

'Certainly not. Let me go, please.'

Mrs Cope released her with a laugh.

'Oh, go by all means – pray don't let me detain you! Shall you go and tell Lady Susan Condit that there's a pair of us – or shall I save you the trouble of enlightening her?'

Lydia stood still in the middle of the path, seeing her antagonist through a mist of terror. Mrs Cope was still laughing.

'Oh, I'm not spiteful by nature, my dear; but you're a little more than flesh and blood can stand! It's impossible, is it? Let you go, indeed! You're too good to be mixed up in my affairs, are you? Why, you little fool, the first day I laid eyes on you I saw that you and I were both in the same box – that's the reason I spoke to you.'

She stepped nearer, her smile dilating on Lydia like a lamp through a fog.

'You can take your choice, you know; I always play fair. If you'll tell I'll promise not to. Now then, which is it to be?'

Lydia, involuntarily, had begun to move away from the pelting storm of words; but at this she turned and sat down again.

'You may go,' she said simply. 'I shall stay here.'

4

She stayed there for a long time, in the hypnotized contemplation, not of Mrs Cope's present, but of her own past. Gannett, early that morning, had gone off on a long walk – he had fallen into the habit of taking these mountain-tramps with various fellow-lodgers; but even had he been within reach she could not have gone to him just then. She had to deal with herself first. She was surprised to find how, in the last months, she had lost the habit of introspection. Since their coming to the Hotel Bellosguardo she and Gannett had tacitly avoided themselves and each other.

She was aroused by the whistle of the three o'clock steamboat as it neared the landing just beyond the hotel gates. Three o'clock! Then Gannett would soon be back – he had told her to expect him before four. She rose hurriedly, her face averted from the inquisitorial façade of the hotel. She could not see him just yet; she could not go indoors. She slipped through one of the overgrown garden-alleys and climbed a steep path to the hills.

It was dark when she opened their sitting-room door. Gannett was sitting on the window-ledge smoking a cigarette. Cigarettes were now his chief resource: he had not written a line during the two months they had spent at the Hotel Bellosguardo. In that respect, it had turned out not to be the right *milieu* after all.

He started up at Lydia's entrance.

'Where have you been? I was getting anxious.'

She sat down in a chair near the door.

'Up the mountain,' she said wearily.

'Alone?'

'Yes.'

Gannett threw away his cigarette: the sound of her voice made him want to see her face.

'Shall we have a little light?' he suggested.

She made no answer and he lifted the globe from the lamp and put a match to the wick. Then he looked at her.

'Anything wrong? You look done up.'

She sat glancing vaguely about the little sitting-room, dimly lit by the pallid-globed lamp, which left in twilight the outlines of the furniture, of his writing-table heaped with books and papers, of the tea-roses and jasmine drooping on the mantelpiece. How like home it had all grown – how like home!

'Lydia, what is wrong?' he repeated.

She moved away from him, feeling for her hatpins and turning to lay her hat and sunshade on the table.

Suddenly she said: 'That woman has been talking to me.'

Gannett stared.

'That woman? What woman?'

'Mrs Linton – Mrs Cope.'

He gave a start of annoyance, still, as she perceived, not grasping the full import of her words.

'The deuce! She told you – ?'

'She told me everything.'

Gannett looked at her anxiously.

'What impudence! I'm so sorry that you should have been exposed to this, dear.'

'Exposed!' Lydia laughed.

Gannett's brow clouded and they looked away from each other.

'Do you know *why* she told me? She had the best of reasons. The first time she laid eyes on me she saw that we were both in the same box.'

'Lydia!'

'So it was natural, of course, that she should turn to me in a difficulty.'

'What difficulty?'

'It seems she has reason to think that Lord Trevenna's people are trying to get him away from her before she gets her divorce—'

'Well?'

'And she fancied he had been consulting with you last night as to – as to the best way of escaping from her.'

Gannett stood up with an angry forehead.

'Well – what concern of yours was all this dirty business? Why should she go to you?'

'Don't you see? It's so simple. I was to wheedle his secret out of you.'

'To oblige that woman?'

'Yes; or, if I was unwilling to oblige her, then to protect myself.'

'To protect yourself? Against whom?'

'Against her telling everyone in the hotel that she and I are in the same box.'

'She threatened that?'

'She left me the choice of telling it myself or of doing it for me.'

'The beast!'

There was a long silence. Lydia had seated herself on the sofa, beyond the radius of the lamp, and he leaned against the window. His next question surprised her.

'When did this happen? At what time, I mean?'

She looked at him vaguely.

'I don't know – after luncheon, I think. Yes, I remember; it must have been at about three o'clock.'

He stepped into the middle of the room and as he approached the light she saw that his brow had cleared.

'Why do you ask?' she said.

'Because when I came in, at about half-past three, the mail was just being distributed, and Mrs Cope was waiting as usual to pounce on her letters; you know she was always watching for the postman. She was standing so close to me that I couldn't help seeing a big official-looking envelope that was handed to her. She tore it open, gave one look at the inside, and rushed off upstairs like a whirlwind, with the director shouting after her that she had left all her other letters behind. I don't believe she ever thought of you again after that paper was put into her hand.'

'Why?'

'Because she was too busy. I was sitting in the window, watching for you, when the five o'clock boat left, and who should go on board, bag and baggage, valet and maid, dressing-bags and poodle, but Mrs Cope and Trevenna. Just an hour and a half to pack up in! And you should have seen her when they started. She was radiant – shaking hands with everybody – waving her handkerchief from the deck – distributing bows and smiles like an empress. If ever a woman got what she wanted just in the nick of time that woman did. She'll be Lady Trevenna within a week, I'll wager.'

'You think she has her divorce?'

'I'm sure of it. And she must have got it just after her talk with you.'

Lydia was silent.

At length she said, with a kind of reluctance, 'She was horribly angry when she left me. It wouldn't have taken long to tell Lady Susan Condit.'

'Lady Susan Condit has not been told.'

'How do you know?'

'Because when I went downstairs half an hour ago I met Lady Susan on the way—'

He stopped, half-smiling.

'Well?'

'And she stopped to ask if I thought you would act as patroness to a charity concert she is getting up.'

In spite of themselves they both broke into a laugh. Lydia's ended in sobs and she sank down with her face hidden. Gannett bent over her, seeking her hands.

'That vile woman – I ought to have warned you to keep away from her; I can't forgive myself! But he spoke to me in confidence; and I never dreamed – well, it's all over now.'

Lydia lifted her head.

'Not for me. It's only just beginning.'

'What do you mean?'

She put him gently aside and moved in her turn to the window. Then she went on, with her face turned toward the shimmering blackness of the lake, 'You see of course that it might happen again at any moment.'

'What?'

'This – this risk of being found out. And we could hardly count again on such a lucky combination of chances, could we?'

He sat down with a groan.

Still keeping her face toward the darkness, she said, 'I want you to go and tell Lady Susan – and the others.'

Gannett, who had moved toward her, paused a few feet off.

'Why do you wish me to do this?' he said at length, with less surprise in his voice than she had been prepared for.

'Because I've behaved basely, abominably, since we came here: letting these people believe we were married – lying with every breath I drew—'

'Yes, I've felt that too,' Gannett exclaimed with sudden energy.

The words shook her like a tempest: all her thoughts seemed to fall about her in ruins.

'You – you've felt so?'

'Of course I have.' He spoke with low-voiced vehemence. 'Do you suppose I like playing the sneak any better than you do? It's damnable.'

He had dropped on the arm of a chair, and they stared at each other like blind people who suddenly see.

'But you have liked it here,' she faltered.

'Oh, I've liked it – I've liked it.' He moved impatiently. 'Haven't you?'

'Yes,' she burst out; 'that's the worst of it – that's what I can't bear. I fancied it was for your sake that I insisted on staying – because you thought you could write here; and perhaps just at first that really was the reason. But afterwards I wanted to stay myself – I loved it.' She broke into a laugh. 'Oh, do you see the full derision of it? These people – the very prototypes of the bores you took me away from, with the same fenced-in view of life, the same keep-off-the-grass morality, the same little cautious virtues and the same little frightened vices – well, I've clung to them, I've delighted in them, I've done my best to please them. I've toadied Lady Susan, I've gossiped with Miss Pinsent, I've pretended to be shocked with Mrs Ainger. Respectability! It was the one thing in life that I was sure I didn't care about, and it's grown so precious to me that I've stolen it because I couldn't get it any other way.'

She moved across the room and returned to his side with another laugh.

'I who used to fancy myself unconventional! I must have been born with a card-case in my hand. You should have seen me with that poor woman in the garden. She came to me for help, poor creature, because she fancied that, having "sinned," as they call it, I might feel some pity for others who had been tempted in the same way. Not I! She didn't know me. Lady Susan would have been kinder, because Lady Susan wouldn't have been afraid. I hated the woman – my one thought was not to be seen with her – I could have killed her for guessing my secret. The one thing that mattered to me at that moment was my standing with Lady Susan!'

Gannett did not speak.

'And you – you've felt it too!' she broke out accusingly. 'You've enjoyed being with these people as much as I have; you've let the chaplain talk to you by the hour about "The Reign of Law" and Professor Drummond. When they asked you to hand the plate in church I was watching you – *you wanted to accept.*'

She stepped close, laying her hand on his arm.

'Do you know, I begin to see what marriage is for. It's to keep people away from each other. Sometimes I think that two people who love each other can be saved from madness only by the things that come between them – children, duties, visits, bores, relations – the things that protect married people from each other. We've been too close together – that has been our sin. We've seen the nakedness of each other's souls.'

She sank again on the sofa, hiding her face in her hands.

Gannett stood above her perplexedly: he felt as though she were being swept away by some implacable current while he stood helpless on its bank.

At length he said, 'Lydia, don't think me a brute – but don't you see yourself that it won't do?'

'Yes, I see it won't do,' she said without raising her head.

His face cleared.

'Then we'll go tomorrow.'

'Go – where?'

'To Paris; to be married.'

For a long time she made no answer; then she asked slowly, 'Would they have us here if we were married?'

'Have us here?'

'I mean Lady Susan – and the others.'

'Have us here? Of course they would.'

'Not if they knew – at least, not unless they could pretend not to know.'

He made an impatient gesture.

'We shouldn't come back here, of course; and other people needn't know – no one need know.'

She sighed. 'Then it's only another form of deception and a meaner one. Don't you see that?'

'I see that we're not accountable to any Lady Susans on earth!'

'Then why are you ashamed of what we are doing here?'

'Because I'm sick of pretending that you're my wife when you're not – when you won't be.'

She looked at him sadly.

'If I were your wife you'd have to go on pretending. You'd have to pretend that I'd never been – anything else. And our friends would have to pretend that they believed what you pretended.'

Gannett pulled off the sofa-tassel and flung it away.

'You're impossible,' he groaned.

'It's not I – it's our being together that's impossible. I only want you to see that marriage won't help it.'

'What will help it then?'

She raised her head.

'My leaving you.'

'Your leaving me?' He sat motionless, staring at the tassel which lay at the other end of the room. At length some impulse of retaliation for the pain she was inflicting made him say deliberately:

'And where would you go if you left me?'

'Oh!' she cried, wincing.

He was at her side in an instant.

'Lydia – Lydia – you know I didn't mean it; I couldn't mean it! But you've driven me out of my senses; I don't know what I'm saying. Can't you get out of this labyrinth of self-torture? It's destroying us both.'

'That's why I must leave you.'

'How easily you say it!' He drew her hands down and made her face him. 'You're very scrupulous about yourself – and others. But have you thought of me? You have no right to leave me unless you've ceased to care—'

'It's because I care—'

'Then I have a right to be heard. If you love me you can't leave me.'

Her eyes defied him.

'Why not?'

He dropped her hands and rose from her side.

'Can you?' he said sadly.

The hour was late and the lamp flickered and sank. She stood up with a shiver and turned toward the door of her room.

5

At daylight a sound in Lydia's room woke Gannett from a troubled sleep. He sat up and listened. She was moving about softly, as though fearful of disturbing him. He heard her push back one of the creaking shutters; then there was a moment's silence, which seemed to indicate that she was waiting to see if the noise had roused him.

Presently she began to move again. She had spent a sleepless night, probably, and was dressing to go down to the garden for a breath of air. Gannett rose also; but some indefinable instinct made his movements as cautious as hers. He stole to his window and looked out through the slats of the shutter.

It had rained in the night and the dawn was gray and lifeless. The cloud-muffled hills across the lake were reflected in its surface as in a tarnished mirror. In the garden, the birds were beginning to shake the drops from the motionless laurustinus-boughs.

An immense pity for Lydia filled Gannett's soul. Her seeming intellectual independence had blinded him for a time to the feminine cast of her mind. He had never thought of her as a woman who wept and clung: there was a lucidity in her intuitions that made them appear to be the result of reasoning. Now he saw the cruelty he had committed in detaching her from the normal conditions of life; he felt, too, the insight with which she had hit upon the real cause of their suffering. Their life was 'impossible,' as she had said – and its worst penalty was that it had made any other life impossible for them. Even had his love lessened, he was bound to her now by a hundred ties of pity and self-reproach; and she, poor child! must turn back to him as Latude returned to his cell . . .

A new sound startled him: it was the stealthy closing of Lydia's door. He crept to his own and heard her footsteps passing down the corridor. Then he went back to the window and looked out.

A minute or two later he saw her go down the steps of the porch and enter the garden. From his post of observation her face was invisible, but something about her appearance struck him. She wore a long travelling cloak and under its folds he detected the outline of a bag or bundle. He drew a deep breath and stood watching her.

She walked quickly down the laurustinus alley toward the gate; there she paused a moment, glancing about the little shady square. The stone benches under the trees were empty, and she seemed to gather resolution from the solitude about her, for she crossed the square to the steamboat landing, and he saw her pause before the ticket-office at the head of the wharf. Now she was buying her ticket. Gannett turned his head a moment to look at the clock: the boat was due in five minutes. He had time to jump into his clothes and overtake her—

He made no attempt to move; an obscure reluctance restrained him. If any thought emerged from the tumult of his sensations, it was that he must let her go if she wished it. He had spoken last night of his rights: what were they? At the last issue, he and she were two separate beings, not made one by the miracle of common forebearances, duties, abnegations, but bound together in a *noyade* of passion that left them resisting yet clinging as they went down.

After buying her ticket, Lydia had stood for a moment looking out across the lake; then he saw her seat herself on one of the benches near the landing. He and she, at that moment, were both listening for the same sound: the whistle of the boat as it rounded the nearest promontory. Gannett turned again to glance at the clock: the boat was due now.

Where would she go? What would her life be when she had left him? She had no near relations and few friends. There was money enough . . . but she asked so much of life, in ways so complex and immaterial. He thought of her as walking barefooted through a stony waste. No one would understand her – no one would pity her – and he, who did both, was powerless to come to her aid . . .

He saw that she had risen from the bench and walked toward the edge of the lake. She stood looking in the direction from which the steamboat was to come; then she turned to the ticket-office, doubtless to ask the cause of the delay. After that she went back to the bench and sat down with bent head. What was she thinking of?

The whistle sounded; she started up, and Gannett involuntarily made a movement toward the door. But he turned back and continued to watch her. She stood motionless, her eyes on the trail of smoke that preceded the appearance of the boat. Then the little craft rounded the point, a dead-white object on the leaden water: a minute later it was puffing and backing at the wharf.

The few passengers who were waiting – two or three peasants and a snuffy priest – were clustered near the ticket-office. Lydia stood apart under the trees.

The boat lay alongside now; the gang-plank was run out and the peasants went on board with their baskets of vegetables, followed by the priest. Still Lydia did not move. A bell began to ring querulously; there was a shriek of steam, and someone must have called to her that she would be late, for she started forward, as though in answer to a summons. She moved waveringly, and at the edge of the wharf she paused. Gannett saw a sailor beckon to her; the bell rang again and she stepped upon the gang-plank.

Half-way down the short incline to the deck she stopped again; then she turned and ran back to the land. The gang-plank was drawn in, the bell ceased to ring, and the boat backed out into the lake. Lydia, with slow steps, was walking toward the garden . . .

As she approached the hotel she looked up furtively and

Gannett drew back into the room. He sat down beside a table; a Bradshaw lay at his elbow, and mechanically, without knowing what he did, he began looking out the trains to Paris . . .

The Other Two

1

Waythorn, on the drawing-room hearth, waited for his wife to come down to dinner.

It was their first night under his own roof, and he was surprised at his thrill of boyish agitation. He was not so old, to be sure – his glass gave him little more than the five-and-thirty years to which his wife confessed – but he had fancied himself already in the temperate zone; yet here he was listening for her step with a tender sense of all it symbolized, with some old trail of verse about the garlanded nuptial door-posts floating through his enjoyment of the pleasant room and the good dinner just beyond it.

They had been hastily recalled from their honeymoon by the illness of Lily Haskett, the child of Mrs Waythorn's first marriage. The little girl, at Waythorn's desire, had been transferred to his house on the day of her mother's wedding, and the doctor, on their arrival, broke the news that she was ill with typhoid, but declared that all the symptoms were favorable. Lily could show twelve years of unblemished health, and the case promised to be a light one. The nurse spoke as reassuringly, and after a moment of alarm Mrs Waythorn had adjusted herself to the situation. She was very fond of Lily – her affection for the child had perhaps been her decisive charm in Waythorn's eyes – but she had the perfectly balanced nerves which her little girl had inherited, and no woman ever wasted less tissue in unproductive worry. Waythorn was therefore quite prepared to see her come in presently, a little late because of a last look at Lily, but as serene and well-appointed as if her good-night kiss had been laid on the brow of health. Her composure was restful to him; it acted as ballast to his somewhat unstable sensibilities. As he pictured her bending over the child's bed he thought how soothing her presence must be in illness; her very step would prognosticate recovery.

His own life had been a gray one, from temperament rather than circumstance, and he had been drawn to her by the unperturbed gaiety which kept her fresh and elastic at an age when most women's activities are growing either slack or febrile. He knew what was said about her; for, popular as she was, there had always been a faint undercurrent of detraction. When she had appeared in New York, nine or ten years earlier, as the pretty Mrs Haskett whom Gus Varick had unearthed somewhere – was it in Pittsburgh or Utica? – society, while promptly accepting her, had reserved the right to cast a doubt on its own indiscrimination. Inquiry, however, established her undoubted connection with a socially reigning family, and explained her recent divorce as the natural result of a runaway match at seventeen; and as nothing was known of Mr Haskett it was easy to believe the worst of him.

Alice Haskett's remarriage with Gus Varick was a passport to the set whose recognition she coveted, and for a few years the Varicks were the most popular couple in town. Unfortunately, the alliance was brief and stormy, and this time the husband had his champions. Still, even Varick's staunchest supporters admitted that he was not meant for matrimony, and Mrs Varick's grievances were of a nature to bear the inspection of the New York courts. A New York divorce is in itself a diploma of virtue, and in the semi-widowhood of this second separation Mrs Varick took on an air of sanctity, and was allowed to confide her wrongs to some of the most scrupulous ears in town. But when it was known that she was to marry Waythorn there was a momentary reaction. Her best friends would have preferred to see her remain in the role of the injured wife, which was as becoming to her as crape to a rosy complexion. True, a decent time had elapsed, and it was not even suggested that Waythorn had supplanted his predecessor. People shook their heads over him, however, and one grudging friend, to whom he affirmed that he took the step with his eyes open, replied oracularly: 'Yes – and with your ears shut.'

Waythorn could afford to smile at these innuendoes. In the Wall Street phrase, he had 'discounted' them. He knew that society has not yet adapted itself to the consequences of divorce, and that till the adaptation takes place every woman who uses the freedom the law accords her must be her own social justification. Waythorn had an amused confidence in his wife's ability to justify herself. His expectations were fulfilled, and before the wedding took place Alice Varick's group had rallied openly to her support.

She took it all imperturbably: she had a way of surmounting obstacles without seeming to be aware of them, and Waythorn looked back with wonder at the trivialities over which he had worn his nerves thin. He had the sense of having found refuge in a richer, warmer nature than his own, and his satisfaction, at the moment, was humorously summed up in the thought that his wife, when she had done all she could for Lily, would not be ashamed to come down and enjoy a good dinner.

The anticipation of such enjoyment was not, however, the sentiment expressed by Mrs Waythorn's charming face when she presently joined him. Though she had put on her most engaging tea-gown she had neglected to assume the smile that went with it, and Waythorn thought he had never seen her look so nearly worried.

'What is it?' he asked. 'Is anything wrong with Lily?'

'No; I've just been in and she's still sleeping.' Mrs Waythorn hesitated. 'But something tiresome has happened.'

He had taken her two hands, and now perceived that he was crushing a paper between them.

'This letter?'

'Yes – Mr Haskett has written – I mean his lawyer has written.'

Waythorn felt himself flush uncomfortably. He dropped his wife's hands.

'What about?'

'About seeing Lily. You know the courts—'

'Yes, yes,' he interrupted nervously.

Nothing was known about Haskett in New York. He was vaguely supposed to have remained in the outer darkness from which his wife had been rescued, and Waythorn was one of the few who were aware that he had given up his business in Utica and followed her to New York in order to be near his little girl. In the days of his wooing, Waythorn had often met Lily on the doorstep, rosy and smiling, on her way 'to see papa.'

'I am so sorry,' Mrs Waythorn murmured.

He roused himself. 'What does he want?'

'He wants to see her. You know she goes to him once a week.'

'Well – he doesn't expect her to go to him now, does he?'

'No – he has heard of her illness; but he expects to come here.'

'*Here?*'

Mrs Waythorn reddened under his gaze. They looked away from each other.

'I'm afraid he has the right. . . . You'll see. . . .' She made a proffer of the letter.

Waythorn moved away with a gesture of refusal. He stood staring about the softly lighted room, which a moment before had seemed so full of bridal intimacy.

'I'm so sorry,' she repeated. 'If Lily could have been moved—'

'That's out of the question,' he returned impatiently.

'I suppose so.'

Her lip was beginning to tremble, and he felt himself a brute.

'He must come, of course,' he said. 'When is – his day?'

'I'm afraid – tomorrow.'

'Very well. Send a note in the morning.'

The butler entered to announce dinner.

Waythorn turned to his wife. 'Come – you must be tired. It's beastly, but try to forget about it,' he said, drawing her hand through his arm.

'You're so good, dear. I'll try,' she whispered back.

Her face cleared at once, and as she looked at him across the flowers, between the rosy candle-shades, he saw her lips waver back into a smile.

'How pretty everything is!' she sighed luxuriously.

He turned to the butler. 'The champagne at once, please. Mrs Waythorn is tired.'

In a moment or two their eyes met above the sparkling glasses. Her own were quite clear and untroubled: he saw that she had obeyed his injunction and forgotten.

2

Waythorn, the next morning, went down town earlier than usual. Haskett was not likely to come till the afternoon, but the instinct of flight drove him forth. He meant to stay away all day – he had thoughts of dining at his club. As his door closed behind him he reflected that before he opened it again it would have admitted another man who had as much right to enter it as himself, and the thought filled him with a physical repugnance.

He caught the 'elevated' at the employees' hour, and found himself crushed between two layers of pendulous humanity. At

Eighth Street the man facing him wriggled out, and another took
his place. Waythorn glanced up and saw that it was Gus Varick.
The men were so close together that it was impossible to ignore
the smile of recognition on Varick's handsome overblown face.
And after all – why not? They had always been on good terms,
and Varick had been divorced before Waythorn's attentions to his
wife began. The two exchanged a word on the perennial
grievance of the congested trains, and when a seat at their side
was miraculously left empty the instinct of self-preservation made
Waythorn slip into it after Varick.

The latter drew the stout man's breath of relief. 'Lord – I was
beginning to feel like a pressed flower.' He leaned back, looking
unconcernedly at Waythorn. 'Sorry to hear that Sellers is
knocked out again.'

'Sellers?' echoed Waythorn, starting at his partner's name.

Varick looked surprised. 'You didn't know he was laid up with
the gout?'

'No. I've been away – I only got back last night.' Waythorn felt
himself reddening in anticipation of the other's smile.

'Ah – yes; to be sure. And Sellers's attack came on two days
ago. I'm afraid he's pretty bad. Very awkward for me, as it
happens, because he was just putting through a rather important
thing for me.'

'Ah?' Waythorn wondered vaguely since when Varick had
been dealing in 'important things.' Hitherto he had dabbled only
in the shallow pools of speculation, with which Waythorn's office
did not usually concern itself.

It occurred to him that Varick might be talking at random, to
relieve the strain of their propinquity. That strain was becoming momentarily more apparent to Waythorn, and when, at
Cortlandt Street, he caught sight of an acquaintance and had a
sudden vision of the picture he and Varick must present to an
initiated eye, he jumped up with a muttered excuse.

'I hope you'll find Sellers better,' said Varick civilly, and he
stammered back: 'If I can be of any use to you—' and let the
departing crowd sweep him to the platform.

At his office he heard that Sellers was in fact ill with the gout,
and would probably not be able to leave the house for some
weeks.

'I'm sorry it should have happened so, Mr Waythorn,' the

senior clerk said with affable significance. 'Mr Sellers was very much upset at the idea of giving you such a lot of extra work just now.'

'Oh, that's no matter,' said Waythorn hastily. He secretly welcomed the pressure of additional business, and was glad to think that, when the day's work was over, he would have to call at his partner's on the way home.

He was late for luncheon, and turned in at the nearest restaurant instead of going to his club. The place was full, and the waiter hurried him to the back of the room to capture the only vacant table. In the cloud of cigar-smoke Waythorn did not at once distinguish his neighbors; but presently, looking about him, he saw Varick seated a few feet off. This time, luckily, they were too far apart for conversation, and Varick, who faced another way, had probably not even seen him; but there was an irony in their renewed nearness.

Varick was said to be fond of good living, and as Waythorn sat despatching his hurried luncheon he looked across half enviously at the other's leisurely degustation of his meal. When Waythorn first saw him he had been helping himself with critical deliberation to a bit of Camembert at the ideal point of liquefaction, and now, the cheese removed, he was just pouring his *café double* from its little two-storied earthen pot. He poured slowly, his ruddy profile bent above the task, and one beringed white hand steadying the lid of the coffee-pot; then he stretched his other hand to the decanter of cognac at his elbow, filled a liqueur-glass, took a tentative sip, and poured the brandy into his coffee-cup.

Waythorn watched him in a kind of fascination. What was he thinking of – only of the flavour of the coffee and the liqueur? Had the morning's meeting left no more trace in his thoughts than on his face? Had his wife so completely passed out of his life that even this odd encounter with her present husband, within a week after her remarriage, was no more than an incident in his day? And as Waythorn mused, another idea struck him: had Haskett ever met Varick as Varick and he had just met? The recollection of Haskett perturbed him, and he rose and left the restaurant, taking a circuitous way out to escape the placid irony of Varick's nod.

It was after seven when Waythorn reached home. He thought the footman who opened the door looked at him oddly.

'How is Miss Lily?' he asked in haste.

'Doing very well, sir. A gentleman—'

'Tell Barlow to put off dinner for half an hour,' Waythorn cut him off, hurrying upstairs.

He went straight to his room and dressed without seeing his wife. When he reached the drawing-room she was there, fresh and radiant. Lily's day had been good; the doctor was not coming back that evening.

At dinner Waythorn told her of Sellers's illness and of the resulting complications. She listened sympathetically, adjuring him not to let himself be overworked, and asking vague feminine questions about the routine of the office. Then she gave him the chronicle of Lily's day; quoted the nurse and doctor, and told him who had called to inquire. He had never seen her more serene and unruffled. It struck him, with a curious pang, that she was very happy in being with him, so happy that she found a childish pleasure in rehearsing the trivial incidents of her day.

After dinner they went to the library, and the servant put the coffee and liqueurs on a low table before her and left the room. She looked singularly soft and girlish in her rosy pale dress, against the dark leather of one of his bachelor armchairs. A day earlier the contrast would have charmed him.

He turned away now, choosing a cigar with affected deliberation.

'Did Haskett come?' he asked, with his back to her.

'Oh, yes – he came.'

'You didn't see him, of course?'

She hesitated a moment. 'I let the nurse see him.'

That was all. There was nothing more to ask. He swung round toward her, applying a match to his cigar. Well, the thing was over for a week, at any rate. He would try not to think of it. She looked up at him, a trifle rosier than usual, with a smile in her eyes.

'Ready for your coffee, dear?'

He leaned against the mantelpiece, watching her as she lifted the coffee-pot. The lamplight struck a gleam from her bracelets and tipped her soft hair with brightness. How light and slender she was, and how each gesture flowed into the next! She seemed a creature all compact of harmonies. As the thought of Haskett receded, Waythorn felt himself yielding again to the joy of possessorship. They were his, those white hands with their flitting motions, his the light haze of hair, the lips and eyes. . . .

She set down the coffee-pot, and reaching for the decanter of cognac, measured off a liqueur-glass and poured it into his cup.

Waythorn muttered a sudden exclamation.

'What is the matter?' she said, startled.

'Nothing; only – I don't take cognac in my coffee.'

'Oh, how stupid of me,' she cried.

Their eyes met, and she blushed a sudden agonized red.

3

Ten days later, Mr Sellers, still house-bound, asked Waythorn to call on his way down town.

The senior partner, with his swaddled foot propped up by the fire, greeted his associate with an air of embarrassment.

'I'm sorry, my dear fellow; I've got to ask you to do an awkward thing for me.'

Waythorn waited, and the other went on, after a pause apparently given to the arrangement of his phrases: 'The fact is, when I was knocked out I had just gone into a rather complicated piece of business for – Gus Varick.'

'Well?' said Waythorn, with an attempt to put him at his ease.

'Well – it's this way: Varick came to me the day before my attack. He had evidently had an inside tip from somebody, and had made about a hundred thousand. He came to me for advice, and I suggested his going in with Vanderlyn.'

'Oh, the deuce!' Waythorn exclaimed. He saw in a flash what had happened. The investment was an alluring one, but required negotiation. He listened quietly while Sellers put the case before him, and, the statement ended, he said: 'You think I ought to see Varick?'

'I'm afraid I can't as yet. The doctor is obdurate. And this thing can't wait. I hate to ask you, but no one else in the office knows the ins and outs of it.'

Waythorn stood silent. He did not care a farthing for the success of Varick's venture, but the honour of the office was to be considered, and he could hardly refuse to oblige his partner.

'Very well,' he said, 'I'll do it.'

That afternoon, apprised by telephone, Varick called at the

office. Waythorn, waiting in his private room, wondered what the others thought of it. The newspapers, at the time of Mrs Waythorn's marriage, had acquainted their readers with every detail of her previous matrimonial ventures, and Waythorn could fancy the clerks smiling behind Varick's back as he was ushered in.

Varick bore himself admirably. He was easy without being undignified, and Waythorn was conscious of cutting a much less impressive figure. Varick had no experience of business, and the talk prolonged itself for nearly an hour while Waythorn set forth with scrupulous precision the details of the proposed transaction.

'I'm awfully obliged to you,' Varick said as he rose. 'The fact is I'm not used to having much money to look after, and I don't want to make an ass of myself—' He smiled, and Waythorn could not help noticing that there was something pleasant about his smile. 'It feels uncommonly queer to have enough cash to pay one's bills. I'd have sold my soul for it a few years ago!'

Waythorn winced at the allusion. He had heard it rumored that a lack of funds had been one of the determining causes of the Varick separation, but it did not occur to him that Varick's words were intentional. It seemed more likely that the desire to keep clear of embarrassing topics had fatally drawn him into one. Waythorn did not wish to be outdone in civility.

'We'll do the best we can for you,' he said. 'I think this is a good thing you're in.'

'Oh, I'm sure it's immense. It's awfully good of you—' Varick broke off, embarrassed. 'I suppose the thing's settled now – but if—'

'If anything happens before Sellers is about, I'll see you again,' said Waythorn quietly. He was glad, in the end, to appear the more self-possessed of the two.

The course of Lily's illness ran smooth, and as the days passed Waythorn grew used to the idea of Haskett's weekly visit. The first time the day came round, he stayed out late, and questioned his wife as to the visit on his return. She replied at once that Haskett had merely seen the nurse downstairs, as the doctor did not wish any one in the child's sick-room till after the crisis.

The following week Waythorn was again conscious of the recurrence of the day, but had forgotten it by the time he came home to dinner. The crisis of the disease came a few days later, with a rapid decline of fever, and the little girl was pronounced out of danger. In the rejoicing which ensued the thought of Haskett passed out of Waythorn's mind, and one afternoon, letting himself into the house with a latchkey, he went straight to his library without noticing a shabby hat and umbrella in the hall.

In the library he found a small effaced-looking man with a thinnish gray beard sitting on the edge of a chair. The stranger might have been a piano-tuner, or one of those mysteriously efficient persons who are summoned in emergencies to adjust some detail of the domestic machinery. He blinked at Waythorn through a pair of gold-rimmed spectacles and said mildly: 'Mr Waythorn, I presume? I am Lily's father.'

Waythorn flushed. 'Oh—' he stammered uncomfortably. He broke off, disliking to appear rude. Inwardly he was trying to adjust the actual Haskett to the image of him projected by his wife's reminiscences. Waythorn had been allowed to infer that Alice's first husband was a brute.

'I am sorry to intrude,' said Haskett, with his over-the-counter politeness.

'Don't mention it,' returned Waythorn, collecting himself. 'I suppose the nurse has been told?'

'I presume so. I can wait,' said Haskett. He had a resigned way of speaking, as though life had worn down his natural powers of resistance.

Waythorn stood on the threshold, nervously pulling off his gloves.

'I'm sorry you've been detained. I will send for the nurse,' he said; and as he opened the door he added with an effort: 'I'm glad we can give you a good report of Lily.' He winced as the *we* slipped out, but Haskett seemed not to notice it.

'Thank you, Mr Waythorn. It's been an anxious time for me.'

'Ah, well, that's past. Soon she'll be able to go to you.' Waythorn nodded and passed out.

In his own room he flung himself down with a groan. He hated the womanish sensibility which made him suffer so acutely from the grotesque chances of life. He had known when he married that his wife's former husbands were both living, and that amid the multiplied contacts of modern existence there

were a thousand chances to one that he would run against one
or the other, yet he found himself as much disturbed by his brief
encounter with Haskett as though the law had not obligingly
removed all difficulties in the way of their meeting.

Waythorn sprang up and began to pace the room nervously.
He had not suffered half as much from his two meetings with
Varick. It was Haskett's presence in his own house that made the
situation so intolerable. He stood still, hearing steps in the
passage.

'This way, please,' he heard the nurse say. Haskett was being
taken upstairs, then: not a corner of the house but was open to
him. Waythorn dropped into another chair, staring vaguely
ahead of him. On his dressing-table stood a photograph of Alice,
taken when he had first known her. She was Alice Varick then –
how fine and exquisite he had thought her! Those were Varick's
pearls about her neck. At Waythorn's instance they had been
returned before her marriage. Had Haskett ever given her any
trinkets – and what had become of them, Waythorn wondered?
He realized suddenly that he knew very little of Haskett's past or
present situation; but from the man's appearance and manner of
speech he could reconstruct with curious precision the surroundings of Alice's first marriage. And it startled him to think that she
had, in the background of her life, a phase of existence so different
from anything with which he had connected her. Varick,
whatever his faults, was a gentleman, in the conventional,
traditional sense of the term: the sense which at that moment
seemed, oddly enough, to have most meaning to Waythorn. He
and Varick had the same social habits, spoke the same language,
understood the same allusions. But this other man . . . it was
grotesquely uppermost in Waythorn's mind that Haskett had
worn a made-up tie attached with an elastic. Why should that
ridiculous detail symbolize the whole man? Waythorn was
exasperated by his own paltriness, but the fact of the tie expanded,
forced itself on him, became as it were the key to Alice's past. He
could see her, as Mrs Haskett, sitting in a 'front parlor' furnished
in plush, with a pianola, and a copy of 'Ben Hur' on the center-
table. He could see her going to the theater with Haskett – or
perhaps even to a 'Church Sociable' – she in a 'picture hat' and
Haskett in a black frock-coat, a little creased, with the made-up tie
on an elastic. On the way home they would stop and look at the

illuminated shop-windows, lingering over the photographs of New York actresses. On Sunday afternoons Haskett would take her for a walk, pushing Lily ahead of them in a white enamelled perambulator, and Waythorn had a vision of the people they would stop and talk to. He could fancy how pretty Alice must have looked, in a dress adroitly constructed from the hints of a New York fashion-paper, and how she must have looked down on the other women, chafing at her life, and secretly feeling that she belonged in a bigger place.

For the moment his foremost thought was one of wonder at the way in which she had shed the phase of existence which her marriage with Haskett implied. It was as if her whole aspect, every gesture, every inflection, every allusion, were a studied negation of that period of her life. If she had denied being married to Haskett she could hardly have stood more convicted of duplicity than in this obliteration of the self which had been his wife.

Waythorn started up, checking himself in the analysis of her motives. What right had he to create a fantastic effigy of her and then pass judgment on it? She had spoken vaguely of her first marriage as unhappy, had hinted, with becoming reticence, that Haskett had wrought havoc among her young illusions. . . . It was a pity for Waythorn's peace of mind that Haskett's very inoffensiveness shed a new light on the nature of those illusions. A man would rather think that his wife has been brutalized by her first husband than that the process has been reversed.

4

'Mr Waythorn, I don't like that French governess of Lily's.'

Haskett, subdued and apologetic, stood before Waythorn in the library, revolving his shabby hat in his hand.

Waythorn, surprised in his armchair over the evening paper, stared back perplexedly at his visitor.

'You'll excuse my asking to see you,' Haskett continued. 'But this is my last visit, and I thought if I could have a word with you it would be a better way than writing to Mrs Waythorn's lawyer.'

Waythorn rose uneasily. He did not like the French governess either; but that was irrelevant.

'I am not so sure of that,' he returned stiffly; 'but since you wish it I will give your message to – my wife.' He always hesitated over the possessive pronoun in addressing Haskett.

The latter sighed. 'I don't know as that will help much. She didn't like it when I spoke to her.'

Waythorn turned red. 'When did you see her?' he asked.

'Not since the first day I came to see Lily – right after she was taken sick. I remarked to her then that I didn't like the governess.'

Waythorn made no answer. He remembered distinctly that, after that first visit, he had asked his wife if she had seen Haskett. She had lied to him then, but she had respected his wishes since; and the incident cast a curious light on her character. He was sure she would not have seen Haskett that first day if she had divined that Waythorn would object, and the fact that she did not divine it was almost as disagreeable to the latter as the discovery that she had lied to him.

'I don't like the woman,' Haskett was repeating with mild persistency. 'She ain't straight, Mr Waythorn – she'll teach the child to be underhand. I've noticed a change in Lily – she's too anxious to please – and she don't always tell the truth. She used to be the straightest child, Mr Waythorn—' He broke off, his voice a little thick. 'Not but what I want her to have a stylish education,' he ended.

Waythorn was touched. 'I'm sorry, Mr Haskett; but frankly, I don't quite see what I can do.'

Haskett hesitated. Then he laid his hat on the table, and advanced to the hearth-rug, on which Waythorn was standing. There was nothing aggressive in his manner, but he had the solemnity of a timid man resolved on a decisive measure.

'There's just one thing you can do, Mr Waythorn,' he said. 'You can remind Mrs Waythorn that, by the decree of the courts, I am entitled to have a voice in Lily's bringing up.' He paused, and went on more deprecatingly: 'I'm not the kind to talk about enforcing my rights, Mr Waythorn. I don't know as I think a man is entitled to rights he hasn't known how to hold on to; but this business of the child is different. I've never let go there – and I never mean to.'

The scene left Waythorn deeply shaken. Shamefacedly, in indirect ways, he had been finding out about Haskett; and all that he had learned was favorable. The little man, in order to be near his daughter, had sold out his share in a profitable business in Utica, and accepted a modest clerkship in a New York manufacturing house. He boarded in a shabby street and had few acquaintances. His passion for Lily filled his life. Waythorn felt that this exploration of Haskett was like groping about with a dark-lantern in his wife's past; but he saw now that there were recesses his lantern had not explored. He had never inquired into the exact circumstances of his wife's first matrimonial rupture. On the surface all had been fair. It was she who had obtained the divorce, and the court had given her the child. But Waythorn knew how many ambiguities such a verdict might cover. The mere fact that Haskett retained a right over his daughter implied an unsuspected compromise. Waythorn was an idealist. He always refused to recognize unpleasant contingencies till he found himself confronted with them, and then he saw them followed by a spectral train of consequences. His next days were thus haunted, and he determined to try to lay the ghosts by conjuring them up in his wife's presence.

When he repeated Haskett's request a flame of anger passed over her face; but she subdued it instantly and spoke with a slight quiver of outraged motherhood.

'It is very ungentlemanly of him,' she said.

The word grated on Waythorn. 'That is neither here nor there. It's a bare question of rights.'

She murmured: 'It's not as if he could ever be a help to Lily—'

Waythorn flushed. This was even less to his taste. 'The question is,' he repeated, 'what authority has he over her?'

She looked downward, twisting herself a little in her seat. 'I am willing to see him – I thought you objected,' she faltered.

In a flash he understood that she knew the extent of Haskett's claims. Perhaps it was not the first time she had resisted them.

'My objecting has nothing to do with it,' he said coldly; 'if Haskett has a right to be consulted you must consult him.'

She burst into tears, and he saw that she expected him to regard her as a victim.

Haskett did not abuse his rights. Waythorn had felt miserably sure that he would not. But the governess was dismissed, and from time to time the little man demanded an interview with Alice. After the first outburst she accepted the situation with her usual adaptability. Haskett had once reminded Waythorn of the piano-tuner, and Mrs Waythorn, after a month or two, appeared to class him with that domestic familiar. Waythorn could not but respect the father's tenacity. At first he had tried to cultivate the suspicion that Haskett might be 'up to' something, that he had an object in securing a foothold in the house. But in his heart Waythorn was sure of Haskett's single-mindedness; he even guessed in the latter a mild contempt for such advantages as his relation with the Waythorns might offer. Haskett's sincerity of purpose made him invulnerable, and his successor had to accept him as a lien on the property.

Mr Sellers was sent to Europe to recover from his gout, and Varick's affairs hung on Waythorn's hands. The negotiations were prolonged and complicated; they necessitated frequent conferences between the two men, and the interests of the firm forbade Waythorn's suggesting that his client should transfer his business to another office.

Varick appeared well in the transaction. In moments of relaxation his coarse streak appeared, and Waythorn dreaded his geniality; but in the office he was concise and clear-headed, with a flattering deference to Waythorn's judgment. Their business relations being so affably established, it would have been absurd for the two men to ignore each other in society. The first time they met in a drawing-room, Varick took up their inter-course in the same easy key, and his hostess's grateful glance obliged Waythorn to respond to it. After that they ran across each other frequently, and one evening at a ball Waythorn, wandering through the remoter rooms, came upon Varick seated beside his wife. She colored a little, and faltered in what she was saying; but Varick nodded to Waythorn without rising, and the latter strolled on.

In the carriage, on the way home, he broke out nervously: 'I didn't know you spoke to Varick.'

Her voice trembled a little. 'It's the first time – he happened to be standing near me; I didn't know what to do. It's so awkward, meeting everywhere – and he said you had been very kind about some business.'

'That's different,' said Waythorn.

She paused a moment. 'I'll do just as you wish,' she returned pliantly. 'I thought it would be less awkward to speak to him when we meet.'

Her pliancy was beginning to sicken him. Had she really no will of her own – no theory about her relation to these men? She had accepted Haskett – did she mean to accept Varick? It was 'less awkward,' as she had said, and her instinct was to evade difficulties or to circumvent them. With sudden vividness Waythorn saw how the instinct had developed. She was 'as easy as an old shoe' – a shoe that too many feet had worn. Her elasticity was the result of tension in too many different directions. Alice Haskett – Alice Varick – Alice Waythorn – she had been each in turn, and had left hanging to each name a little of her privacy, a little of her personality, a little of the inmost self where the unknown god abides.

'Yes – it's better to speak to Varick,' said Waythorn wearily.

5

The winter wore on, and society took advantage of the Waythorns' acceptance of Varick. Harassed hostesses were grateful to them for bridging over a social difficulty, and Mrs Waythorn was held up as a miracle of good taste. Some experimental spirits could not resist the diversion of throwing Varick and his former wife together, and there were those who thought he found a zest in the propinquity. But Mrs Waythorn's conduct remained irreproachable. She neither avoided Varick nor sought him out. Even Waythorn could not but admit that she had discovered the solution of the newest social problem.

He had married her without giving much thought to that problem. He had fancied that a woman can shed her past like a man. But now he saw that Alice was bound to hers both by the circumstances which forced her into continued relation with it, and by the traces it had left on her nature. With grim irony Waythorn compared himself to a member of a syndicate. He held so many shares in his wife's personality and his predecessors were his partners in the business. If there had been any element of passion in the transaction he would have felt less deteriorated by it. The fact that Alice took her change of husbands like a change of weather reduced the situation to mediocrity. He could have forgiven her for blunders, for excesses; for resisting Haskett, for yielding to Varick; for anything but her acquiescence and her tact. She reminded him of a juggler tossing knives; but the knives were blunt and she knew they would never cut her.

And then, gradually, habit formed a protecting surface for his sensibilities. If he paid for each day's comfort with the small change of his illusions, he grew daily to value the comfort more and set less store upon the coin. He had drifted into a dulling propinquity with Haskett and Varick and he took refuge in the cheap revenge of satirizing the situation. He even began to reckon up the advantages which accrued from it, to ask himself if it were not better to own a third of a wife who knew how to make a man happy than a whole one who had lacked opportunity to acquire the art. For it *was* an art, and made up, like all others, of concessions, eliminations and embellishments; of lights judiciously thrown and shadows skilfully softened. His wife knew exactly how to manage the lights, and he knew exactly to what training she owed her skill. He even tried to trace the source of his obligations, to discriminate between the influences which had combined to produce his domestic happiness: he perceived that Haskett's commonness had made Alice worship good breeding, while Varick's liberal construction of the marriage bond had taught her to value the conjugal virtues; so that he was directly indebted to his predecessors for the devotion which made his life easy if not inspiring.

From this phase he passed into that of complete acceptance. He ceased to satirize himself because time dulled the irony of the situation and the joke lost its humor with its sting. Even the sight of Haskett's hat on the hall table had ceased to touch the springs of epigram. The hat was often seen there now, for it had been decided that it was better for Lily's father to visit her than for the little girl to go to his boarding-house. Waythorn, having acquiesced in this arrangement, had been surprised to find how little difference it made. Haskett was never obtrusive, and the few visitors who met him on the stairs were unaware of his identity. Waythorn did not know how often he saw Alice, but with himself Haskett was seldom in contact.

One afternoon, however, he learned on entering that Lily's father was waiting to see him. In the library he found Haskett occupying a chair in his usual provisional way. Waythorn always felt grateful to him for not leaning back.

'I hope you'll excuse me, Mr Waythorn,' he said rising. 'I wanted to see Mrs Waythorn about Lily, and your man asked me to wait here till she came in.'

'Of course,' said Waythorn, remembering that a sudden leak had that morning given over the drawing-room to the plumbers.

He opened his cigar-case and held it out to his visitor, and Haskett's acceptance seemed to mark a fresh stage in their intercourse. The spring evening was chilly, and Waythorn invited his guest to draw up his chair to the fire. He meant to find an excuse to leave Haskett in a moment; but he was tired and cold, and after all the little man no longer jarred on him.

The two were enclosed in the intimacy of their blended cigar-smoke when the door opened and Varick walked into the room. Waythorn rose abruptly. It was the first time that Varick had come to the house, and the surprise of seeing him, combined with the singular inopportuneness of his arrival, gave a new edge to Waythorn's blunted sensibilities. He stared at his visitor without speaking.

Varick seemed too preoccupied to notice his host's embarrassment.

'My dear fellow,' he exclaimed in his most expansive tone. 'I must apologize for tumbling in on you in this way, but I was too late to catch you down town, and so I thought—'

He stopped short, catching sight of Haskett, and his sanguine color deepened to a flush which spread vividly under his scant blond hair. But in a moment he recovered himself and nodded slightly. Haskett returned the bow in silence, and Waythorn was still groping for speech when the footman came in carrying a tea-table.

The intrusion offered a welcome vent to Waythorn's nerves. 'What the deuce are you bringing this here for?' he said sharply.

'I beg your pardon, sir, but the plumbers are still in the drawing-room, and Mrs Waythorn said she would have tea in the library.' The footman's perfectly respectful tone implied a reflection on Waythorn's reasonableness.

'Oh, very well,' said the latter resignedly, and the footman proceeded to open the folding tea-table and set out its complicated appointments. While this interminable process continued the three men stood motionless, watching it with a fascinated stare, till Waythorn, to break the silence, said to Varick: 'Won't you have a cigar?'

He held out the case he had just tendered to Haskett, and Varick helped himself with a smile. Waythorn looked about for a match, and finding none, proffered a light from his own cigar. Haskett, in the background, held his ground mildly, examining his cigar-tip now and then, and stepping forward at the right moment to knock its ashes into the fire.

The footman at last withdrew, and Varick immediately began: 'If I could just say half a word to you about this business—'

'Certainly,' stammered Waythorn; 'in the dining-room—'

But as he placed his hand on the door it opened from without, and his wife appeared on the threshold.

She came in fresh and smiling, in her street dress and hat, shedding a fragrance from the boa which she loosened in advancing.

'Shall we have tea in here, dear?' she began; and then she caught sight of Varick. Her smile deepened, veiling a slight tremor of surprise.

'Why, how do you do?' she said with a distinct note of pleasure.

As she shook hands with Varick she saw Haskett standing behind him. Her smile faded for a moment, but she recalled it quickly, with a scarcely perceptible side-glance at Waythorn.

'How do you do, Mr Haskett?' she said, and shook hands with him a shade less cordially.

The three men stood awkwardly before her, till Varick, always the most self-possessed, dashed into an explanatory phrase.

'We – I had to see Waythorn a moment on business,' he stammered, brick-red from chin to nape.

Haskett stepped forward with his air of mild obstinacy. 'I am sorry to intrude; but you appointed five o'clock' – he directed his resigned glance to the time-piece on the mantel.

She swept aside their embarrassment with a charming gesture of hospitality.

'I'm so sorry – I'm always late; but the afternoon was so lovely.' She stood drawing off her gloves, propitiatory and graceful, diffusing about her a sense of ease and familiarity in which the situation lost its grotesqueness. 'But before talking business,' she added brightly, 'I'm sure every one wants a cup of tea.'

She dropped into her low chair by the tea-table, and the two visitors, as if drawn by her smile, advanced to receive the cups she held out.

She glanced about for Waythorn, and he took the third cup with a laugh.

The Mission of Jane

Lethbury, surveying his wife across the dinner-table, found his transient glance arrested by an indefinable change in her appearance.

'How smart you look! Is that a new gown?' he asked.

Her answering look seemed to deprecate his charging her with the extravagance of wasting a new gown on him, and he now perceived that the change lay deeper than any accident of dress. At the same time, he noticed that she betrayed her consciousness of it by a delicate, almost frightened blush. It was one of the compensations of Mrs Lethbury's protracted childishness that she still blushed as prettily as at eighteen. Her body had been privileged not to outstrip her mind, and the two, as it seemed to Lethbury, were destined to travel together through an eternity of girlishness.

'I don't know what you mean,' she said.

Since she never did, he always wondered at her bringing this out as a fresh grievance against him; but his wonder was unresentful, and he said good-humoredly: 'You sparkle so that I thought you had on your diamonds.'

She sighed and blushed again.

'It must be,' he continued, 'that you've been to a dressmaker's opening. You're absolutely brimming with illicit enjoyment.'

She stared again, this time at the adjective. His adjectives always embarrassed her; their unintelligibleness savored of impropriety.

'In short,' he summed up, 'you've been doing something that you're thoroughly ashamed of.'

To his surprise she retorted: 'I don't see why I should be ashamed of it!'

Lethbury leaned back with a smile of enjoyment. When there was nothing better going he always liked to listen to her explanations.

'Well – ?' he said.

She was becoming breathless and ejaculatory. 'Of course you'll laugh – you laugh at everything!'

'That rather blunts the point of my derision, doesn't it?' he interjected; but she pushed on without noticing:

'It's so easy to laugh at things.'

'Ah,' murmured Lethbury with relish, 'that's Aunt Sophronia's, isn't it?'

Most of his wife's opinions were heirlooms, and he took a quaint pleasure in tracing their descent. She was proud of their age, and saw no reason for discarding them while they were still serviceable. Some, of course, were so fine that she kept them for state occasions, like her great-grandmother's Crown Derby; but from the lady known as Aunt Sophronia she had inherited a stout set of everyday prejudices that were practically as good as new; whereas her husband's, as she noticed, were always having to be replaced. In the early days she had fancied there might be a certain satisfaction in taxing him with the fact; but she had long since been silenced by the reply: 'My dear, I'm not a rich man, but I never use an opinion twice if I can help it.'

She was reduced, therefore, to dwelling on his moral deficiencies; and one of the most obvious of these was his refusal to take things seriously. On this occasion, however, some ulterior purpose kept her from taking up his taunt.

'I'm not in the least ashamed!' she repeated, with the air of shaking a banner to the wind; but the domestic atmosphere being calm, the banner drooped unheroically.

'That,' said Lethbury judicially, 'encourages me to infer that you ought to be, and that, consequently, you've been giving yourself the unusual pleasure of doing something I shouldn't approve of.'

She met this with an almost solemn directness.

'No,' she said. 'You won't approve of it. I've allowed for that.'

'Ah,' he exclaimed, setting down his liqueur glass. 'You've worked out the whole problem, eh?'

'I believe so.'

'That's uncommonly interesting. And what is it?'

She looked at him quietly. 'A baby.'

If it was seldom given her to surprise him, she had attained the distinction for once.

'A baby?'

'Yes.'

'A – human baby?'

'Of course!' she cried, with the virtuous resentment of the woman who has never allowed dogs in the house.

Lethbury's puzzled stare broke into a fresh smile. 'A baby I shan't approve of? Well, in the abstract I don't think much of them, I admit. Is this an abstract baby?'

Again she frowned at the adjective; but she had reached a pitch of exaltation at which such obstacles could not deter her.

'It's the loveliest baby—' she murmured.

'Ah, then it's concrete. It exists. In this harsh world it draws its breath in pain—'

'It's the healthiest child I ever saw!' she indignantly corrected.

'You've seen it, then?'

Again the accusing blush suffused her. 'Yes – I've seen it.'

'And to whom does the paragon belong?'

And here indeed she confounded him. 'To me – I hope,' she declared.

He pushed his chair back with an articulate murmur. 'To you – ?'

'To *us*,' she corrected.

'Good Lord!' he said. If there had been the least hint of hallucination in her transparent gaze – but no; it was as clear, as shallow, as easily fathomable as when he had first suffered the sharp surprise of striking bottom in it.

It occurred to him that perhaps she was trying to be funny: he knew that there is nothing more cryptic than the humor of the unhumorous.

'Is it a joke?' he faltered.

'Oh, I hope not. I want it so much to be a reality—'

He paused to smile at the limitations of a world in which jokes were not realities, and continued gently: 'But since it is one already—'

'To us, I mean: to you and me. I want—' her voice wavered, and her eyes with it. 'I have always wanted so dreadfully . . . it has been such a disappointment . . . not to . . .'

'I see,' said Lethbury slowly.

But he had not seen before. It seemed curious now that he had never thought of her taking it in that way, had never surmised any hidden depths beneath her outspread obviousness. He felt as though he had touched a secret spring in her mind.

There was a moment's silence, moist and tremulous on her part, awkward and slightly irritated on his.

'You've been lonely, I suppose?' he began. It was odd, having suddenly to reckon with the stranger who gazed at him out of her trivial eyes.

'At times,' she said.

'I'm sorry.'

'It was not your fault. A man has so many occupations; and women who are clever – or very handsome – I suppose that's an occupation too. Sometimes I've felt that when dinner was ordered I had nothing to do till the next day.'

'Oh,' he groaned.

'It wasn't your fault,' she insisted. 'I never told you – but when I chose that rosebud paper for the front room upstairs, I always thought—'

'Well – ?'

'It would be such a pretty paper – for a baby – to wake up in. That was years ago, of course; but it was rather an expensive paper . . . and it hasn't faded in the least . . .' she broke off incoherently.

'It hasn't faded?'

'No – and so I thought . . . as we don't use the room for anything . . . now that Aunt Sophronia is dead . . . I thought I might . . . you might . . . oh, Julian, if you could only have seen it just waking up in its crib!'

'Seen what – where? You haven't got a baby upstairs?'

'Oh, no – not *yet*,' she said, with her rare laugh – the girlish bubbling of merriment that had seemed one of her chief graces in the early days. It occurred to him that he had not given her enough things to laugh about lately. But then she needed such very elementary things: she was as difficult to amuse as a savage. He concluded that he was not sufficiently simple.

'Alice,' he said almost solemnly, 'what *do* you mean?'

She hesitated a moment: he saw her gather her courage for a supreme effort. Then she said slowly, gravely, as though she were pronouncing a sacramental phrase:

'I'm so lonely without a little child – and I thought perhaps you'd let me adopt one. . . . It's at the hospital . . . its mother is

dead . . . and I could . . . pet it, and dress it, and do things for
it . . . and it's such a good baby . . . you can ask any of the
nurses . . . it would never, *never* bother you by crying. . . .'

2

Lethbury accompanied his wife to the hospital in a mood of
chastened wonder. It did not occur to him to oppose her wish.
He knew, of course, that he would have to bear the brunt of the
situation: the jokes at the club, the inquiries, the explanations.
He saw himself in the comic role of the adopted father and
welcomed it as an expiation. For in his rapid reconstruction of
the past he found himself cutting a shabbier figure than he cared
to admit. He had always been intolerant of stupid people, and it
was his punishment to be convicted of stupidity. As his mind
traversed the years between his marriage and this unexpected
assumption of paternity, he saw, in the light of an overheated
imagination, many signs of unwonted crassness. It was not that
he had ceased to think his wife stupid: she *was* stupid, limited,
inflexible; but there was a pathos in the struggles of her
swaddled mind, in its blind reachings toward the primal
emotions. He had always thought she would have been happier
with a child; but he had thought it mechanically, because it had
so often been thought before, because it was in the nature of
things to think it of every woman, because his wife was so
eminently one of a species that she fitted into all the generalizations of the sex. But he had regarded this generalization as
merely typical of the triumph of tradition over experience.
Maternity was no doubt the supreme function of primitive
woman, the one end to which her whole organism tended; but
the law of increasing complexity had operated in both sexes, and
he had not seriously supposed that, outside the world of
Christmas fiction and anecdotic art, such truisms had any special
hold on the feminine imagination. Now he saw that the arts in
question were kept alive by the vitality of the sentiments they
appealed to.

Lethbury was in fact going through a rapid process of readjustment. His marriage had been a failure, but he had preserved
toward his wife the exact fidelity of act that is sometimes supposed
to excuse any divagation of feeling; so that, for years, the tie

between them had consisted mainly in his abstaining from making love to other women. The abstention had not always been easy, for the world is surprisingly well stocked with the kind of woman one ought to have married but did not; and Lethbury had not escaped the solicitation of such alternatives. His immunity had been purchased at the cost of taking refuge in the somewhat rarefied atmosphere of his perceptions; and his world being thus limited, he had given unusual care to its details, compensating himself for the narrowness of his horizon by the minute finish of his foreground. It was a world of fine shadings and the nicest proportions, where impulse seldom set a blundering foot, and the feast of reason was undisturbed by an intemperate flow of soul. To such a banquet his wife naturally remained uninvited. The diet would have disagreed with her, and she would probably have objected to the other guests. But Lethbury, miscalculating her needs, had hitherto supposed that he had made ample provision for them, and was consequently at liberty to enjoy his own fare without any reproach of mendicancy at his gates. Now he beheld her pressing a starved face against the windows of his life, and in his imaginative reaction he invested her with a pathos borrowed from the sense of his own shortcomings.

In the hospital the imaginative process continued with increasing force. He looked at his wife with new eyes. Formerly she had been to him a mere bundle of negations, a labyrinth of dead walls and bolted doors. There was nothing behind the walls, and the doors led no whither: he had sounded and listened often enough to be sure of that. Now he felt like a traveller who, exploring some ancient ruin, comes on an inner cell, intact amid the general dilapidation, and painted with images which reveal the forgotten use of the building.

His wife stood by a white crib in one of the wards. In the crib lay a child, a year old, the nurse affirmed, but to Lethbury's eye a mere dateless fragment of humanity projected against a background of conjecture. Over this anonymous particle of life Mrs Lethbury leaned, such ecstasy reflected in her face as strikes up, in Correggio's 'Nightpiece,' from the child's body to the mother's countenance. It was a light that irradiated and dazzled her. She looked up at an inquiry of Lethbury's, but as their glances met he perceived that she no longer saw him, that he had become as invisible to her as she had long been to him. He had to transfer his question to the nurse.

'What is the child's name?' he asked.

'We call her Jane,' said the nurse.

3

Lethbury, at first, had resisted the idea of a legal adoption; but when he found that his wife could not be brought to regard the child as hers till it had been made so by process of law, he promptly withdrew his objection. On one point only he remained inflexible; and that was the changing of the waif's name. Mrs Lethbury, almost at once, had expressed a wish to rechristen it: she fluctuated between Muriel and Gladys, deferring the moment of decision like a lady wavering between two bonnets. But Lethbury was unyielding. In the general surrender of his prejudices this one alone held out.

'But Jane is so dreadful,' Mrs Lethbury protested.

'Well, we don't know that *she* won't be dreadful. She may grow up a Jane.'

His wife exclaimed reproachfully. 'The nurse says she's the loveliest—'

'Don't they always say that?' asked Lethbury patiently. He was prepared to be inexhaustibly patient now that he had reached a firm foothold of opposition.

'It's cruel to call her Jane,' Mrs Lethbury pleaded.

'It's ridiculous to call her Muriel.'

'The nurse is *sure* she must be a lady's child.'

Lethbury winced: he had tried, all along, to keep his mind off the question of antecedents.

'Well, let her prove it,' he said, with a rising sense of exasperation. He wondered how he could ever have allowed himself to be drawn into such a ridiculous business; for the first time he felt the full irony of it. He had visions of coming home in the afternoon to a house smelling of linseed and paregoric, and of being greeted by a chronic howl as he went upstairs to dress for dinner. He had never been a club man, but he saw himself becoming one now.

The worst of his anticipations were unfulfilled. The baby was surprisingly well and surprisingly quiet. Such infantile remedies as she absorbed were not potent enough to be perceived beyond the nursery; and when Lethbury could be induced to enter that sanctuary, there was nothing to jar his nerves in the mild pink presence of his adopted daughter. Jars there were, indeed: they were probably inevitable in the disturbed routine of the household; but they occurred between Mrs Lethbury and the nurses, and Jane contributed to them only a placid stare which might have served as a rebuke to the combatants.

In the reaction from his first impulse of atonement, Lethbury noted with sharpened perceptions the effect of the change of his wife's character. He saw already the error of supposing that it could work any transformation in her. It simply magnified her existing qualities. She was like a dried sponge put in water: she expanded, but she did not change her shape. From the standpoint of scientific observation it was curious to see how her stored instincts responded to the pseudo-maternal call. She overflowed with the petty maxims of the occasion. One felt in her the epitome, the consummation, of centuries of animal maternity, so that this little woman, who screamed at a mouse and was nervous about burglars, came to typify the cave mother rending her prey for her young.

It was less easy to regard philosophically the practical effects of her borrowed motherhood. Lethbury found with surprise that she was becoming assertive and definite. She no longer represented the negative side of his life; she showed, indeed, a tendency to inconvenient affirmations. She had gradually expanded her assumption of motherhood till it included his own share in the relation, and he suddenly found himself regarded as the father of Jane. This was a contingency he had not foreseen, and it took all his philosophy to accept it; but there were moments of compensation. For Mrs Lethbury was undoubtedly happy for the first time in years; and the thought that he had tardily contributed to this end reconciled him to the irony of the means.

At first he was inclined to reproach himself for still viewing the situation from the outside, for remaining a spectator instead of a participant. He had been allured, for a moment, by the vision of severed hands meeting over a cradle, as the whole body of domestic fiction bears witness to their doing; and the fact that no such conjunction took place he could explain only on the ground that it was a borrowed cradle. He did not dislike the little girl. She still remained to him a hypothetical presence, a query rather than a fact; but her nearness was not unpleasant, and there were moments when her tentative utterances, her groping steps, seemed to loosen the dry accretions enveloping his inner self. But even at such moments – moments which he invited and caressed – she did not bring him nearer to his wife. He now perceived that he had made a certain place in his life for Mrs Lethbury, and that she no longer fitted into it. It was too late to enlarge the space, and so she overflowed and encroached. Lethbury struggled against the sense of submergence. He let down barrier after barrier, yielding privacy after privacy; but his wife's personality continued to dilate. She was no longer herself alone: she was herself and Jane. Gradually, a monstrous fusion of identity, she became herself, himself and Jane; and instead of trying to adapt her to a spare crevice of his character, he found himself carelessly squeezed into the smallest compartment of the domestic economy.

4

He continued to tell himself that he was satisfied if his wife was happy; and it was not till the child's tenth year that he felt a doubt of her happiness.

Jane had been a preternaturally good child. During the eight years of her adoption she had caused her foster parents no anxiety beyond those connected with the usual succession of youthful diseases. But her unknown progenitors had given her a robust constitution, and she passed unperturbed through measles, chicken pox and whooping cough. If there was any suffering it was endured vicariously by Mrs Lethbury, whose temperature rose and fell with the patient's, and who could not hear Jane sneeze without visions of a marble angel weeping over a broken column. But though Jane's prompt recoveries contin- ued to belie such premonitions, though her existence continued to move forward on an even keel of good health and good conduct, Mrs Lethbury's satisfaction showed no corresponding advance. Lethbury, at first, was disposed to add her disappoint- ment to the long list of feminine inconsistencies with which the sententious observer of life builds up his favorable induction; but circumstances presently led him to take a kindlier view of the case.

Hitherto his wife had regarded him as a negligible factor in Jane's evolution. Beyond providing for his adopted daughter, and effacing himself before her, he was not expected to contribute to her well-being. But as time passed he appeared to his wife in a new light. It was he who was to educate Jane. In matters of the intellect, Mrs Lethbury was the first to declare her deficiencies – to proclaim them, even, with a certain virtuous superiority. She said she did not pretend to be clever, and there was no denying the truth of the assertion. Now, however, she seemed less ready, not to own her limitations, but to glory in them. Confronted with the problem of Jane's instruction she stood in awe of the child.

'I have always been stupid, you know,' she said to Lethbury with a new humility, 'and I'm afraid I shan't know what is best for Jane. I'm sure she has a wonderfully good mind, and I should reproach myself if I didn't give her every opportunity.' She looked at him helplessly. 'You must tell me what ought to be done.'

Lethbury was not unwilling to oblige her. Somewhere in his mental lumber room there rusted a theory of education such as usually lingers among the impedimenta of the childless. He brought this out, refurbished it, and applied it to Jane. At first he thought his wife had not overrated the quality of the child's mind. Jane seemed extraordinarily intelligent. Her precocious definiteness of mind was encouraging to her inexperienced preceptor. She had no difficulty in fixing her attention, and he felt that every fact he imparted was being etched in metal. He helped his wife to engage the best teachers, and for a while continued to take an ex-official interest in his adopted daughter's studies. But gradually his interest waned. Jane's ideas did not increase with her acquisitions. Her young mind remained a mere receptacle for facts: a kind of cold storage from which anything which had been put there could be taken out at a moment's notice, intact but congealed. She developed, moreover, an inordinate pride in the capacity of her mental storehouse, and a tendency to pelt her public with its contents. She was overheard to jeer at her nurse for not knowing when the Saxon Heptarchy had fallen, and she alternately dazzled and depressed Mrs Lethbury by the wealth of her chronological allusions. She showed no interest in the significance of the facts she amassed: she simply collected dates as another child might have collected stamps or marbles. To her foster mother she seemed a prodigy of wisdom; but Lethbury saw, with a secret movement of sympathy, how the aptitudes in which Mrs Lethbury gloried were slowly estranging her from her child.

'She is getting too clever for me,' his wife said to him, after one of Jane's historical flights, 'but I am so glad that she will be a companion to you.'

Lethbury groaned in spirit. He did not look forward to Jane's companionship. She was still a good little girl: but there was something automatic and formal in her goodness, as though it were a kind of moral callisthenics which she went through for the sake of showing her agility. An early consciousness of virtue had moreover constituted her the natural guardian and adviser of her elders. Before she was fifteen she had set about reforming the household. She took Mrs Lethbury in hand first; then she extended her efforts to the servants, with consequences more disastrous to the domestic harmony; and lastly she applied herself to Lethbury. She proved to him by statistics that he smoked too much, and that it was injurious to the optic nerve to read in bed. She took him to task for not going to church more regularly, and pointed out to him the evils of desultory reading. She suggested that a regular course of study encourages mental concentration, and hinted that inconsecutiveness of thought is a sign of approaching age.

To her adopted mother her suggestions were equally pertinent. She instructed Mrs Lethbury in an improved way of making beef stock, and called her attention to the unhygienic qualities of carpets. She poured out distracting facts about bacilli and vegetable mold, and demonstrated that curtains and picture frames are a hotbed of animal organisms. She learned by heart the nutritive ingredients of the principal articles of diet, and revolutionized the cuisine by an attempt to establish a scientific average between starch and phosphates. Four cooks left during this experiment, and Lethbury fell into the habit of dining at the club.

Once or twice, at the outset, he had tried to check Jane's ardor; but his efforts resulted only in hurting his wife's feelings. Jane remained impervious, and Mrs Lethbury resented any attempt to protect her from her daughter. Lethbury saw that she was

consoled for the sense of her own inferiority by the thought of
what Jane's intellectual companionship must be to him; and he
tried to keep up the illusion by enduring with what grace he
might the blighting edification of Jane's discourse.

5

As Jane grew up he sometimes avenged himself by wondering if
his wife was still sorry that they had not called her Muriel. Jane
was not ugly; she developed, indeed, a kind of categorical
prettiness which might have been a projection of her mind. She
had a creditable collection of features, but one had to take an
inventory of them to find out that she was good-looking. The
fusing grace had been omitted.

Mrs Lethbury took a touching pride in her daughter's first steps
in the world. She expected Jane to take by her complexion those
whom she did not capture by her learning. But Jane's rosy
freshness did not work any perceptible ravages. Whether the
young men guessed the axioms on her lips and detected the
encyclopedia in her eyes, or whether they simply found no
intrinsic interest in these features, certain it is, that, in spite of
her mother's heroic efforts, and of incessant calls on Lethbury's
purse, Jane, at the end of her first season, had dropped hopelessly
out of the running. A few duller girls found her interesting, and
one or two young men came to the house with the object of
meeting other young women; but she was rapidly becoming one
of the social supernumeraries who are asked out only because
they are on people's lists.

The blow was bitter to Mrs Lethbury; but she consoled herself
with the idea that Jane had failed because she was too clever. Jane
probably shared this conviction; at all events she betrayed no
consciousness of failure. She had developed a pronounced taste
for society, and went out, unweariedly and obstinately, winter
after winter, while Mrs Lethbury toiled in her wake, showering
attentions on oblivious hostesses. To Lethbury there was something at once tragic and exasperating in the sight of their two
figures, the one conciliatory, the other dogged, both pursuing
with unabated zeal the elusive prize of popularity. He even began
to feel a personal stake in the pursuit, not as it concerned Jane but
as it affected his wife. He saw that the latter was the victim of

Jane's disappointment: that Jane was not above the crude satisfaction of 'taking it out' of her mother. Experience checked the impulse to come to his wife's defense; and when his resentment was at its height, Jane disarmed him by giving up the struggle.

Nothing was said to mark her capitulation; but Lethbury noticed that the visiting ceased and that the dressmaker's bills diminished. At the same time Mrs Lethbury made it known that Jane had taken up charities; and before long Jane's conversation confirmed this announcement. At first Lethbury congratulated himself on the change; but Jane's domesticity soon began to weigh on him. During the day she was sometimes absent on errands of mercy; but in the evening she was always there. At first she and Mrs Lethbury sat in the drawing-room together, and Lethbury smoked in the library; but presently Jane formed the habit of joining him there, and he began to suspect that he was included among the objects of her philanthropy.

Mrs Lethbury confirmed the suspicion. 'Jane has grown very serious-minded lately,' she said. 'She imagines that she used to neglect you and she is trying to make up for it. Don't discourage her,' she added innocently.

Such a plea delivered Lethbury helpless to his daughter's ministrations; and he found himself measuring the hours he spent with her by the amount of relief they must be affording her mother. There were even moments when he read a furtive gratitude in Mrs Lethbury's eye.

But Lethbury was no hero, and he had nearly reached the limit of vicarious endurance when something wonderful happened. They never quite knew afterward how it had come about, or who first perceived it; but Mrs Lethbury one day gave tremulous voice to their discovery.

'Of course,' she said, 'he comes here because of Elise.' The young lady in question, a friend of Jane's, was possessed of attractions which had already been found to explain the presence of masculine visitors.

Lethbury risked a denial. 'I don't think he does,' he declared.

'But Elise is thought very pretty,' Mrs Lethbury insisted.

'I can't help that,' said Lethbury doggedly.

He saw a faint light in his wife's eyes; but she remarked carelessly, 'Mr Budd would be a very good match for Elise.'

Lethbury could hardly repress a chuckle: he was so exquisitely aware that she was trying to propitiate the gods.

For a few weeks neither said a word; then Mrs Lethbury once more reverted to the subject.

'It is a month since Elise went abroad,' she said.

'Is it?'

'And Mr Budd seems to come here just as often—'

'Ah,' said Lethbury with heroic indifference; and his wife hastily changed the subject.

Mr Winstanley Budd was a young man who suffered from an excess of manner. Politeness gushed from him in the driest seasons. He was always performing feats of drawing-room chivalry, and the approach of the most unobtrusive female threw him into attitudes which endangered the furniture. His features, being of the cherubic order, did not lend themselves to this role; but there were moments when he appeared to dominate them, to force them into compliance with an aquiline ideal. The range of Mr Budd's social benevolence made its object hard to distinguish. He spread his cloak so indiscriminately that one could not always interpret the gesture, and Jane's impassive manner had the effect of increasing his demonstrations: she threw him into paroxysms of politeness.

At first he filled the house with his amenities; but gradually it became apparent that his most dazzling effects were directed exclusively to Jane. Lethbury and his wife held their breath and looked away from each other. They pretended not to notice the frequency of Mr Budd's visits, they struggled against an imprudent inclination to leave the young people too much alone. Their conclusions were the result of indirect observation, for neither of them dared to be caught watching Mr Budd: they behaved like naturalists on the trail of a rare butterfly.

In his efforts not to notice Mr Budd, Lethbury centered his attentions on Jane; and Jane, at this crucial moment, wrung from him a reluctant admiration. While her parents went about dissembling their emotions, she seemed to have none to conceal. She betrayed neither eagerness nor surprise; so complete was her unconcern that there were moments when Lethbury feared it was obtuseness, when he could hardly help whispering to her that now was the moment to lower the net.

Meanwhile the velocity of Mr Budd's gyrations increased with the ardor of courtship; his politeness became incandescent, and Jane found herself the center of a pyrotechnical display culminating in the 'set piece' of an offer of marriage.

Mrs Lethbury imparted the news to her husband one evening after their daughter had gone to bed. The announcement was made and received with an air of detachment, as though both feared to be betrayed into unseemly exultation; but Lethbury, as his wife ended, could not repress the inquiry, 'Have they decided on a day?'

Mrs Lethbury's superior command of her features enabled her to look shocked. 'What can you be thinking of? He only offered himself at five!'

'Of course – of course – ' stammered Lethbury ' – but nowadays people marry after such short engagements—'

'Engagement!' said his wife solemnly. 'There is no engagement.'

Lethbury dropped his cigar. 'What on earth do you mean?'

'Jane is thinking it over.'

'*Thinking it over?*'

'She has asked for a month before deciding.'

Lethbury sank back with a gasp. Was it genius or was it madness? He felt incompetent to decide; and Mrs Lethbury's next words showed that she shared his difficulty.

'Of course I don't want to hurry Jane—'

'Of course not,' he acquiesced.

'But I pointed out to her that a young man of Mr Budd's impulsive temperament might – might be easily discouraged—'

'Yes; and what did she say?'

'She said that if she was worth winning she was worth waiting for.'

6

The period of Mr Budd's probation could scarcely have cost him as much mental anguish as it caused his would-be parents-in-law.

Mrs Lethbury, by various ruses, tried to shorten the ordeal, but Jane remained inexorable; and each morning Lethbury came down to breakfast with the certainty of finding a letter of withdrawal from her discouraged suitor.

When at length the decisive day came, and Mrs Lethbury, at its close, stole into the library with an air of chastened joy, they stood for a moment without speaking; then Mrs Lethbury paid a fitting tribute to the proprieties by faltering out: 'It will be dreadful to have to give her up—'

Lethbury could not repress a warning gesture; but even as it escaped him he realized that his wife's grief was genuine.

'Of course, of course,' he said, vainly sounding his own emotional shallows for an answering regret. And yet it was his wife who had suffered most from Jane!

He had fancied that these sufferings would be effaced by the milder atmosphere of their last weeks together; but felicity did not soften Jane. Not for a moment did she relax her dominion; she simply widened it to include a new subject. Mr Budd found himself under orders with the others; and a new fear assailed Lethbury as he saw Jane assume prenuptial control of her betrothed. Lethbury had never felt any strong personal interest in Mr Budd; but as Jane's prospective husband the young man excited his sympathy. To his surprise he found that Mrs Lethbury shared the feeling.

'I'm afraid he may find Jane a little exacting,' she said, after an evening dedicated to a stormy discussion of the wedding arrangements. 'She really ought to make some concessions. If he *wants* to be married in a black frock coat instead of a dark gray one – ' She paused and looked doubtfully at Lethbury.

'What can I do about it?' he said.

'You might explain to him – tell him that Jane's isn't always—'

Lethbury made an impatient gesture. 'What are you afraid of? His finding her out or his not finding her out?'

Mrs Lethbury flushed. 'You put it so dreadfully!'

Her husband mused for a moment; then he said with an air of cheerful hypocrisy: 'After all, Budd is old enough to take care of himself.'

But the next day Mrs Lethbury surprised him. Late in the afternoon she entered the library, so breathless and inarticulate that he scented a catastrophe.

'I've done it!' she cried.

'Done what?'

'Told him.' She nodded toward the door. 'He's just gone. Jane is out, and I had a chance to talk to him alone.'

Lethbury pushed a chair forward and she sank into it.

'What did you tell him? That she is *not* always—'

Mrs Lethbury lifted a tragic eye. 'No; I told him that she always *is*—'

'Always *is*—'

'Yes.'

There was a pause. Lethbury made a call on his hoarded philosophy. He saw Jane suddenly reinstated in her evening seat by the library fire; but an answering chord in him thrilled at his wife's heroism.

'Well – what did he say?'

Mrs Lethbury's agitation deepened. It was clear that the blow had fallen.

'He . . . he said . . . that we . . . had never understood Jane . . . or appreciated her . . .' The final syllables were lost in her handkerchief, and she left him marvelling at the mechanism of woman.

After that, Lethbury faced the future with an undaunted eye. They had done their duty – at least his wife had done hers – and they were reaping the usual harvest of ingratitude with zest seldom accorded to such reaping. There was a marked change in Mr Budd's manner, and his increasing coldness sent a genial glow through Lethbury's system. It was easy to bear with Jane in the light of Mr Budd's disapproval.

There was a good deal to be borne in the last days, and the brunt of it fell on Mrs Lethbury. Jane marked her transition to the married state by a seasonable but incongruous display of nerves. She became sentimental, hysterical and reluctant. She quarrelled with her betrothed and threatened to return the ring. Mrs Lethbury had to intervene, and Lethbury felt the hovering sword of destiny. But the blow was suspended. Mr Budd's chivalry was proof against all his bride's caprices and his devotion throve on her cruelty. Lethbury feared that he was too faithful, too enduring, and longed to urge him to vary his tactics. Jane presently reappeared with the ring on her finger, and consented to try on the wedding dress; but her uncertainties, her reactions, were prolonged till the final day.

When it dawned, Lethbury was still in an ecstasy of apprehension. Feeling reasonably sure of the principal actors he had centered his fears on incidental possibilities. The clergyman might have a stroke, or the church might burn down, or there might be something wrong with the license. He did all that was humanly possible to avert such contingencies, but there remained that incalculable factor known as the hand of God. Lethbury seemed to feel it groping for him.

At the altar it almost had him by the nape. Mr Budd was late; and for five immeasurable minutes Lethbury and Jane faced a churchful of conjecture. Then the bridegroom appeared, flushed but chivalrous, and explaining to his father-in-law under cover of the ritual that he had torn his glove and had to go back for another.

'You'll be losing the ring next,' muttered Lethbury; but Mr Budd produced this article punctually, and a moment or two later was bearing its wearer captive down the aisle.

At the wedding breakfast Lethbury caught his wife's eye fixed on him in mild disapproval, and understood that his hilarity was exceeding the bounds of fitness. He pulled himself together and tried to subdue his tone; but his jubilation bubbled over like a champagne glass perpetually refilled. The deeper his draughts the higher it rose.

It was at the brim when, in the wake of the dispersing guests, Jane came down in her travelling dress and fell on her mother's neck.

'I can't leave you!' she wailed, and Lethbury felt as suddenly sobered as a man under a shower. But if the bride was reluctant her captor was relentless. Never had Mr Budd been more dominant, more aquiline. Lethbury's last fears were dissipated as the young man snatched Jane from her mother's bosom and bore her off to the brougham.

The brougham rolled away, the last milliner's girl forsook her post by the awning, the red carpet was folded up, and the house door closed. Lethbury stood alone in the hall with his wife. As he turned toward her, he noticed the look of tired heroism in her eyes, the deepened lines of her face. They reflected his own symptoms too accurately not to appeal to him. The nervous tension had been horrible. He went up to her, and an answering impulse made her lay a hand on his arm. He held it there a moment.

'Let us go off and have a jolly little dinner at a restaurant,' he proposed.

There had been a time when such a suggestion would have surprised her to the verge of disapproval; but now she agreed to it at once.

'Oh, that would be so nice,' she murmured with a great sigh of relief and assuagement.

Jane had fulfilled her mission after all: she had drawn them together at last.

The Reckoning

'The marriage law of the new dispensation will be: *Thou shalt not be unfaithful – to thyself.*'

A discreet murmur of approval filled the studio, and through the haze of cigarette smoke Mrs Clement Westall, as her husband descended from his improvised platform, saw him merged in a congratulatory group of ladies. Westall's informal talks on 'The New Ethics' had drawn about him an eager following of the mentally unemployed – those who, as he had once phrased it, liked to have their brain food cut up for them. The talks had begun by accident. Westall's ideas were known to be 'advanced,' but hitherto their advance had not been in the direction of publicity. He had been, in his wife's opinion, almost pusillanimously careful not to let his personal views endanger his professional standing. Of late, however, he had shown a puzzling tendency to dogmatize, to throw down the gauntlet, to flaunt his private code in the face of society; and the relation of the sexes being a topic always sure of an audience, a few admiring friends had persuaded him to give his after-dinner opinions a larger circulation by summing them up in a series of talks at the Van Sideren studio.

The Herbert Van Siderens were a couple who subsisted, socially, on the fact that they had a studio. Van Sideren's pictures were chiefly valuable as accessories to the *mise en scène* which differentiated his wife's 'afternoons' from the blighting functions held in long New York drawing-rooms, and permitted her to offer their friends whiskey and soda instead of tea. Mrs Van Sideren, for her part, was skilled in making the most of the kind of atmosphere which a lay figure and an easel create; and if at times she found the illusion hard to maintain, and lost courage to the extent of almost wishing that Herbert could paint, she promptly overcame such moments of weakness by calling in some fresh talent, some extraneous re-enforcement of the 'artistic' impression. It was in quest of such aid that she had seized on Westall, coaxing him, somewhat to his wife's surprise, into a flattered participation in her fraud. It was vaguely felt, in the Van Sideren circle, that all the audacities were artistic, and that a teacher who pronounced marriage immoral was somehow as distinguished as a painter who depicted purple grass and a green sky. The Van Sideren set were tired of the conventional color scheme in art and conduct.

Julia Westall had long had her own views on the immorality of marriage; she might indeed have claimed her husband as a disciple. In the early days of their union she had secretly resented his disinclination to proclaim himself a follower of the new creed; had been inclined to tax him with moral cowardice, with a failure to live up to the convictions for which their marriage was supposed to stand. That was in the first burst of propagandism, when, womanlike, she wanted to turn her disobedience into a law. Now she felt differently. She could hardly account for the change, yet being a woman who never allowed her impulses to remain unaccounted for, she tried to do so by saying that she did not care to have the articles of her faith misinterpreted by the vulgar. In this connection, she was beginning to think that almost everyone was vulgar; certainly there were few to whom she would have cared to intrust the defence of so esoteric a doctrine. And it was precisely at this point that Westall, discarding his unspoken principles, had chosen to descend from the heights of privacy, and stand hawking his convictions at the street corner!

It was Una Van Sideren who, on this occasion, unconsciously focused upon herself Mrs Westall's wandering resentment. In the first place, the girl had no business to be there. It was 'horrid' – Mrs Westall found herself slipping back into the old feminine vocabulary – simply 'horrid' to think of a young girl's being allowed to listen to such talk. The fact that Una smoked cigarettes and sipped an occasional cocktail did not in the least tarnish a certain radiant innocency which made her appear the victim, rather than the accomplice, of her parents' vulgarities. Julia Westall felt in a hot helpless way that something ought to be done – that someone ought to speak to the girl's mother. And just then Una glided up.

'Oh, Mrs Westall, how beautiful it was!' Una fixed her with large limpid eyes. 'You believe it all, I suppose?' she asked with seraphic gravity.

'All – what, my dear child?'

The girl shone on her. 'About the higher life – the freer expansion of the individual – the law of fidelity to one's self,' she glibly recited.

Mrs Westall, to her own wonder, blushed a deep and burning blush.

'My dear Una,' she said, 'you don't in the least understand what it's all about!'

Miss Van Sideren stared, with a slowly answering blush! 'Don't *you*, then?' she murmured.

Mrs Westall laughed. 'Not always – or altogether! But I should like some tea, please.'

Una led her to the corner where innocent beverages were dispensed. As Julia received her cup she scrutinized the girl more carefully. It was not such a girlish face, after all – definite lines were forming under the rosy haze of youth. She reflected that Una must be six-and-twenty, and wondered why she had not married. A nice stock of ideas she would have as her dowry! If *they* were to be a part of the modern girl's trousseau—

Mrs Westall caught herself up with a start. It was as though someone else had been speaking – a stranger who had borrowed her own voice: she felt herself the dupe of some fantastic mental ventriloquism. Concluding suddenly that the room was stifling and Una's tea too sweet, she set down her cup and looked about for Westall: to meet his eyes had long been her refuge from every uncertainty. She met them now, but only, as she felt, in transit; they included her parenthetically in a larger flight. She followed the flight, and it carried her to a corner to which Una had withdrawn – one of the palmy nooks to which Mrs Van Sideren attributed the success of her Saturdays. Westall, a moment later, had overtaken his look, and found a place at the girl's side. She bent forward, speaking eagerly; he leaned back, listening, with the depreciatory smile which acted as a filter to flattery, enabling him to swallow the strongest doses without apparent grossness of appetite. Julia winced at her own definition of the smile.

On the way home, in the deserted winter dusk, Westall surprised his wife by a sudden boyish pressure of her arm. 'Did I open their eyes a bit? Did I tell them what you wanted me to?' he asked gaily.

Almost unconsciously, she let her arm slip from his. 'What *I* wanted – ?'

'Why, haven't you – all this time?' She caught the honest wonder of his tone. 'I somehow fancied you'd rather blamed me for not talking more openly before. You almost made me feel, at times, that I was sacrificing principles to expediency.'

She paused a moment over her reply; then she asked quietly: 'What made you decide not to – any longer?'

She felt again the vibration of a faint surprise. 'Why – the wish to please you!' he answered, almost too simply.

'I wish you would not go on, then,' she said abruptly.

He stopped in his quick walk, and she felt his stare through the darkness.

'Not go on – ?'

'Call a hansom, please. I'm tired,' broke from her with a sudden rush of physical weariness.

Instantly his solicitude enveloped her. The room had been infernally hot – and then that confounded cigarette smoke – he had noticed once or twice that she looked pale – she mustn't come to another Saturday. She felt herself yielding, as she always did, to the warm influence of his concern for her, the feminine in her leaning on the man in him with a conscious intensity of abandonment. He put her in the hansom, and her hand stole into his in the darkness. A tear or two rose, and she let them fall. It was so delicious to cry over imaginary troubles!

That evening, after dinner, he surprised her by reverting to the subject of his talk. He combined a man's dislike of uncomfortable questions with an almost feminine skill in eluding them; and she knew that if he returned to the subject he must have some special reason for doing so.

'You seem not to have cared for what I said this afternoon. Did I put the case badly?'

'No – you put it very well.'

'Then what did you mean by saying that you would rather not have me go on with it?'

She glanced at him nervously, her ignorance of his intention deepening her sense of helplessness.

'I don't think I care to hear such things discussed in public.'

'I don't understand you,' he exclaimed. Again the feeling that his surprise was genuine gave an air of obliquity to her own attitude. She was not sure that she understood herself.

'Won't you explain?' he said with a tingle of impatience.

Her eyes wandered about the familiar drawing-room which had been the scene of so many of their evening confidences. The shaded lamps, the quiet-colored walls hung with mezzotints, the pale spring flowers scattered here and there in Venice glasses and bowls of old Sèvres, recalled she hardly knew why, the apartment in which the evenings of her first marriage had been passed – a wilderness of rosewood and upholstery, with a picture of a Roman peasant above the mantelpiece, and a Greek slave in statuary marble between the folding doors of the back drawing-room. It was a room with which she had never been able to establish any closer relation than that between a traveller and a railway station; and now, as she looked about at the surroundings which stood for her deepest affinities – the room for which she had left that other room – she was startled by the same sense of strangeness and unfamiliarity. The prints, the flowers, the subdued tones of the old porcelains, seemed to typify a superficial refinement which had no relation to the deeper significances of life.

Suddenly she heard her husband repeating his question.

'I don't know that I can explain,' she faltered.

He drew his armchair forward so that he faced her across the hearth. The light of a reading lamp fell on his finely drawn face, which had a kind of surface sensitiveness akin to the surface refinement of its setting.

'Is it that you no longer believe in our ideas?' he asked.

'In our ideas – ?'

'The ideas I am trying to teach. The ideas you and I are supposed to stand for.' He paused a moment. 'The ideas on which our marriage was founded.'

The blood rushed to her face. He had his reasons, then – she was sure now that he had his reasons! In the ten years of their marriage, how often had either of them stopped to consider the ideas on which it was founded? How often does a man dig about the basement of his house to examine its foundation? The foundation is there, of course – the house rests on it – but one lives abovestairs and not in the cellar. It was she, indeed, who in the beginning had insisted on reviewing the situation now and then, on recapitulating the reasons which justified her course, on proclaiming, from time to time, her adherence to the religion of personal independence; but she had long ceased to feel the want of any such ideal standards, and had accepted her marriage as frankly and naturally as though it had been based on the primitive needs of the heart, and required no special sanction to explain or justify it.

'Of course I still believe in our ideas!' she exclaimed.

'Then I repeat that I don't understand. It was a part of your theory that the greatest possible publicity should be given to our view of marriage. Have you changed your mind in that respect?'

She hesitated. 'It depends on circumstances – on the public one is addressing. The set of people that the Van Siderens get about them don't care for the truth or falseness of a doctrine. They are attracted simply by its novelty.'

'And yet it was in just such a set of people that you and I met, and learned the truth from each other.'

'That was different.'

'In what way?'

'I was not a young girl, to begin with. It is perfectly unfitting that young girls should be present at – at such times – should hear such things discussed—'

'I thought you considered it one of the deepest social wrongs that such things never *are* discussed before young girls; but that is beside the point, for I don't remember seeing any young girl in my audience today—'

'Except Una Van Sideren!'

He turned slightly and pushed back the lamp at his elbow.

'Oh, Miss Van Sideren – naturally—'

'Why naturally?'

'The daughter of the house – would you have had her sent out with her governess?'

'If I had a daughter I should not allow such things to go on in my house!'

Westall, stroking his mustache, leaned back with a faint smile. 'I fancy Miss Van Sideren is quite capable of taking care of herself.'

'No girl knows how to take care of herself – till it's too late.'

'And yet you would deliberately deny her the surest means of self-defence?'

'What do you call the surest means of self-defence?'

'Some preliminary knowledge of human nature in its relation to the marriage tie.'

She made an impatient gesture. 'How should you like to marry that kind of a girl?'

'Immensely – if she were my kind of girl in other respects.'

She took up the argument at another point.

'You are quite mistaken if you think such talk does not affect young girls. Una was in a state of the most absurd exaltation—' She broke off, wondering why she had spoken.

Westall reopened a magazine which he had laid aside at the beginning of their discussion. 'What you tell me is immensely flattering to my oratorical talent – but I fear you overrate its effect. I can assure you that Miss Van Sideren doesn't have to have her thinking done for her. She's quite capable of doing it herself.'

'You seem very familiar with her mental processes!' flashed unguardedly from his wife.

He looked up quietly from the pages he was cutting.

'I should like to be,' he answered. 'She interests me.'

2

If there be a distinction in being misunderstood, it was one denied to Julia Westall when she left her first husband. Everyone was ready to excuse and even to defend her. The world she adorned agreed that John Arment was 'impossible,' and hostesses gave a sigh of relief at the thought that it would no longer be necessary to ask him to dine.

There had been no scandal connected with the divorce: neither side had accused the other of the offence euphemistically described as 'statutory.' The Arments had indeed been obliged to transfer their allegiance to a state which recognized desertion as a cause for divorce, and construed the term so liberally that the seeds of desertion were shown to exist in every union. Even Mrs Arment's second marriage did not make traditional morality stir in its sleep. It was known that she had not met her second husband till after she had parted from the first, and she had, moreover, replaced a rich man by a poor one. Though Clement Westall was acknowledged to be a rising lawyer, it was generally felt that his fortunes would not rise as rapidly as his reputation. The Westalls would probably always have to live quietly and go out to dinner in cabs. Could there be better evidence of Mrs Arment's complete disinterestedness?

If the reasoning by which her friends justified her course was somewhat cruder and less complex than her own elucidation of the matter, both explanations led to the same conclusion: John Arment was impossible. The only difference was that, to his wife, his impossibility was something deeper than a social disqualification. She had once said, in ironical defence of her marriage, that it had at least preserved her from the necessity of sitting next to him at dinner; but she had not then realized at what cost the immunity was purchased. John Arment was impossible; but the sting of his impossibility lay in the fact that he made it impossible for those about him to be other than himself. By an unconscious process of elimination he had excluded from the world everything of which he did not feel a personal need: had become, as it were, a climate in which only his own requirements survived. This might seem to imply a deliberate selfishness; but there was nothing deliberate about Arment. He was as instinctive as an animal or a child. It was this childish element in his nature which sometimes for a moment unsettled his wife's estimate of him. Was it possible that he was simply undeveloped, that he had delayed, somewhat longer than is usual, the laborious process of growing up? He had the kind of sporadic shrewdness which causes it to be said of a dull man that he is 'no fool'; and it was this quality that his wife found most trying. Even to the naturalist it is annoying to have his deductions disturbed by some unforeseen aberrancy of form or function; and how much more so to the wife whose estimate of herself is inevitably bound up with her judgment of her husband!

Arment's shrewdness did not, indeed, imply any latent intellectual power; it suggested, rather, potentialities of feeling, of suffering, perhaps, in a blind rudimentary way, on which Julia's sensibilities naturally declined to linger. She so fully understood her own reasons for leaving him that she disliked to think they were not as comprehensible to her husband. She was haunted, in her analytic moments, by the look of perplexity, too inarticulate for words, with which he had acquiesced in her explanations.

These moments were rare with her, however. Her marriage had been too concrete a misery to be surveyed philosophically. If she had been unhappy for complex reasons, the unhappiness was as real as though it had been uncomplicated. Soul is more bruisable than flesh, and Julia was wounded in every fiber of her spirit. Her husband's personality seemed to be closing gradually in on her, obscuring the sky and cutting off the air, till she felt herself shut up among the decaying bodies of her starved hopes. A sense of having been decoyed by some world-old conspiracy into this bondage of body and soul filled her with despair. If marriage was the slow lifelong acquittal of a debt contracted in ignorance, then marriage was a crime against human nature. She, for one, would have no share in maintaining the pretense of which she had been a victim: the pretense that a man and a woman, forced into the narrowest of personal relations, must remain there till the end, though they may have outgrown the span of each other's natures as the mature tree outgrows the iron brace about the sapling.

It was in the first heat of her moral indignation that she had met Clement Westall. She had seen at once that he was 'interested,' and had fought off the discovery, dreading any influence that should draw her back into the bondage of conventional relations. To ward off the peril she had, with an almost crude precipitancy, revealed her opinions to him. To her surprise, she found that he shared them. She was attracted by the frankness of a suitor who, while pressing his suit, admitted that he did not believe in marriage. Her worst audacities did not seem to surprise him: he had thought out all that she had felt, and they had reached the same conclusion. People grew at varying rates, and the yoke that was an easy fit for the one might soon become galling to the other. That was what divorce was for: the readjustment of personal relations. As soon as their necessarily transitive nature was recognized they would gain in dignity as well as in harmony. There would be no further need of the ignoble concessions and connivances, the perpetual sacrifice of personal delicacy and moral pride, by means of which imperfect marriages were now held together. Each partner to the contract would be on his mettle, forced to live up to the highest standard of self-development, on pain of losing the other's respect and affection. The low nature could no longer drag the higher down, but must struggle to rise, or remain alone on its inferior level. The only necessary condition to a harmonious marriage was a frank recognition of this truth, and a solemn agreement between the contracting parties to keep faith with themselves, and not to live together for a moment after complete accord had ceased to exist between them. The new adultery was unfaithfulness to self.

It was, as Westall had just reminded her, on this understanding that they had married. The ceremony was an unimportant concession to social prejudice: now that the door of divorce stood open, no marriage need be an imprisonment, and the contract therefore no longer involved any diminution of self-respect. The nature of their attachment placed them so far beyond the reach of such contingencies that it was easy to discuss them with an open mind; and Julia's sense of security made her dwell with a tender insistence on Westall's promise to claim his release when he should cease to love her. The exchange of these vows seemed to make them, in a sense, champions of the new law, pioneers in the forbidden realm of individual freedom: they felt that they had somehow achieved beatitude without martyrdom.

This, as Julia now reviewed the past, she perceived to have been her theoretical attitude toward marriage. It was unconsciously, insidiously, that her ten years of happiness with Westall had developed another conception of the tie; a reversion, rather, to the old instinct of passionate dependency and possessorship that now made her blood revolt at the mere hint of change. Change? Renewal? Was that what they had called it, in their foolish jargon? Destruction, extermination, rather – this rending of a myriad fibers interwoven with another's being! Another? But he was not other! He and she were one, one in the mystic sense which alone gave marriage its significance. The new law was not for them, but for the disunited creatures forced into a mockery of union. The gospel she had felt called on to proclaim had no bearing on her own case. . . . She sent for the doctor and told him she was sure she needed a nerve tonic.

She took the nerve tonic diligently, but it failed to act as a sedative to her fears. She did not know what she feared; but that made her anxiety the more pervasive. Her husband had not reverted to the subject of his Saturday talks. He was unusually kind and considerate, with a softening of his quick manner, a touch of shyness in his consideration, that sickened her with new fears. She told herself that it was because she looked badly – because he knew about the doctor and the nerve tonic – that he showed this deference to her wishes, this eagerness to screen her from moral drafts; but the explanation simply cleared the way for fresh inferences.

The week passed slowly, vacantly, like a prolonged Sunday. On Saturday the morning post brought a note from Mrs Van Sideren.

Would dear Julia ask Mr Westall to come half an hour earlier than usual, as there was to be some music after his 'talk'? Westall was just leaving for his office when his wife read the note. She opened the drawing-room door and called him back to deliver the message.

He glanced at the note and tossed it aside. 'What a bore! I shall have to cut my game of racquets. Well, I suppose it can't be helped. Will you write and say it's all right?'

Julia hesitated a moment, her hand stiffening on the chair back against which she leaned.

'You mean to go on with these talks?' she asked.

'I – why not?' he returned; and this time it struck her that his surprise was not quite unfeigned. The perception helped her to find words.

'You said you had started them with the idea of pleasing me—'

'Well?'

'I told you last week that they didn't please me.'

'Last week? – Oh—' He seemed to make an effort of memory. 'I thought you were nervous then; you sent for the doctor the next day.'

'It was not the doctor I needed; it was your assurance—'

'My assurance?'

Suddenly she felt the floor fail under her. She sank into the chair with a choking throat, her words, her reasons slipping away from her like straws down a whirling flood.

'Clement,' she cried, 'isn't it enough for you to know that I hate it?'

He turned to close the door behind them; then he walked toward her and sat down. 'What is it that you hate?' he asked gently.

She had made a desperate effort to rally her routed argument.

'I can't bear to have you speak as if – as if – our marriage – were like the other kind – the wrong kind. When I heard you there, the other afternoon, before all those inquisitive gossiping people, proclaiming that husbands and wives had a right to leave each other whenever they were tired – or had seen someone else—'

Westall sat motionless, his eyes fixed on a pattern of the carpet.

'You *have* ceased to take this view, then?' he said as she broke off. 'You no longer believe that husbands and wives *are* justified in separating – under such conditions?'

'Under such conditions?' she stammered. 'Yes – I still believe that – but how can we judge for others? What can we know of the circumstances—?'

He interrupted her. 'I thought it was a fundamental article of our creed that the special circumstances produced by marriage were not to interfere with the full assertion of individual liberty.' He paused a moment. 'I thought that was your reason for leaving Arment.'

She flushed to the forehead. It was not like him to give a personal turn to the argument.

'It was my reason,' she said simply.

'Well, then – why do you refuse to recognize its validity now?'

'I don't – I don't – I only say that one can't judge for others.'

He made an impatient movement. 'This is mere hairsplitting. What you mean is that, the doctrine having served your purpose when you needed it, you now repudiate it.'

'Well,' she exclaimed, flushing again, 'what if I do? What does it matter to us?'

Westall rose from his chair. He was excessively pale, and stood before his wife with something of the formality of a stranger.

'It matters to me,' he said in a low voice, 'because I do *not* repudiate it.'

'Well – ?'

'And because I had intended to invoke it as—'

He paused and drew his breath deeply. She sat silent, almost deafened by her heartbeats.

'—as a complete justification of the course I am about to take.'

Julia remained motionless. 'What course is that?' she asked.

He cleared his throat. 'I mean to claim the fulfilment of your promise.'

For an instant the room wavered and darkened; then she recovered a torturing acuteness of vision. Every detail of her surroundings pressed upon her: the tick of the clock, the slant of sunlight on the wall, the hardness of the chair arms that she grasped, were a separate wound to each sense.

'My promise—' she faltered.

'Your part of our mutual agreement to set each other free if one or the other should wish to be released.'

She was silent again. He waited a moment, shifting his position nervously; then he said, with a touch of irritability: 'You acknowledge the agreement?'

The question went through her like a shock. She lifted her head to it proudly. 'I acknowledge the agreement,' she said.

'And – you don't mean to repudiate it?'

A log on the hearth fell forward, and mechanically he advanced and pushed it back.

'No,' she answered slowly, 'I don't mean to repudiate it.'

There was a pause. He remained near the hearth, his elbow resting on the mantelshelf. Close to his hand stood a little cup of jade that he had given her on one of their wedding anniversaries. She wondered vaguely if he noticed it.

'You intend to leave me, then?' she said at length.

His gesture seemed to deprecate the crudeness of the allusion.

'To marry someone else?'

Again his eye and hand protested. She rose and stood before him.

'Why should you be afraid to tell me? Is it Una Van Sideren?'

He was silent.

'I wish you good luck,' she said.

3

She looked up, finding herself alone. She did not remember when or how he had left the room, or how long afterward she had sat there. The fire still smoldered on the hearth, but the slant of sunlight had left the wall.

Her first conscious thought was that she had not broken her word, that she had fulfilled the very letter of their bargain. There had been no crying out, no vain appeal to the past, no attempt at temporizing or evasion. She had marched straight up to the guns.

Now that it was over, she was sickened to find herself alive. She looked about her, trying to recover her hold on reality. Her identity seemed to be slipping from her, as it disappears in a physical swoon. 'This is my room – this is my house,' she heard herself saying. Her room? Her house? She could almost hear the walls laugh back at her.

She stood up, weariness in every bone. The silence of the room frightened her. She remembered, now, having heard the front door close a long time ago: the sound suddenly re-echoed through her brain. Her husband must have left the house, then – her *husband?* She no longer knew in what terms to think: the simplest phrases had a poisoned edge. She sank back into her chair, overcome by a strange weakness. The clock struck ten – it was only ten o'clock! Suddenly she remembered that she had not ordered dinner . . . or were they dining out that evening? *Dinner – dining out* – the old meaningless phraseology pursued her! She must try to think of herself as she would think of someone else, a someone dissociated from all the familiar routine of the past, whose wants and habits must gradually be learned, as one might spy out the ways of a strange animal. . . .

The clock struck another hour – eleven. She stood up again and walked to the door: she thought she would go upstairs to her room. *Her* room? Again the word derided her. She opened the door, crossed the narrow hall, and walked up the stairs. As she passed, she noticed Westall's sticks and umbrellas: a pair of his gloves lay on the hall table. The same stair carpet mounted between the same walls; the same old French print, in its narrow black frame, faced her on the landing. This visual continuity was intolerable. Within, a gaping chasm; without, the same un-troubled and familiar surface. She must get away from it before she could attempt to think. But, once in her room, she sat down on the lounge, a stupor creeping over her. . . .

Gradually her vision cleared. A great deal had happened in the interval – a wild marching and countermarching of emotions, arguments, ideas – a fury of insurgent impulses that fell back spent upon themselves. She had tried, at first, to rally, to organize these chaotic forces. There must be help somewhere, if only she could master the inner tumult. Life could not be broken off short like this, for a whim, a fancy; the law itself would side with her, would defend her. The law? What claim had she upon it? She was the prisoner of her own choice: she had been her own legislator, and she was the predestined victim of the code she had devised. But this was grotesque, intolerable – a mad mistake, for which she could not be held accountable! The law she had despised was still there, might still be invoked . . . invoked, but to what end? Could she ask it to chain Westall to her side? *She* had been allowed to go free when she claimed her freedom – should she show less magnanimity than she had exacted? Magnanimity? The word lashed her with its irony – one does not strike an attitude when one is fighting for life! She would threaten, grovel, cajole . . . she would yield anything to keep her hold on happiness. Ah, but the difficulty lay deeper! The law could not help her – her own apostasy could not help her. She was the victim of the theories she renounced. It was as though some giant machine of her own making had caught her up in its wheels and was grinding her to atoms. . . .

It was afternoon when she found herself out of doors. She walked with an aimless haste, fearing to meet familiar faces. The day was radiant, metallic: one of those searching American days so calculated to reveal the shortcomings of our street-cleaning and the excesses of our architecture. The streets looked bare and hideous; everything stared and glittered. She called a passing hansom, and gave Mrs Van Sideren's address. She did not know what had led up to the act; but she found herself suddenly resolved to speak, to cry out a warning. It was too late to save herself – but the girl might still be told. The hansom rattled up Fifth Avenue; she sat with her eyes fixed, avoiding recognition. At the Van Siderens' door she sprang out and rang the bell. Action had cleared her brain, and she felt calm and self-possessed. She knew now exactly what she meant to say.

The ladies were both out . . . the parlormaid stood waiting for a card. Julia, with a vague murmur, turned away from the door and lingered a moment on the sidewalk. Then she remembered that she had not paid the cab driver. She drew a dollar from her purse and handed it to him. He touched his hat and drove off, leaving her alone in the long empty street. She wandered away westward, toward strange thoroughfares, where she was not likely to meet acquaintances. The feeling of aimlessness had returned. Once she found herself in the afternoon torrent of Broadway, swept past tawdry shops and flaming theatrical posters, with a succession of meaningless faces gliding by in the opposite direction. . . .

A feeling of faintness reminded her that she had not eaten since morning. She turned into a side street of shabby houses, with rows of ash barrels behind bent area railings. In a basement window she saw the sign 'Ladies' Restaurant': a pie and a dish of doughnuts lay against the dusty pane like petrified food in an ethnological museum. She entered and a young woman with a weak mouth and a brazen eye cleared a table for her near the window. The table was covered with a red-and-white cotton

cloth and adorned with a bunch of celery in a thick tumbler and
a saltcellar full of grayish lumpy salt. Julia ordered tea, and sat a
long time waiting for it. She was glad to be away from the noise
and confusion of the streets. The low-ceilinged room was empty,
and two or three waitresses with thin pert faces lounged in the
background staring at her and whispering together. At last the
tea was brought in a discolored metal teapot. Julia poured a cup
and drank it hastily. It was black and bitter, but it flowed through
her veins like an elixir. She was almost dizzy with exhilaration.
Oh, how tired, how unutterably tired she had been!

She drank a second cup, blacker and bitterer, and now her
mind was once more working clearly. She felt as vigorous, as
decisive, as when she had stood on the Van Siderens' doorstep –
but the wish to return there had subsided. She saw now the
futility of such an attempt – the humiliation to which it might
have exposed her. . . . The pity of it was that she did not know
what to do next. The short winter day was fading, and she realized
that she could not remain much longer in the restaurant without
attracting notice. She paid for her tea and went out into the street.
The lamps were alight, and here and there a basement shop cast
an oblong of gaslight across the fissured pavement. In the dusk
there was something sinister about the aspect of the street, and
she hastened back toward Fifth Avenue. She was not used to
being out alone at that hour.

At the corner of Fifth Avenue she paused and stood watching
the stream of carriages. At last a policeman caught sight of her
and signed to her that he would take her across. She had not
meant to cross the street, but she obeyed automatically, and
presently found herself on the farther corner. There she paused
again for a moment; but she fancied the policeman was watching
her, and this sent her hastening down the nearest side street. . . .
After that she walked a long time, vaguely. . . . Night had fallen,
and now and then, through the windows of a passing carriage,
she caught the expanse of an evening waistcoat or the shimmer of
an opera cloak. . . .

Suddenly she found herself in a familiar street. She stood still a
moment, breathing quickly. She had turned the corner without
noticing whither it led; but now, a few yards ahead of her, she saw
the house in which she had once lived – her first husband's house.
The blinds were drawn, and only a faint translucence marked the

windows and the transom above the door. As she stood there she
heard a step behind her, and a man walked by in the direction of
the house. He walked slowly, with a heavy middle-aged gait, his
head sunk a little between the shoulders, the red crease of his neck
visible above the fur collar of his overcoat. He crossed the street,
went up the steps of the house, drew forth a latchkey, and let
himself in. . . .

There was no one else in sight. Julia leaned for a long time
against the area rail at the corner, her eyes fixed on the front of
the house. The feeling of physical weariness had returned, but the
strong tea still throbbed in her veins and lit her brain with an
unnatural clearness. Presently she heard another step draw near,
and moving quickly away, she too crossed the street and mounted
the steps of the house. The impulse which had carried her there
prolonged itself in a quick pressure of the electric bell – then she
felt suddenly weak and tremulous, and grasped the balustrade for
support. The door opened and a young footman with a fresh
inexperienced face stood on the threshold. Julia knew in an
instant that he would admit her.

'I saw Mr Arment going in just now,' she said. 'Will you ask
him to see me for a moment?'

The footman hesitated. 'I think Mr Arment has gone up to dress
for dinner, madam.'

Julia advanced into the hall. 'I am sure he will see me – I will
not detain him long,' she said. She spoke quietly, authoritatively,
in the tone which a good servant does not mistake. The footman
had his hand on the drawing-room door.

'I will tell him, madam. What name, please?'

Julia trembled: she had not thought of that. 'Merely say a lady,'
she returned carelessly.

The footman wavered and she fancied herself lost; but at that
instant the door opened from within and John Arment stepped
into the hall. He drew back sharply as he saw her, his florid face
turning sallow with the shock; then the blood poured back to it,
swelling the veins on his temples and reddening the lobes of his
thick ears.

It was long since Julia had seen him, and she was startled at
the change in his appearance. He had thickened, coarsened,
settled down into the enclosing flesh. But she noted this in-
sensibly: her one conscious thought was that, now she was face

to face with him, she must not let him escape till he had heard her. Every pulse in her body throbbed with the urgency of her message.

She went up to him as he drew back. 'I must speak to you,' she said.

Arment hesitated, red and stammering. Julia glanced at the footman, and her look acted as a warning. The instinctive shrinking from a scene predominated over every other impulse, and Arment said slowly: 'Will you come this way?'

He followed her into the drawing-room and closed the door. Julia, as she advanced, was vaguely aware that the room at least was unchanged: time had not mitigated its horrors. The contadina still lurched from the chimney breast, and the Greek slave obstructed the threshold of the inner room. The place was alive with memories: they started out from every fold of the yellow satin curtains and glided between the angles of the rosewood furniture. But while some subordinate agency was carrying these impressions to her brain, her whole conscious effort was centered in the act of dominating Arment's will. The fear that he would refuse to hear her mounted like fever to her brain. She felt her purpose melt before it, words and arguments running into each other in the heat of her longing. For a moment her voice failed her, and she imagined herself thrust out before she could speak; but as she was struggling for a word Arment pushed a chair forward, and said quietly: 'You are not well.'

The sound of his voice steadied her. It was neither kind nor unkind – a voice that suspended judgment, rather, awaiting unforeseen developments. She supported herself against the back of the chair and drew a deep breath.

'Shall I send for something?' he continued, with a cold embarrassed politeness.

Julia raised an entreating hand. 'No – no – thank you. I am quite well.'

He paused midway toward the bell, and turned on her. 'Then may I ask—?'

'Yes,' she interrupted him. 'I came here because I wanted to see you. There is something I must tell you.'

Arment continued to scrutinize her. 'I am surprised at that,' he said. 'I should have supposed that any communication you may wish to make could have been made through our lawyers.'

'Our lawyers!' She burst into a little laugh. 'I don't think they could help me – this time.'

Arment's face took on a barricaded look. 'If there is any question of help – of course—'

It struck her, whimsically, that she had seen that look when some shabby devil called with a subscription book. Perhaps he thought she wanted him to put his name down for so much in sympathy – or even in money. . . . The thought made her laugh again. She saw his look change slowly to perplexity. All his facial changes were slow, and she remembered, suddenly, how it had once diverted her to shift that lumbering scenery with a word. For the first time it struck her that she had been cruel. 'There *is* a question of help,' she said in a softer key; 'you can help me; but only by listening. . . . I want to tell you something. . . .'

Arment's resistance was not yielding. 'Would it not be easier to – write?' he suggested.

She shook her head. 'There is no time to write . . . and it won't take long.' She raised her head and their eyes met. 'My husband has left me,' she said.

'Westall – ?' he stammered, reddening again.

'Yes. This morning. Just as I left you. Because he was tired of me.'

The words, uttered scarcely above a whisper, seemed to dilate to the limit of the room. Arment looked toward the door; then his embarrassed glance returned to Julia.

'I am very sorry,' he said awkwardly.

'Thank you,' she murmured.

'But I don't see—'

'No – but you will – in a moment. Won't you listen to me? Please!' Instinctively she had shifted her position, putting herself between him and the door. 'It happened this morning,' she went on in short breathless phrases. 'I never suspected anything – I thought we were – perfectly happy. . . . Suddenly he told me he was tired of me . . . there is a girl he likes better. . . . He has gone to her. . . .' As she spoke, the lurking anguish rose upon her, possessing her once more to the exclusion of every other emotion. Her eyes ached, her throat swelled with it, and two painful tears ran down her face.

Arment's constraint was increasing visibly. 'This – this is very unfortunate,' he began. 'But I should say the law—'

'The law?' she echoed ironically. 'When he asks for his freedom?'

'You are not obliged to give it.'

'You were not obliged to give me mine – but you did.'

He made a protesting gesture.

'You saw that the law couldn't help you – didn't you?' she went on. 'That is what I see now. The law represents material rights – it can't go beyond. If we don't recognize an inner law . . . the obligation that love creates . . . being loved as well as loving . . . there is nothing to prevent our spreading ruin unhindered . . . is there?' She raised her head plaintively, with the look of a bewildered child. 'That is what I see now . . . what I wanted to tell you. He leaves me because he's tired . . . but *I* was not tired; and I don't understand why he is. That's the dreadful part of it – the not understanding: I hadn't realized what it meant. But I've been thinking of it all day, and things have come back to me – things I hadn't noticed . . . when you and I . . .' She moved closer to him, and fixed her eyes on his with the gaze which tries to reach beyond words. 'I see now that *you* didn't understand – did you?'

Their eyes met in a sudden shock of comprehension: a veil seemed to be lifted between them. Arment's lip trembled.

'No,' he said, 'I didn't understand.'

She gave a little cry, almost of triumph. 'I knew it! I knew it! You wondered – you tried to tell me – but no words came. . . . You saw your life falling in ruins . . . the world slipping from you . . . and you couldn't speak or move!'

She sank down on the chair against which she had been leaning. 'Now I know – now I know,' she repeated.

'I am very sorry for you,' she heard Arment stammer.

She looked up quickly. 'That's not what I came for. I don't want you to be sorry. I came to ask you to forgive me . . . for not understanding that *you* didn't understand. . . . That's all I wanted to say.' She rose with a vague sense that the end had come, and put out a groping hand toward the door.

Arment stood motionless. She turned to him with a faint smile.

'You forgive me?'

'There is nothing to forgive—'

'Then you will shake hands for good-bye?' She felt his hand in hers: it was nerveless, reluctant.

'Good-bye,' she repeated. 'I understand now.'

She opened the door and passed out into the hall. As she did so, Arment took an impulsive step forward; but just then the footman, who was evidently alive to his obligations, advanced from the background to let her out. She heard Arment fall back. The footman threw open the door, and she found herself outside in the darkness.

The Long Run

The shade of those our days that had no tongue.

1

It was last winter, after a twelve years' absence from New York, that I saw again, at one of the Jim Cumnors' dinners, my old friend Halston Merrick.

The Cumnors' house is one of the few where, even after such a lapse of time, one can be sure of finding familiar faces and picking up old threads; where for a moment one can abandon one's self to the illusion that New York humanity is a shade less unstable than its bricks and mortar. And that evening in particular I remember feeling that there could be no pleasanter way of re-entering the confused and careless world to which I was returning than through the quiet softly-lit dining-room in which Mrs Cumnor, with a characteristic sense of my needing to be broken in gradually, had contrived to assemble so many friendly faces.

I was glad to see them all, including the three or four I did not know, or failed to recognize, that had no difficulty in passing as in the tradition and of the group; but I was most of all glad – as I rather wonderingly found – to set eyes again on Halston Merrick.

He and I had been at Harvard together, for one thing, and had shared there curiosities and ardors a little outside the current tendencies: had, on the whole, been more critical than our comrades, and less amenable to the accepted. Then, for the next following years, Merrick had been a vivid and promising figure in young American life. Handsome, careless, and free, he had wandered and tasted and compared. After leaving Harvard he had spent two years at Oxford; then he had accepted a private secretaryship to our Ambassador in England, and had come back from this adventure with a fresh curiosity about public affairs at home, and the conviction that men of his kind should play a larger part in them. This led, first, to his running for a State

Senatorship which he failed to get, and ultimately to a few months of intelligent activity in a municipal office. Soon after being deprived of this post by a change of party he had published a small volume of delicate verse, and, a year later, an odd uneven brilliant book on Municipal Government. After that one hardly knew where to look for his next appearance; but chance rather disappointingly solved the problem by killing off his father and placing Halston at the head of the Merrick Iron Foundry at Yonkers.

His friends had gathered that, whenever this regrettable contingency should occur, he meant to dispose of the business and continue his life of free experiment. As often happens in just such cases, however, it was not the moment for a sale, and Merrick had to take over the management of the foundry. Some two years later he had a chance to free himself; but when it came he did not choose to take it. This tame sequel to an inspiriting start was disappointing to some of us, and I was among those disposed to regret Merrick's drop to the level of the prosperous. Then I went away to a big engineering job in China, and from there to Africa, and spent the next twelve years out of sight and sound of New York doings.

During that long interval I heard of no new phase in Merrick's evolution, but this did not surprise me, as I had never expected from him actions resonant enough to cross the globe. All I knew – and this did surprise me – was that he had not married, and that he was still in the iron business. All through those years, however, I never ceased to wish, in certain situations and at certain turns of thought, that Merrick were in reach, that I could tell this or that to Merrick. I had never, in the interval, found any one with just his quickness of perception and just his sureness of response.

After dinner, therefore, we irresistibly drew together. In Mrs Cumnor's big easy drawing-room cigars were allowed, and there was no break in the communion of the sexes; and, this being the case, I ought to have sought a seat beside one of the ladies among whom we were allowed to remain. But, as had generally happened of old when Merrick was in sight, I found myself steering straight for him past all minor ports of call.

There had been no time, before dinner, for more than the barest expression of satisfaction at meeting, and our seats had been at

opposite ends of the longish table, so that we got our first real look
at each other in the secluded corner to which Mrs Cumnor's
vigilance now directed us.

Merrick was still handsome in his stooping tawny way:
handsomer perhaps, with thinnish hair and more lines in his
face, than in the young excess of his good looks. He was very glad
to see me and conveyed his gladness by the same charming smile;
but as soon as we began to talk I felt a change. It was not merely
the change that years and experience and altered values bring.
There was something more fundamental the matter with Merrick,
something dreadful, unforeseen, unaccountable: Merrick had
grown conventional and dull.

In the glow of his frank pleasure in seeing me I was ashamed to
analyze the nature of the change; but presently our talk began to
flag – fancy a talk with Merrick flagging! – and self-deception
became impossible as I watched myself handing out platitudes
with the gesture of the salesman offering something to a
purchaser 'equally good.' The worst of it was that Merrick –
Merrick, who had once felt everything! – didn't seem to feel the
lack of spontaneity in my remarks, but hung on them with a
harrowing faith in the resuscitating power of our past. It was as if
he hugged the empty vessel of our friendship without perceiving
that the last drop of its essence was dry.

But after all, I am exaggerating. Through my surprise and
disappointment I felt a certain sense of well-being in the mere
physical presence of my old friend. I liked looking at the way
his dark hair waved away from the forehead, at the tautness of
his dry brown cheek, the thoughtful backward tilt of his head,
the way his brown eyes mused upon the scene through lowered
lids. All the past was in his way of looking and sitting, and I
wanted to stay near him, and felt that he wanted me to stay;
but the devil of it was that neither of us knew what to talk
about.

It was this difficulty which caused me, after a while, since I
could not follow Merrick's talk, to follow his eyes in their roaming
circuit of the room.

At the moment when our glances joined, his had paused on a
lady seated at some distance from our corner. Immersed, at first,
in the satisfaction of finding myself again with Merrick, I had been
only half aware of this lady, as of one of the few persons present

whom I did not know, or had failed to remember. There was nothing in her appearance to challenge my attention or to excite my curiosity, and I don't suppose I should have looked at her again if I had not noticed that my friend was doing so.

She was a woman of about forty-seven, with fair faded hair and a young figure. Her gray dress was handsome but ineffective, and her pale and rather serious face wore a small unvarying smile which might have been pinned on with her ornaments. She was one of the women in whom increasing years show rather what they have taken than what they have bestowed, and only on looking closely did one see that what they had taken must have been good of its kind.

Jim Cumnor and another man were talking to her, and the very intensity of the attention she bestowed on them betrayed the straining of rebellious thoughts. She never let her eyes stray or her smile drop; and at the proper moment I saw she was ready with the proper sentiment.

The party, like most of those that Mrs Cumnor gathered about her, was not composed of exceptional beings. The people of the old vanished New York set were not exceptional: they were mostly cut on the same convenient and unobtrusive pattern; but they were often exceedingly 'nice.' And this obsolete quality marked every look and gesture of the lady I was scrutinizing.

While these reflections were passing through my mind I was aware that Merrick's eyes rested still on her. I took a cross-section of his look and found in it neither surprise nor absorption, but only a certain sober pleasure just about at the emotional level of the rest of the room. If he continued to look at her, his expression seemed to say, it was only because, all things considered, there were fewer reasons for looking at anybody else.

This made me wonder what were the reasons for looking at *her*; and as a first step toward enlightenment I said: 'I'm sure I've seen the lady over there in gray—'

Merrick detached his eyes and turned them on me with a wondering look.

'Seen her? You know her.' He waited. '*Don't* you know her? It's Mrs Reardon.'

I wondered that he should wonder, for I could not remember, in the Cumnor group or elsewhere, having known any one of the name he mentioned.

'But perhaps,' he continued, 'you hadn't heard of her marriage? You knew her as Mrs Trant.'

I gave him back his stare. 'Not Mrs Philip Trant?'

'Yes; Mrs Philip Trant.'

'Not Paulina?'

'Yes – Paulina,' he said, with a just perceptible delay before the name.

In my surprise I continued to stare at him. He averted his eyes from mine after a moment, and I saw that they had strayed back to her. 'You find her so changed?' he asked.

Something in his voice acted as a warning signal, and I tried to reduce my astonishment to less unbecoming proportions. 'I don't find that she looks much older.'

'No. Only different?' he suggested, as if there were nothing new to him in my perplexity.

'Yes – awfully different.'

'I suppose we're all awfully different. To you, I mean – coming from so far?'

'I recognized all the rest of you,' I said, hesitating. 'And she used to be the one who stood out most.'

There was a flash, a wave, a stir of something deep down in his eyes. 'Yes,' he said. '*That's* the difference.'

'I see it is. She – she looks worn down. Soft but blurred, like the figures in that tapestry behind her.'

He glanced at her again, as if to test the exactness of my analogy.

'Life wears everybody down,' he said.

'Yes – except those it makes more distinct. They're the rare ones, of course; but she *was* rare.'

He stood up suddenly, looking old and tired. 'I believe I'll be off. I wish you'd come down to my place for Sunday. . . . No, don't shake hands – I want to slide away unawares.'

He had backed away to the threshold and was turning the noiseless doorknob. Even Mrs Cumnor's doorknobs had tact and didn't tell.

'Of course I'll come,' I promised warmly. In the last ten minutes he had begun to interest me again.

'All right. Good-bye.' Half through the door he paused to add: '*She* remembers you. You ought to speak to her.'

'I'm going to. But tell me a little more.' I thought I saw

a shade of constraint on his face, and did not add as I had meant to: 'Tell me – because she interests me – what wore her down?' Instead, I asked: 'How soon after Trant's death did she remarry?'

He seemed to make an effort of memory. 'It was seven years ago, I think.'

'And is Reardon here tonight?'

'Yes; over there, talking to Mrs Cumnor.'

I looked across the broken groupings and saw a large glossy man with straw-colored hair and red face, whose shirt and shoes and complexion seemed all to have received a coat of the same expensive varnish.

As I looked there was a drop in the talk about us, and I heard Mr Reardon pronounce in a big booming voice: 'What I say is: what's the good of disturbing things? Thank the Lord, I'm content with what I've got!'

'Is *that* her husband? What's he like?'

'Oh, the best fellow in the world,' said Merrick, going.

2

Merrick had a little place at Riverdale, where he went occasionally to be near the Iron Works, and where he hid his weekends when the world was too much with him.

Here, on the following Saturday afternoon, I found him awaiting me in a pleasant setting of books and prints and faded parental furniture.

We dined late, and smoked and talked afterward in his book-walled study till the terrier on the hearth-rug stood up and yawned for bed. When we took the hint and moved toward the staircase I felt, not that I had found the old Merrick again, but that I was on his track, had come across traces of his passage here and there in the thick jungle that had grown up between us. But I had a feeling that when I finally came on the man himself he might be dead. . . .

As we started upstairs he turned back with one of his abrupt shy movements, and walked into the study.

'Wait a bit!' he called to me.

I waited, and he came out in a moment carrying a limp folio.

'It's typewritten. Will you take a look at it? I've been trying to get to work again,' he explained, thrusting the manuscript into my hand.

'What? Poetry, I hope?' I exclaimed.

He shook his head with a gleam of derision. 'No – just general considerations. The fruit of fifty years of inexperience.'

He showed me to my room and said good night.

The following afternoon we took a long walk inland, across the hills, and I said to Merrick what I could of his book. Unluckily there wasn't much to say. The essays were judicious, polished and cultivated; but they lacked the freshness and audacity of his youthful work. I tried to conceal my opinion behind the usual generalizations, but he broke through these feints with a quick thrust to the heart of my meaning.

'It's worn down – blurred? Like the figures in the Cumnors' tapestry?'

I hesitated. 'It's a little too damned resigned,' I said.

'Ah,' he exclaimed, 'so am I. Resigned.' He switched the bare brambles by the roadside. 'A man can't serve two masters.'

'You mean business and literature?'

'No; I mean theory and instinct. The gray tree and the green. You've got to choose which fruit you'll try; and you don't know till afterward which of the two has the dead core.'

'How can anybody be sure that only one of them has?'

'I'm sure,' said Merrick sharply.

We turned back to the subject of his essays, and I was astonished at the detachment with which he criticized and demolished them. Little by little, as we talked, his old perspective, his old standards came back to him; but with the difference that they no longer seemed like functions of his mind but merely like attitudes assumed or dropped at will. He could still, with an effort, put himself at the angle from which he had formerly seen things; but it was with the effort of a man climbing mountains after a sedentary life in the plain.

I tried to cut the talk short, but he kept coming back to it with nervous insistence, forcing me into the last retrenchments of hypocrisy, and anticipating the verdict I held back. I perceived that a great deal – immensely more than I could see a reason for – had hung for him on my opinion of his book.

Then, as suddenly, his insistence dropped and, as if ashamed of

having forced himself so long on my attention, he began to talk
rapidly and uninterestingly of other things.

We were alone again that evening, and after dinner, wishing to
efface the impression of the afternoon, and above all to show that
I wanted him to talk about himself, I reverted to his work. 'You
must need an outlet of that sort. When a man's once had it in
him, as you have – and when other things begin to dwindle—'

He laughed. 'Your theory is that a man ought to be able to
return to the Muse as he comes back to his wife after he's ceased
to interest other women?'

'No; as he comes back to his wife after the day's work is done.'
A new thought came to me as I looked at him. 'You ought to have
had one,' I added.

He laughed again. 'A wife, you mean? So that there'd have
been someone waiting for me even if the Muse decamped?' He
went on after a pause: 'I've a notion that the kind of woman
worth coming back to wouldn't be much more patient than the
Muse. But as it happens I never tried – because, for fear they'd
chuck me, I put them both out of doors together.'

He turned his head and looked past me with a queer expression
at the low-panelled door at my back. 'Out of that very door they
went – the two of 'em, on a rainy night like this: and one stopped
and looked back, to see if I wasn't going to call her – and I didn't –
and so they both went.'

3

'The Muse?' (said Merrick, refilling my glass and stooping to pat
the terrier as he went back to his chair) 'Well, you've met the
Muse in the little volume of sonnets you used to like; and you've
met the woman too, and you used to like *her*; though you didn't
know her when you saw her the other evening. . . .

'No, I won't ask you how she struck you when you talked to
her: I know. She struck you like that stuff I gave you to read last
night. She's conformed – I've conformed – the mills have caught
us and ground us: ground us, oh, exceedingly small!

'But you remember what she was; and that's the reason why
I'm telling you this now. . . .

'You may recall that after my father's death I tried to sell the
Works. I was impatient to free myself from anything that would

keep me tied to New York. I don't dislike my trade, and I've made, in the end, a fairly good thing of it; but industrialism was not, at that time, in the line of my tastes, and I know now that it wasn't what I was meant for. Above all, I wanted to get away, to see new places and rub up against different ideas. I had reached a time of life – the top of the first hill, so to speak – where the distance draws one, and everything in the foreground seems tame and stale. I was sick to death of the particular set of conformities I had grown up among; sick of being a pleasant popular young man with a long line of dinners on my list, and the dead certainty of meeting the same people, or their prototypes, at all of them.

'Well – I failed to sell the Works, and that increased my discontent. I went through moods of cold unsociability, alternating with sudden flushes of curiosity, when I gloated over stray scraps of talk overheard in railway stations and omnibuses, when strange faces that I passed in the street tantalized me with fugitive promises. I wanted to be among things that were unexpected and unknown; and it seemed to me that nobody about me understood in the least what I felt, but that somewhere just out of reach there was someone who *did*, and whom I must find or despair. . . .

'It was just then that, one evening, I saw Mrs Trant for the first time.

'Yes: I know – you wonder what I mean. I'd known her, of course, as a girl; I'd met her several times after her marriage; and I'd lately been thrown with her, quite intimately and continuously, during a succession of country-house visits. But I had never, as it happened, really *seen* her. . . .

'It was at a dinner at the Cumnors'; and there she was, in front of the very tapestry we saw her against the other evening, with people about her, and her face turned from me, and nothing noticeable or different in her dress or manner; and suddenly she stood out for me against the familiar unimportant background, and for the first time I saw a meaning in the stale phrase of a picture's walking out of its frame. For, after all, most people *are* just that to us: pictures, furniture, the inanimate accessories of our little island area of sensation. And then sometimes one of these graven images moves and throws out live filaments toward us, and the line they make draws us across the world as the moon track seems to draw a boat across the water. . . .

'There she stood; and as this queer sensation came over me I felt that she was looking steadily at me, that her eyes were voluntarily, consciously resting on me with the weight of the very question I was asking.

'I went over and joined her, and she turned and walked with me into the music room. Earlier in the evening someone had been singing, and there were low lights there, and a few couples still sitting in those confidential corners of which Mrs Cumnor has the art; but we were under no illusion as to the nature of these presences. We knew that they were just painted in, and that the whole of life was in us two, flowing back and forward between us. We talked, of course; we had the attitudes, even the words, of the others: I remember her telling me her plans for the spring and asking me politely about mine! As if there were the least sense in plans, now that this thing had happened!

'When we went back into the drawing-room I had said nothing to her that I might not have said to any other woman of the party; but when we shook hands I knew we should meet the next day – and the next. . . .

'That's the way, I take it, that Nature has arranged the beginning of the great enduring loves; and likewise of the little epidermal flurries. And how is a man to know where he is going?

'From the first my feeling for Paulina Trant seemed to me a grave business; but then the Enemy is given to producing that illusion. Many a man – I'm talking of the kind with imagination – has thought he was seeking a soul when all he wanted was a closer view of its tenement. And I tried – honestly tried – to make myself think I was in the latter case. Because, in the first place, I didn't, just then, want a big disturbing influence in my life; and because I didn't want to be a dupe; and because Paulina Trant was not, according to hearsay, the kind of woman for whom it was worthwhile to bring up the big batteries. . . .

'But my resistance was only half-hearted. What I really felt – *all* I really felt – was the flood of joy that comes of heightened emotion. She had given me that, and I wanted her to give it to me again. That's as near as I've ever come to analyzing my state in the beginning.

'I knew her story, as no doubt you know it: the current version, I mean. She had been poor and fond of enjoyment, and she had married that pompous stick Philip Trant because she needed a home, and perhaps also because she wanted a little luxury. Queer how we sneer at women for wanting the thing that gives them half their attraction!

'People shook their heads over the marriage, and divided, prematurely, into Philip's partisans and hers: for no one thought it would work. And they were almost disappointed when, after all, it did. She and her wooden consort seemed to get on well enough. There was a ripple, at one time, over her friendship with young Jim Dalham, who was always with her during a summer at Newport and an autumn in Italy; then the talk died out, and she and Trant were seen together, as before, on terms of apparent good fellowship.

'This was the more surprising because, from the first, Paulina had never made the least attempt to change her tone or subdue her colors. In the gray Trant atmosphere she flashed with prismatic fires. She smoked, she talked subversively, she did as she liked and went where she chose, and danced over the Trant prejudices and the Trant principles as if they'd been a ballroom floor; and all without apparent offence to her solemn husband and his cloud of cousins. I believe her frankness and directness struck them dumb. She moved like a kind of primitive Una through the virtuous rout, and never got a finger mark on her freshness.

'One of the finest things about her was the fact that she never, for an instant, used her situation as a means of enhancing her attraction. With a husband like Trant it would have been so easy! He was a man who always saw the small sides of big things. He thought most of life compressible into a set of bylaws and the rest unmentionable; and with his stiff frock-coated and tall-hatted mind, instinctively distrustful of intelligences in another dress, with his arbitrary classification of whatever he didn't understand into "the kind of thing I don't approve of," "the kind of thing that isn't done," and – deepest depth of all – "the kind of thing I'd rather not discuss," he lived in bondage to a shadowy moral etiquette of which the complex rites and awful penalties had cast an abiding gloom upon his manner.

'A woman like his wife couldn't have asked a better foil; yet I'm sure she never consciously used his dullness to relieve her brilliancy. She may have felt that the case spoke for itself. But I believe her reserve was rather due to a lively sense of justice, and to the rare habit (you said she was rare) of looking at facts as they are, without any throwing of sentimental limelights. She knew Trant could no more help being Trant than she could help being herself – and there was an end of it. I've never known a woman who "made up" so little mentally. . . .

'Perhaps her very reserve, the fierceness of her implicit rejection of sympathy, exposed her the more to – well, to what happened when we met. She said afterward that it was like having been shut up for months in the hold of a ship, and coming suddenly on deck on a day that was all flying blue and silver. . . .

'I won't try to tell you what she was. It's easier to tell you what her friendship made of me; and I can do that best by adopting her metaphor of the ship. Haven't you, sometimes, at the moment of starting on a journey, some glorious plunge into the unknown, been tripped up by the thought: "If only one hadn't to come back"? Well, with her one had the sense that one would never have to come back; that the magic ship would always carry one farther. And what an air one breathed on it! And, oh, the wind, and the islands, and the sunsets!

'I said just now "her friendship"; and I used the word advisedly. Love is deeper than friendship, but friendship is a good deal wider. The beauty of our relation was that it included both dimensions. Our thoughts met as naturally as our eyes: it was almost as if we loved each other because we liked each other. The quality of a love may be tested by the amount of friendship it contains, and in our case there was no dividing line between loving and liking, no disproportion between them, no barrier against which desire beat in vain or from which thought fell back unsatisfied. Ours was a robust passion that could give an open-eyed account of itself, and not a beautiful madness shrinking away from the proof. . . .

'For the first months friendship sufficed us, or rather gave us so much by the way that we were in no hurry to reach what we knew it was leading to. But we were moving there nevertheless, and one day we found ourselves on the borders. It came about through a sudden decision of Trant's to start on a long tour with his wife. We had never foreseen that: he seemed rooted in his New York habits and convinced that the whole social and financial machinery of the metropolis would cease to function if he did not keep an eye on it through the columns of his morning paper, and pronounce judgment on it in the afternoon at his club. But something new had happened to him: he caught a cold, which was followed by a touch of pleurisy, and instantly he perceived the intense interest and importance which ill-health may add to life. He took the fullest advantage of it. A discerning doctor recommended travel in a warm climate; and suddenly, the morning paper, the afternoon club, Fifth Avenue, Wall Street, all the complex phenomena of the metropolis, faded into insignificance, and the rest of the terrestrial globe, from being a mere geographical hypothesis, useful in enabling one to determine the latitude of New York, acquired reality and magnitude as a factor in the convalescence of Mr Philip Trant.

'His wife was absorbed in preparations for the journey. To move him was like mobilizing an army, and weeks before the date set for their departure it was almost as if she were already gone.

'This foretaste of separation showed us what we were to each other. Yet I was letting her go – and there was no help for it, no way of preventing it. Resistance was as useless as the vain struggles in a nightmare. She was Trant's and not mine: part of his luggage when he travelled as she was part of his household furniture when he stayed at home. . . .

'The day she told me that their passages were taken – it was on a November afternoon, in her drawing-room in town – I turned away from her and, going to the window, stood looking out at the torrent of traffic interminably pouring down Fifth Avenue. I watched the senseless machinery of life revolving in the rain and mud, and tried to picture myself performing my small function in it after she had gone from me.

' "It can't be – it can't be!" I exclaimed.

' "What can't be?"

'I came back into the room and sat down by her. "This – this—" I hadn't any words. "Two weeks!" I said. "What's two weeks?"

'She answered, vaguely, something about their thinking of Spain for the spring—

' "Two weeks – two weeks!" I repeated. "And the months we've lost – the days that belonged to us!"

' "Yes," she said, "I'm thankful it's settled."

'Our words seemed irrelevant, haphazard. It was as if each were answering a secret voice, and not what the other was saying.

'"Don't you *feel* anything at all?" I remember bursting out at her. As I asked it the tears were streaming down her face. I felt angry with her, and was almost glad to note that her lids were red and that she didn't cry becomingly. I can't express my sensation to you except by saying that she seemed part of life's huge league against me. And suddenly I thought of an afternoon we had spent together in the country, on a ferny hillside, when we had sat under a beech tree, and her hand had lain palm upward in the moss, close to mine, and I had watched a little black and red beetle creeping over it. . . .

'The bell rang, and we heard the voice of a visitor and the click of an umbrella in the umbrella stand.

'She rose to go into the inner drawing-room, and I caught her suddenly by the wrist. "You understand," I said, "that we can't go on like this?"

'"I understand," she answered, and moved away to meet her visitor. As I went out I heard her saying in the other room: "Yes, we're really off on the twelfth."

4

'I wrote her a long letter that night, and waited two days for a reply.

'On the third day I had a brief line saying that she was going to spend Sunday with some friends who had a place near Riverdale, and that she would arrange to see me while she was there. That was all.

'It was on a Saturday night that I received the note and I came out here the same night. The next morning was rainy, and I was in despair, for I had counted on her asking me to take her for a drive or a long walk. It was hopeless to try to say what I had to say to her in the drawing-room of a crowded country house. And only eleven days were left!

'I stayed indoors all the morning, fearing to go out lest she should telephone me. But no sign came, and I grew more and more restless and anxious. She was too free and frank for coquetry, but her silence and evasiveness made me feel that, for some reason, she did not wish to hear what she knew I meant to say. Could it be that she was, after all, more conventional, less genuine, than I had thought? I went again and again over the whole maddening round of conjecture; but the only conclusion I could rest in was that, if she loved me as I loved her, she would be as determined as I was to let no obstacle come between us during the days that were left.

'The luncheon hour came and passed, and there was no word from her. I had ordered my trap to be ready, so that I might drive over as soon as she summoned me; but the hours dragged on, the early twilight came, and I sat here in this very chair, or measured up and down, up and down, the length of this very rug – and still there was no message and no letter.

'It had grown quite dark, and I had ordered away, impatiently, the servant who came in with the lamps: I couldn't *bear* any definite sign that the day was over! And I was standing there on the rug, staring at the door, and noticing a bad crack in its panel, when I heard the sound of wheels on the gravel. A word at last, no doubt – a line to explain. . . . I didn't seem to care much for her reasons, and I stood where I was and continued to stare at the door. And suddenly it opened and she came in.

'The servant followed her with a light, and then went out and closed the door. Her face looked pale in lamplight, but her voice was as clear as a bell.

' "Well," she said, "you see I've come."

'I started toward her with hands outstretched. "You've come – you've come!" I stammered.

'Yes; it was like her to come in that way – without dissimulation or explanation or excuse. It was like her, if she gave at all, to give not furtively or in haste, but openly, deliberately, without stinting the measure or counting the cost. But her quietness and serenity disconcerted me. She did not look like a woman who has yielded impetuously to an uncontrollable impulse. There was something almost solemn in her face.

'The effect of it stole over me as I looked at her, suddenly subduing the huge flush of gratified longing.

' "You're here, here, here!" I kept repeating, like a child singing over a happy word.

' "You said," she continued, in her grave clear voice, "that we couldn't go on as we were—"

'"Ah, it's divine of you!" I held out my arms to her.

'She didn't draw back from them, but her faint smile said, "Wait," and lifting her hands she took the pins from her hat, and laid the hat on the table.

'As I saw her dear head bare in the lamplight, with the thick hair waving away from the parting, I forgot everything but the bliss and wonder of her being here – here, in my house, on my hearth – that fourth rose from the corner of the rug is the exact spot where she was standing. . . .

'I drew her to the fire, and made her sit down in the chair you're in, and knelt down by her, and hid my face on her knees. She put her hand on my head, and I was happy to the depths of my soul.

'"Oh, I forgot—" she exclaimed suddenly. I lifted my head and our eyes met. Hers were smiling.

'She reached out her hand, opened the little bag she had tossed down with her hat, and drew a small object from it. "I left my trunk at the station. Here's the check. Can you send for it?" she asked.

'Her trunk – she wanted me to send for her trunk! Oh, yes – I see your smile, your "lucky man!" Only, you see, I didn't love her in that way. I knew she couldn't come to my house without running a big risk of discovery, and my tenderness for her, my impulse to shield her, was stronger, even then, than vanity or desire. Judged from the point of view of those emotions I fell terribly short of my part. I hadn't any of the proper feelings. Such an act of romantic folly was so unlike her that it almost irritated me, and I found myself desperately wondering how I could get her to reconsider her plan without – well, without seeming to want her to.

'It's not the way a novel hero feels; it's probably not the way a man in real life ought to have felt. But it's the way I felt – and she saw it.

'She put her hands on my shoulders and looked at me with deep, deep eyes. "Then you didn't expect me to stay?" she asked.

'I caught her hands and pressed them to me, stammering out that I hadn't dared to dream. . . .

'"You thought I'd come – just for an hour?"

'"How could I dare think more? I adore you, you know, for what you've done! But it would be known if you – if you stayed

on. My servants – everybody about here knows you. I've no right
to expose you to the risk." She made no answer, and I went on
tenderly: "Give me, if you will, the next few hours: there's a train
that will get you to town by midnight. And then we'll arrange
something – in town – where it's safer for you – more easily
managed. . . . It's beautiful, it's heavenly of you to have come;
but I love you too much – I must take care of you and think for
you—"

'I don't suppose it ever took me so long to say so few words, and
though they were profoundly sincere they sounded unutterably
shallow, irrelevant and grotesque. She made no effort to help me
out, but sat silent, listening, with her meditative smile. "It's my
duty, dearest, as a man," I rambled on. "The more I love you the
more I'm bound—"

' "Yes; but you don't understand," she interrupted.

'She rose as she spoke, and I got up also, and we stood and
looked at each other.

' "I haven't come for a night; if you want me I've come for
always," she said.

'Here again, if I give you an honest account of my feelings I
shall write myself down as the poor-spirited creature I suppose
I am. There wasn't, I swear, at the moment, a grain of selfishness, of personal reluctance, in my feeling. I worshiped every
hair of her head – when we were together I was happy, when
I was away from her something was gone from every good
thing; but I had always looked on our love for each other, our
possible relation to each other, as such situations are looked on
in what is called society. I had supposed her, for all her freedom and originality, to be just as tacitly subservient to that
view as I was: ready to take what she wanted on the terms on
which society concedes such taking, and to pay for it by the
usual restrictions, concealments and hypocrisies. In short, I
supposed that she would "play the game" – look out for her
own safety, and expect me to look out for it. It sounds cheap
enough, put that way – but it's the rule we live under, all of
us. And the amazement of finding her suddenly outside of it,
oblivious of it, unconscious of it, left me, for an awful minute,
stammering at her like a graceless dolt. . . . Perhaps it wasn't
even a minute; but in it she had gone the whole round of my
thoughts.

' "It's raining," she said, very low. "I suppose you can telephone for a trap?"

'There was no irony or resentment in her voice. She walked slowly across the room and paused before the Brangwyn etching over there. "That's a good impression. *Will* you telephone, please?" she repeated.

'I found my voice again, and with it the power of movement. I followed her and dropped at her feet. "You can't go like this!" I cried.

'She looked down on me from heights and heights. "I can't stay like this," she answered.

'I stood up and we faced each other like antagonists. "You don't know," I accused her passionately, "in the least what you're asking me to ask of you!"

' "Yes, I do: *everything*," she breathed.

' "And it's got to be that or nothing?"

' "Oh, on both sides," she reminded me.

' "*Not* on both sides. It's not fair. That's why—"

' "Why you won't?"

' "Why I cannot – may not!"

' "Why you'll take a night and not a life?"

'The taunt, for a woman usually so sure of her aim, fell so short of the mark that its only effect was to increase my conviction of her helplessness. The very intensity of my longing for her made me tremble where she was fearless. I had to protect her first, and think of my own attitude afterward.

'She was too discerning not to see this too. Her face softened, grew inexpressibly appealing, and she dropped again into that chair you're in, leaned forward, and looked up with her grave smile.

' "You think I'm beside myself – raving? (You're not thinking of yourself, I know.) I'm not: I never was saner. Since I've known you I've often thought this might happen. This thing between us isn't an ordinary thing. If it had been we shouldn't, all these months, have drifted. We should have wanted to skip to the last page – and then throw down the book. We shouldn't have felt we could *trust* the future as we did. We were in no hurry because we knew we shouldn't get tired; and when two people feel that about each other they must live together – or part. I don't see what else they can do. A little trip along the coast won't answer. It's the high seas – or else being tied up to Lethe wharf. And I'm for the high seas, my dear!"

'Think of sitting here – here, in this room, in this chair – and listening to that, and seeing the light on her hair, and hearing the sound of her voice! I don't suppose there ever was a scene just like it. . . .

'She was astounding – inexhaustible; through all my anguish of resistance I found a kind of fierce joy in following her. It was lucidity at white heat: the last sublimation of passion. She might have been an angel arguing a point in the empyrean if she hadn't been, so completely, a woman pleading for her life. . . .

'Her life: that was the thing at stake! She couldn't do with less of it than she was capable of; and a woman's life is inextricably part of the man's she cares for.

'That was why, she argued, she couldn't accept the usual solution: couldn't enter into the only relation that society tolerates between people situated like ourselves. Yes: she knew all the arguments on *that* side: didn't I suppose she'd been over them and over them? She knew (for hadn't she often said it of others?) what is said of the woman who, by throwing in her lot with her lover's, binds him to a lifelong duty which has the irksomeness without the dignity of marriage. Oh, she could talk on that side with the best of them: only she asked me to consider the other – the side of the man and woman who love each other deeply and completely enough to want their lives enlarged, and not diminished, by their love. What, in such a case – she reasoned – must be the inevitable effect of concealing, denying, disowning, the central fact, the motive power of one's existence? She asked me to picture the course of such a love: first working as a fever in the blood, distorting and deflecting everything, making all other interests insipid, all other duties irksome, and then, as the acknowledged claims of life regained their hold, gradually dying – the poor starved passion! – for want of the wholesome necessary food of common living and doings, yet leaving life impoverished by the loss of all it might have been.

'"I'm not talking, dear—" I see her now, leaning toward me with shining eyes: "I'm not talking of the people who haven't enough to fill their days, and to whom a little mystery, a little maneuvering, gives an illusion of importance that they can't afford to miss; I'm talking of you and me, with all our tastes and curiosities and activities; and I ask you what our love would become if we had to keep it apart from our lives, like a pretty useless animal that we went to peep at and feed with sweetmeats through its cage?"

'I won't, my dear fellow, go into the other side of our strange duel: the arguments I used were those that most men in my situation would have felt bound to use, and that most women in Paulina's accept instinctively, without even formulating them. The exceptionalness, the significance, of the case lay wholly in the fact that she had formulated them all and then rejected them. . . .

'There was one point I didn't, of course, touch on; and that was the popular conviction (which I confess I shared) that when a man and a woman agree to defy the world together the man really sacrifices much more than the woman. I was not even conscious of thinking of this at the time, though it may have lurked somewhere in the shadow of my scruples for her; but she dragged it out into the daylight and held me face to face with it.

'"Remember, I'm not attempting to lay down any general rule," she insisted; "I'm not theorizing about Man and Woman, I'm talking about you and me. How do I know what's best for the woman in the next house? Very likely she'll bolt when it would have been better for her to stay at home. And it's the same with the man: he'll probably do the wrong thing. It's generally the weak heads that commit follies, when it's the strong ones that ought to: and my point is that you and I are both strong enough to behave like fools if we want to. . . .

'"Take your own case first – because, in spite of the sentimentalists, it's the man who stands to lose most. You'll have to give up the Iron Works: which you don't much care about – because it won't be particularly agreeable for us to live in New York: which you don't care much about either. But you won't be sacrificing what is called 'a career.' You made up your mind long ago that your best chance of self-development, and consequently of general usefulness, lay in thinking rather than doing; and, when we first met, you were already planning to sell out your business, and travel and write. Well! Those ambitions are of a kind that won't be harmed by your dropping out of your social setting. On the contrary, such work as you want to do ought to gain by it, because you'll be brought nearer to life-as-it-is, in contrast to life-as-a-visiting-list. . . ."

'She threw back her head with a sudden laugh. "And the joy of not having any more visits to make! I wonder if you've ever thought of *that*? Just at first, I mean; for society's getting so deplorably lax that, little by little, it will edge up to us – you'll see! I don't want to idealize the situation, dearest, and I won't conceal from you that in time we shall be called on. But, oh, the fun we shall have had in the interval! And then, for the first time we shall be able to dictate our own terms, one of which will be that no bores need apply. Think of being cured of all one's chronic bores! We shall feel as jolly as people do after a successful operation."

'I don't know why this nonsense sticks in my mind when some of the graver things we said are less distinct. Perhaps it's because of a certain iridescent quality of feeling that made gaiety seem like sunshine through a shower. . . .

' "You ask me to think of myself?" she went on. "But the beauty of our being together will be that, for the first time, I shall dare to! Now I have to think of all the tedious trifles I can pack the days with, because I'm afraid – I'm afraid – to hear the voice of the real me, down below, in the windowless underground hole where I keep her. . . .

' "Remember again, please, it's not Woman, it's Paulina Trant, I'm talking of. The woman in the next house may have all sorts of reasons – honest reasons – for staying there. There may be some- one there who needs her badly: for whom the light would go out if she went. Whereas to Philip I've been simply – well, what New York was before he decided to travel: the most important thing in life till he made up his mind to leave it; and now merely the starting place of several lines of steamers. Oh, I didn't have to love you to know that! I only had to live with *him*. . . . If he lost his eyeglasses he'd think it was the fault of the eyeglasses; he'd really feel that the eyeglasses had been careless. And he'd be convinced that no others would suit him quite as well. But at the optician's he'd probably be told that he needed something a little different, and after that he'd feel that the old eyeglasses had never suited him at all, and that *that* was their fault too. . . ."

'At one moment – but I don't recall when – I remember she

stood up with one of her quick movements, and came toward me, holding out her arms. "Oh, my dear, I'm pleading for my life; do you suppose I shall ever want for arguments?" she cried. . . .

'After that, for a bit, nothing much remains with me except a sense of darkness and of conflict. The one spot of daylight in my whirling brain was the conviction that I couldn't – whatever happened – profit by the sudden impulse she had acted on, and allow her to take, in a moment of passion, a decision that was to shape her whole life. I couldn't so much as lift my little finger to keep her with me then, unless I were prepared to accept for her as well as for myself the full consequences of the future she had planned for us. . . .

'Well – there's the point: I wasn't. I felt in her – poor fatuous idiot that I was! – that lack of objective imagination which had always seemed to me to account, at least in part, for many of the so-called heroic qualities in women. When their feelings are involved they simply can't look ahead. Her unfaltering logic notwithstanding, I felt this about Paulina as I listened. She had a specious air of knowing where she was going, but she didn't. She seemed the genius of logic and understanding, but the demon of illusion spoke through her lips. . . .

'I said just now that I hadn't, at the outset, given my own side of the case a thought. It would have been truer to say that I hadn't given it a *separate* thought. But I couldn't think of her without seeing myself as a factor – the chief factor – in her problem, and without recognizing that whatever the experiment made of me, it must fatally, in the end, make of her. If I couldn't carry the thing through she must break down with me: we should have to throw our separate selves into the melting pot of this mad adventure, and be "one" in a terrible indissoluble completeness of which marriage is only an imperfect counterpart. . . .

'There could be no better proof of her extraordinary power over me, and of the way she had managed to clear the air of sentimental illusion, than the fact that I presently found myself putting this before her with a merciless precision of touch.

'"If we love each other enough to do a thing like this, we must love each other enough to see just what it is we're going to do."

'So I invited her to the dissecting table, and I see now the fearless eye with which she approached the cadaver. "For that's what it is, you know," she flashed out at me, at the end of my long demonstration. "It's a dead body, like all the instances and examples and hypothetical cases that ever were! What do you expect to learn from *that?* The first great anatomist was the man who stuck his knife in a heart that was beating; and the only way to find out what doing a thing will be like is to do it!"

'She looked away from me suddenly, as if she were fixing her eyes on some vision on the outer rim of consciousness. "No: there's one other way," she exclaimed, "and that is, *not* to do it! To abstain and refrain; and then see what we become, or what we don't become, in the long run, and to draw our inferences. That's the game that almost everybody about us is playing, I suppose; there's hardly one of the dull people one meets at dinner who hasn't had, just once, the chance of a berth on a ship that was off for the Happy Isles, and hasn't refused it for fear of sticking on a sandbank!

' "I'm doing my best, you know," she continued, "to see the sequel as you see it, as you believe it's your duty to me to see it. I know the instances you're thinking of: the listless couples wearing out their lives in shabby watering places, and hanging on the favor of hotel acquaintances; or the proud quarrelling wretches shut up alone in a fine house because they're too good for the only society they can get, and trying to cheat their boredom by squabbling with their tradesmen and spying on their servants. No doubt there are such cases; but I don't recognize either of us in those dismal figures. Why, to do it would be to admit that our life, yours and mine, is in the people about us and not in ourselves; that we're parasites and not self-sustaining creatures; and that the lives we're leading now are so brilliant, full and satisfying that what we should have to give up would surpass even the blessedness of being together!"

'At that stage, I confess, the solid ground of my resistance began to give way under me. It was not that my convictions were shaken, but that she had swept me into a world whose laws were different, where one could reach out in directions that the slave of gravity hasn't pictured. But at the same time my opposition hardened from reason into instinct. I knew it was her voice, and not her logic, that was unsettling me. I knew that if she'd written out her thesis and sent it to me by post I should have made short work of it; and again the part of me which I called by all the finest names: my chivalry, my unselfishness, my superior masculine experience, cried out with one voice: "You can't let a woman use her graces to her own undoing – you can't, for her own sake, let her eyes convince you when her reasons don't!"

'And then, abruptly, and for the first time, a doubt entered me: a doubt of her perfect moral honesty. I don't know how else to describe my feeling that she wasn't playing fair, that in coming to my house, in throwing herself at my head (I called things by their names), she had perhaps not so much obeyed an irresistible impulse as deeply, deliberately reckoned on the dissolvent effect of her generosity, her rashness and her beauty. . . .

'From the moment that this mean doubt raised its head in me I was once more the creature of all the conventional scruples: I was repeating, before the looking glass of my self-consciousness, all the stereotyped gestures of the "man of honor." . . . Oh, the sorry figure I must have cut! You'll understand my dropping the curtain on it as quickly as I can. . . .

'Yet I remember, as I made my point, being struck by its impressiveness. I was suffering and enjoying my own suffering. I told her that, whatever step we decided to take, I owed it to her to insist on its being taken soberly, deliberately—

'("No: it's 'advisedly,' isn't it? Oh, I was thinking of the Marriage Service," she interposed with a faint laugh.)

'—That if I accepted, there, on the spot, her headlong beautiful gift of herself, I should feel I had taken an unfair advantage of her, an advantage which she would be justified in reproaching me with afterward; that I was not afraid to tell her this because she was intelligent enough to know that my scruples were the surest proof of the quality of my love; that I refused to owe my happiness to an unconsidered impulse; that we must see each other again, in her own house, in less agitating circumstances, when she had had time to reflect on my words, to study her heart and look into the future. . . .

'The factitious exhilaration produced by uttering these beautiful sentiments did not last very long, as you may imagine. It fell, little by little, under her quiet gaze, a gaze in which there was neither contempt nor irony nor wounded pride, but only a tender wistfulness of interrogation; and I think the acutest point in my suffering was reached when she said, as I ended: "Oh; yes, of course I understand."

'"If only you hadn't come to me here!" I blurted out in the torture of my soul.

'She was on the threshold when I said it, and she turned and laid her hand gently on mine. "There was no other way," she said; and at the moment it seemed to me like some hackneyed phrase in a novel that she had used without any sense of its meaning.

'I don't remember what I answered or what more we either of us said. At the end a desperate longing to take her in my arms and keep her with me swept aside everything else, and I went up to her, pleading, stammering, urging I don't know what. . . . But she held me back with a quiet look, and went. I had ordered the carriage, as she asked me to; and my last definite recollection is of watching her drive off in the rain. . . .

'I had her promise that she would see me, two days later, at her house in town, and that we should then have what I called "a decisive talk"; but I don't think that even at the moment I was the dupe of my phrase. I knew, and she knew, that the end had come. . . .

5

'It was about that time (Merrick went on after a long pause) that I definitely decided not to sell the Works, but to stick to my job and conform my life to it.

'I can't describe to you the rage of conformity that possessed me. Poetry, ideas – all the picture-making processes stopped. A kind of dull self-discipline seemed to me the only exercise worthy of a reflecting mind. I *had* to justify my great refusal, and I tried to do it by plunging myself up to the eyes into the very conditions I had been instinctively struggling to get away from. The only possible consolation would have been to find in a life of business routine and social submission such moral compensations as may reward the citizen if they fail the man; but to attain to these I should have had to accept the old delusion that the social and the individual man are two. Now, on the contrary, I found soon enough that I couldn't get one part of my machinery to work effectively while another wanted feeding: and that in rejecting what had seemed to me a negation of action I had made all my action negative.

'The best solution, of course, would have been to fall in love with another woman; but it was long before I could bring myself to wish that this might happen to me. . . . Then, at length, I suddenly and violently desired it; and as such impulses are seldom without some kind of imperfect issue I contrived, a year or two later, to work myself up into the wished-for state. . . . She was a woman in society, and with all the awe of that institution that Paulina lacked. Our relation was consequently one of those unavowed affairs in which triviality is the only alternative to tragedy. Luckily we had, on both sides, risked only as much as prudent people stake in a drawing-room game; and when the match was over I take it that we came out fairly even.

'My gain, at all events, was of an unexpected kind. The adventure had served only to make me understand Paulina's abhorrence of such experiments, and at every turn of the slight intrigue I had felt how exasperating and belittling such a relation was bound to be between two people who, had they been free, would have mated openly. And so from a brief phase of imperfect forgetting I was driven back to a deeper and more understanding remembrance. . . .

'This second incarnation of Paulina was one of the strangest episodes of the whole strange experience. Things she had said during our extraordinary talk, things I had hardly heard at the time, came back to me with singular vividness and a fuller meaning. I hadn't any longer the cold consolation of believing in my own perspicacity: I saw that her insight had been deeper and keener than mine.

'I remember, in particular, starting up in bed one sleepless night as there flashed into my head the meaning of her last words: "There was no other way"; the phrase I had half-smiled at at the time, as a parrot-like echo of the novel heroine's stock farewell. I had never, up to that moment, wholly understood why Paulina had come to my house that night. I had never been able to make that particular act – which could hardly, in the light of her subsequent conduct, be dismissed as a blind surge of passion – square with my conception of her character. She was at once the most spontaneous and the steadiest-minded woman I had ever known, and the last to wish to owe any advantage to surprise, to unpreparedness, to any play on the spring of sex. The better I came, retrospectively, to know her, the more sure I was of this, and the less intelligible her act appeared. And then, suddenly, after a night of hungry restless thinking, the flash of enlightenment came. She had come to my house, had brought her trunk with her, had thrown herself at my head with all possible violence and publicity, in order to give me a pretext, a loophole, an honorable excuse, for doing and saying – why, precisely what I had said and done!

'As the idea came to me it was as if some ironic hand had touched an electric button, and all my fatuous phrases had leapt out on me in fire.

'Of course she had known all along just the kind of thing I should say if I didn't at once open my arms to her; and to save my pride, my dignity, my conception of the figure I was cutting in her eyes, she had recklessly and magnificently provided me with the decentest pretext a man could have for doing a pusillanimous thing. . . .

'With that discovery the whole case took a different aspect. It hurt less to think of Paulina – and yet it hurt more. The tinge of bitterness, of doubt, in my thoughts of her had had a tonic quality. It was harder to go on persuading myself that I had done right as, bit by bit, my theories crumbled under the test of time. Yet, after all, as she herself had said, one could judge of results only in the long run. . . .

'The Trants stayed away for two years; and about a year after they got back, you may remember, Trant was killed in a railway accident. You know Fate's way of untying a knot after everybody has given up tugging at it!

'Well – there I was, completely justified: all my weaknesses turned into merits! I had "saved" a weak woman from herself, I had kept her to the path of duty, I had spared her the humiliation of scandal and the misery of self-reproach; and now I had only to put out my hand and take my reward.

'I had avoided Paulina since her return, and she had made no effort to see me. But after Trant's death I wrote her a few lines, to which she sent a friendly answer; and when a decent interval had elapsed, and I asked if I might call on her, she answered at once that she would see me.

'I went to her house with the fixed intention of asking her to

marry me – and I left it without having done so. Why? I don't
know that I can tell you. Perhaps you would have had to sit there
opposite her, knowing what I did and feeling as I did, to understand why. She was kind, she was compassionate – I could see she
didn't want to make it hard for me. Perhaps she even wanted to
make it easy. But there, between us, was the memory of the
gesture I hadn't made, forever parodying the one I was attempting! There wasn't a word I could think of that hadn't an echo in it
of words of hers I had been deaf to; there wasn't an appeal I could
make that didn't mock the appeal I had rejected. I sat there and
talked of her husband's death, of her plans, of my sympathy; and I
knew she understood; and knowing that, in a way, made it
harder. . . . The doorbell rang and the footman came in to ask if
she would receive other visitors. She looked at me a moment and
said "Yes," and I got up and shook hands and went away.

'A few days later she sailed for Europe, and the next time we
met she had married Reardon. . . .'

6

It was long past midnight, and the terrier's hints became
imperious.

Merrick rose from his chair, pushed back a fallen log and put up
the fender. He walked across the room and stared a moment at the
Brangwyn etching before which Paulina Trant had paused at a
memorable turn of their talk. Then he came back and laid his
hand on my shoulder.

'She summed it all up, you know, when she said that one way
of finding out whether a risk is worth taking is *not* to take it, and
then to see what one becomes in the long run, and draw one's
inferences. The long run – well, we've run it, she and I. I know
what I've become, but that's nothing to the misery of knowing
what she's become. She had to have some kind of life, and she
married Reardon. Reardon's a very good fellow in his way; but the
worst of it is that it's not her way. . . .

'No: the worst of it is that now she and I meet as friends. We
dine at the same houses, we talk about the same people, we play
bridge together, and I lend her books. And sometimes Reardon
slaps me on the back and says: "Come in and dine with us, old
man! What you want is to be cheered up!" And I go and dine with

them, and he tells me how jolly comfortable she makes him, and what an ass I am not to marry; and she presses on me a second helping of *poulet Maryland*, and I smoke one of Reardon's cigars, and at half-past ten I get into my overcoat, and walk back alone to my rooms. . . .'

Xingu

1

Mrs Ballinger is one of the ladies who pursue Culture in bands, as though it were dangerous to meet alone. To this end she had founded the Lunch Club, an association composed of herself and several other indomitable huntresses of erudition. The Lunch Club after three or four winters of lunching and debate, had acquired such local distinction that the entertainment of distinguished strangers became one of its accepted functions; in recognition of which it duly extended to the celebrated 'Osric Dane,' on the day of her arrival in Hillbridge, an invitation to be present at the next meeting.

The club was to meet at Mrs Ballinger's. The other members, behind her back, were of one voice in deploring her unwillingness to cede her rights in favor of Mrs Plinth, whose house made a more impressive setting for the entertainment of celebrities; while, as Mrs Leveret observed, there was always the picture-gallery to fall back on.

Mrs Plinth made no secret of sharing this view. She had always regarded it as one of her obligations to entertain the Lunch Club's distinguished guests. Mrs Plinth was almost as proud of her obligations as she was of her picture-gallery; she was in fact fond of implying that the one possession implied the other, and that only a woman of her wealth could afford to live up to a standard as high as that which she had set herself. An all-round sense of duty, roughly adaptable to various ends, was, in her opinion, all that Providence exacted of the more humbly stationed; but the power which had predestined Mrs Plinth to keep a footman clearly intended her to maintain an equally specialized staff of responsibilities. It was the more to be regretted that Mrs Ballinger, whose obligations to society were bounded by the narrow scope of two parlormaids, should have been so tenacious of the right to entertain Osric Dane.

The question of that lady's reception had for a month past

profoundly moved the members of the Lunch Club. It was not that they felt themselves unequal to the task, but that their sense of the opportunity plunged them into the agreeable uncertainty of the lady who weighs the alternatives of a well-stocked wardrobe. If such subsidiary members as Mrs Leveret were fluttered by the thought of exchanging ideas with the author of 'The Wings of Death,' no forebodings disturbed the conscious adequacy of Mrs Plinth, Mrs Ballinger and Miss Van Vluyck. 'The Wings of Death' had, in fact, at Miss Van Vluyck's suggestion, been chosen as the subject of discussion at the last club meeting, and each member had thus been enabled to express her own opinion or to appropriate whatever sounded well in the comments of the others.

Mrs Roby alone had abstained from profiting by the opportunity; but it was now openly recognized that, as a member of the Lunch Club, Mrs Roby was a failure. 'It all comes,' as Miss Van Vluyck put it, 'of accepting a woman on a man's estimation.' Mrs Roby, returning to Hillbridge from a prolonged sojourn in exotic lands – the other ladies no longer took the trouble to remember where – had been heralded by the distinguished biologist, Professor Foreland, as the most agreeable woman he had ever met; and the members of the Lunch Club, impressed by an encomium that carried the weight of a diploma, and rashly assuming that the Professor's social sympathies would follow the line of his professional bent, had seized the chance of annexing a biological member. Their disillusionment was complete. At Miss Van Vluyck's first off-hand mention of the pterodactyl Mrs Roby had confusedly murmured: 'I know so little about metres—' and after that painful betrayal of incompetence she had prudently withdrawn from further participation in the mental gymnastics of the club.

'I suppose she flattered him,' Miss Van Vluyck summed up – 'or else it's the way she does her hair.'

The dimensions of Miss Van Vluyck's dining-room having restricted the membership of the club to six, the non-conductiveness of one member was a serious obstacle to the exchange of ideas, and some wonder had already been expressed that Mrs Roby should care to live, as it were, on the intellectual bounty of the others. This feeling was increased by the discovery that she had not yet read 'The Wings of Death.' She owned to having

heard the name of Osric Dane; but that – incredible as it appeared
– was the extent of her acquaintance with the celebrated novelist.
The ladies could not conceal their surprise; but Mrs Ballinger,
whose pride in the club made her wish to put even Mrs Roby in
the best possible light, gently insinuated that, though she had not
had time to acquaint herself with 'The Wings of Death,' she must
at least be familiar with its equally remarkable predecessor, 'The
Supreme Instant.'

Mrs Roby wrinkled her sunny brows in a conscientious effort of
memory, as a result of which she recalled that, oh, yes, she *had*
seen the book at her brother's, when she was staying with him in
Brazil, and had even carried it off to read one day on a boating
party; but they had all got to shying things at each other in the
boat, and the book had gone overboard, so she had never had the
chance—

The picture evoked by this anecdote did not increase Mrs
Roby's credit with the club, and there was a painful pause,
which was broken by Mrs Plinth's remarking: 'I can understand that, with all your other pursuits, you should not find
much time for reading; but I should have thought you might at
least have *got up* "The Wings of Death" before Osric Dane's
arrival.'

Mrs Roby took this rebuke good-humoredly. She had meant,
she owned, to glance through the book; but she had been so
absorbed in a novel of Trollope's that—

'No one reads Trollope now,' Mrs Ballinger interrupted.

Mrs Roby looked pained. 'I'm only just beginning,' she
confessed.

'And does he interest you?' Mrs Plinth inquired.

'He amuses me.'

'Amusement,' said Mrs Plinth, 'is hardly what I look for in my
choice of books.'

'Oh, certainly, "The Wings of Death" is not amusing,' ventured
Mrs Leveret, whose manner of putting forth an opinion was like
that of an obliging salesman with a variety of other styles to
submit if his first selection does not suit.

'Was it *meant* to be?' inquired Mrs Plinth, who was fond of
asking questions that she permitted no one but herself to answer.
'Assuredly not.'

'Assuredly not – that is what I was going to say,' assented Mrs

Leveret, hastily rolling up her opinion and reaching for another. 'It was meant to – to elevate.'

Miss Van Vluyck adjusted her spectacles as though they were the black cap of condemnation. 'I hardly see,' she interposed, 'how a book steeped in the bitterest pessimism can be said to elevate, however much it may instruct.'

'I meant of course, to instruct,' said Mrs Leveret, flurried by the unexpected distinction between two terms which she had supposed to be synonymous. Mrs Leveret's enjoyment of the Lunch Club was frequently marred by such surprise; and not knowing her own value to the other ladies as a mirror for their mental complacency she was sometimes troubled by a doubt of her worthiness to join in their debates. It was only the fact of having a dull sister who thought her clever that saved her from a sense of hopeless inferiority.

'Do they get married in the end?' Mrs Roby interposed.

'They – who?' the Lunch Club collectively exclaimed.

'Why, the girl and man. It's a novel, isn't it? I always think that's the one thing that matters. If they're parted it spoils my dinner.'

Mrs Plinth and Mrs Ballinger exchanged scandalized glances, and the latter said: 'I should hardly advise you to read "The Wings of Death" in that spirit. For my part, when there are so many books one *has* to read, I wonder how any one can find time for those that are merely amusing.'

'The beautiful part of it,' Laura Glyde murmured, 'is surely just this – that no one can tell *how* "The Wings of Death" ends. Osric Dane, overcome by the awful significance of her own meaning, has mercifully veiled it – perhaps even from herself – as Apelles, in representing the sacrifice of Iphigenia, veiled the face of Agamemnon.'

'What's that? Is it poetry?' whispered Mrs Leveret to Mrs Plinth, who, disdaining a definite reply, said coldly: 'You should look it up. I always make it a point to look things up.' Her tone added – 'though I might easily have it done for me by the footman.'

'I was about to say,' Miss Van Vluyck resumed, 'that it must always be a question whether a book *can* instruct unless it elevates.'

'Oh—' murmured Mrs Leveret, now feeling herself hopelessly astray.

'I don't know,' said Mrs Ballinger, scenting in Miss Van Vluyck's tone a tendency to depreciate the coveted distinction of entertaining Osric Dane; 'I don't know that such a question can seriously be raised as to a book which has attracted more attention among thoughtful people than any novel since "Robert Elsmere."'

'Oh, but don't you see,' exclaimed Laura Glyde, 'that it's just the dark hopelessness of it all – the wonderful tone-scheme of black on black – that makes it such an artistic achievement? It reminded me when I read it of Prince Rupert's *manière noire* . . . the book is etched, not painted, yet one feels the color-values so intensely. . . .'

'Who is *he*?' Mrs Leveret whispered to her neighbor. 'Some one she's met abroad?'

'The wonderful part of the book,' Mrs Ballinger conceded, 'is that it may be looked at from so many points of view. I hear that as a study of determinism Professor Lupton ranks it with "The Data of Ethics."'

'I'm told that Osric Dane spent ten years in preparatory studies before beginning to write it,' said Mrs Plinth. 'She looks up everything – verifies everything. It has always been my principle, as you know. Nothing would induce me, now, to put aside a book before I'd finished it, just because I can buy as many more as I want.'

'And what do *you* think of "The Wings of Death"?' Mrs Roby abruptly asked her.

It was the kind of question that might be termed out of order, and the ladies glanced at each other as though disclaiming any share in such a breach of discipline. They all knew there was nothing Mrs Plinth so much disliked as being asked her opinion of a book. Books were written to be read; if one read them what more could be expected? To be questioned in detail regarding the contents of a volume seemed to her as great an outrage as being searched for smuggled laces at the Custom House. The club had always respected this idiosyncrasy of Mrs Plinth's. Such opinions as she had were imposing and substantial: her mind, like her house, was furnished with monumental 'pieces' that were not meant to be disarranged; and it was one of the unwritten rules of the Lunch Club that, within her own province, each member's habits of thought should be respected. The meeting therefore closed with an increased sense, on the part of the other ladies, of Mrs Roby's hopeless unfitness to be one of them.

2

Mrs Leveret, on the eventful day, arrived early at Mrs Ballinger's, her volume of Appropriate Allusions in her pocket.

It always flustered Mrs Leveret to be late at the Lunch Club: she liked to collect her thoughts and gather a hint, as the others assembled, of the turn the conversation was likely to take. Today, however, she felt herself completely at a loss; and even the familiar contact of Appropriate Allusions, which stuck into her as she sat down, failed to give her any reassurance. It was an admirable little volume, compiled to meet all the social emergencies; so that, whether on the occasion of Anniversaries, joyful or melancholy (as the classification ran), of Banquets, social or municipal, or of Baptisms, Church of England or sectarian, its student need never be at a loss for a pertinent reference. Mrs Leveret, though she had for years devoutly conned its pages, valued it, however, rather for its moral support than for its practical services; for though in the privacy of her own room she commanded an army of quotations, these invariably deserted her at the critical moment, and the only phrase she retained – *Canst thou draw out leviathan with a hook?* – was one she had never yet found occasion to apply.

Today she felt that even the complete mastery of the volume would hardly have insured her self-possession; for she thought it probable that, even if she *did*, in some miraculous way, remember an Allusion, it would be only to find that Osric Dane used a different volume (Mrs Leveret was convinced that literary people always carried them), and would consequently not recognize her quotations.

Mrs Leveret's sense of being adrift was intensified by the appearance of Mrs Ballinger's drawing-room. To a careless eye its aspect was unchanged; but those acquainted with Mrs Ballinger's way of arranging her books would instantly have detected the marks of recent perturbation. Mrs Ballinger's province, as a member of the Lunch Club, was the Book of the Day. On that, whatever it was, from a novel to a treatise on experimental psychology, she was confidently, authoritatively 'up.' What became of last year's books, or last week's even; what she did with the 'subjects' she had previously professed with equal authority; no one had ever yet discovered. Her mind was an hotel where facts came and went like transient lodgers, without leaving their address behind, and frequently without paying for their board. It was Mrs Ballinger's boast that she was 'abreast with the Thought of the Day,' and her pride that this advanced position should be expressed by the books on her table. These volumes, frequently renewed, and almost always damp from the press, bore names generally unfamiliar to Mrs Leveret, and giving her, as she furtively scanned them, a disheartened glimpse of new fields of knowledge to be breathlessly traversed in Mrs Ballinger's wake. But today a number of maturer-looking volumes were adroitly mingled with the *primeurs* of the press – Karl Marx jostled Professor Bergson, and the 'Confessions of St Augustine' lay beside the last work on 'Mendelism'; so that even to Mrs Leveret's fluttered perceptions it was clear that Mrs Ballinger didn't in the least know what Osric Dane was likely to talk about, and had taken measures to be prepared for anything. Mrs Leveret felt like a passenger on an ocean steamer who is told that there is no immediate danger, but that she had better put on her life-belt.

It was a relief to be roused from these forebodings by Miss Van Vluyck's arrival.

'Well, my dear,' the newcomer briskly asked her hostess, 'what subjects are we to discuss today?'

Mrs Ballinger was furtively replacing a volume of Wordsworth by a copy of Verlaine. 'I hardly know,' she said, somewhat nervously. 'Perhaps we had better leave that to circumstances.'

'Circumstances?' said Miss Van Vluyck drily. 'That means, I suppose, that Laura Glyde will take the floor as usual, and we shall be deluged with literature.'

Philanthropy and statistics were Miss Van Vluyck's province, and she resented any tendency to divert their guest's attention from these topics.

Mrs Plinth at this moment appeared.

'Literature?' she protested in a tone of remonstrance. 'But this is perfectly unexpected. I understood we were to talk of Osric Dane's novel.'

Mrs Ballinger winced at the discrimination, but let it pass. 'We hardly make that our chief subject – at least not *too* intentionally,' she suggested. 'Of course we can let our talk *drift* in that direction, but we ought to have some other topic as an introduction, and that is what I wanted to consult you about. The fact is, we know so little of Osric Dane's tastes and interests that it is difficult to make any special preparation.'

'It may be difficult,' said Mrs Plinth with decision, 'but it is necessary. I know what that happy-go-lucky principle leads to. As I told one of my nieces the other day, there are certain emergencies for which a lady should always be prepared. It's in shocking taste to wear colors when one pays a visit of condolence, or a last year's dress when there are reports that one's husband is on the wrong side of the market; and so it is with conversation. All I ask is that I should know beforehand what is to be talked about; then I feel sure of being able to say the proper thing.'

'I quite agree with you,' Mrs Ballinger assented: 'but—'

And at that instant, heralded by the fluttered parlormaid, Osric Dane appeared upon the threshold.

Mrs Leveret told her sister afterward that she had known at a glance what was coming. She saw that Osric Dane was not going to meet them half-way. That distinguished personage had indeed entered with an air of compulsion not calculated to promote the easy exercise of hospitality. She looked as though she were about to be photographed for a new edition of her books.

The desire to propitiate a divinity is generally in inverse ratio to its responsiveness, and the sense of discouragement produced by Osric Dane's entrance visibly increased the Lunch Club's eagerness to please her. Any lingering idea that she might consider herself under an obligation to her entertainers was at once dispelled by her manner: as Mrs Leveret said afterward to her sister, she had a way of looking at you that made you feel as if there was something wrong with your hat. This evidence of greatness produced such an immediate impression on the ladies that a shudder of awe ran through them when Mrs Roby, as their hostess led the great personage into the dining-room, turned back to whisper to the others: 'What a brute she is!'

The hour about the table did not tend to revise this verdict. It was passed by Osric Dane in the silent deglutition of Mrs Ballinger's menu, and by the members of the club in the emission of tentative platitudes which their guest seemed to swallow as perfunctorily as the successive courses of the luncheon.

Mrs Ballinger's reluctance to fix a topic had thrown the club into a mental disarray which increased with the return to the drawing-room, where the actual business of discussion was to open. Each lady waited for the other to speak; and there was a general shock of disappointment when their hostess opened the conversation by the painfully commonplace inquiry: 'Is this your first visit to Hillbridge?'

Even Mrs Leveret was conscious that this was a bad beginning; and a vague impulse of deprecation made Miss Glyde interject: 'It is a very small place indeed.'

Mrs Plinth bristled. 'We have a great many representative people,' she said, in the tone of one who speaks for her order.

Osric Dane turned to her. 'What do they represent?' she asked.

Mrs Plinth's constitutional dislike to being questioned was intensified by her sense of unpreparedness; and her reproachful glance passed the question on to Mrs Ballinger.

'Why,' said that lady, glancing in turn at the other members, 'as a community I hope it is not too much to say that we stand for culture.'

'For art—' Miss Glyde interjected.

'For art and literature,' Mrs Ballinger emended.

'And for sociology, I trust,' snapped Miss Van Vluyck.

'We have a standard,' said Mrs Plinth, feeling herself suddenly secure on the vast expanse of a generalization; and Mrs Leveret, thinking there must be room for more than one on so broad a statement, took courage to murmur: 'Oh, certainly; we have a standard.'

'The object of our little club,' Mrs Ballinger continued, 'is to concentrate the highest tendencies of Hillbridge – to centralize and focus its intellectual effort.'

This was felt to be so happy that the ladies drew an almost audible breath of relief.

'We aspire,' the President went on, 'to be in touch with whatever is highest in art, literature and ethics.'

Osric Dane again turned to her. 'What ethics?' she asked.

A tremor of apprehension encircled the room. None of the ladies required any preparation to pronounce on a question of morals; but when they were called ethics it was different. The club, when fresh from the 'Encyclopaedia Britannica,' the 'Reader's Handbook' or Smith's 'Classical Dictionary,' could deal confidently with any subject; but when taken unawares it had been known to define agnosticism as a heresy of the Early Church and Professor Froude as a distinguished histologist; and such minor members as Mrs Leveret still secretly regarded ethics as something vaguely pagan.

Even to Mrs Ballinger, Osric Dane's question was unsettling, and there was a general sense of gratitude when Laura Glyde leaned forward to say, with her most sympathetic accent: 'You must excuse us, Mrs Dane, for not being able, just at present, to talk of anything but "The Wings of Death." '

'Yes,' said Miss Van Vluyck, with a sudden resolve to carry the war into the enemy's camp. 'We are so anxious to know the exact purpose you had in mind in writing your wonderful book.'

'You will find,' Mrs Plinth interposed, 'that we are not super-ficial readers.'

'We are eager to hear from you,' Miss Van Vluyck continued, 'if the pessimistic tendency of the book is an expression of your own convictions or—'

'Or merely,' Miss Glyde thrust in, 'a sombre background brushed in to throw your figures into more vivid relief. *Are* you not primarily plastic?'

'*I* have always maintained,' Mrs Ballinger interposed, 'that you represent the purely objective method—'

Osric Dane helped herself critically to coffee. 'How do you define objective?' she then inquired.

There was a flurried pause before Laura Glyde intensely murmured: 'In reading *you* we don't define, we feel.'

Osric Dane smiled. 'The cerebellum,' she remarked, 'is not infrequently the seat of the literary emotions.' And she took a second lump of sugar.

The sting that this remark was vaguely felt to conceal was almost neutralized by the satisfaction of being addressed in such technical language.

'Ah, the cerebellum,' said Miss Van Vluyck complacently. 'The club took a course in psychology last winter.'

'Which psychology?' asked Osric Dane.

There was an agonizing pause, during which each member of the club secretly deplored the distressing inefficiency of the others. Only Mrs Roby went on placidly sipping her chartreuse. At last Mrs Ballinger said, with an attempt at a high tone: 'Well, really, you know, it was last year that we took psychology, and this winter we have been so absorbed in—'

She broke off, nervously trying to recall some of the club's discussions; but her faculties seemed to be paralysed by the petrifying stare of Osric Dane. What *had* the club been absorbed in? Mrs Ballinger, with a vague purpose of gaining time, repeated slowly: 'We've been so intensely absorbed in—'

Mrs Roby put down her liqueur glass and drew near the group with a smile.

'In Xingu?' she gently prompted.

A thrill ran through the other members. They exchanged confused glances, and then, with one accord, turned a gaze of mingled relief and interrogation on their rescuer. The expression of each denoted a different phase of the same emotion. Mrs Plinth was the first to compose her features to an air of reassurance: after a moment's hasty adjustment her look almost implied that it was she who had given the word to Mrs Ballinger.

'Xingu, of course!' exclaimed the latter with her accustomed promptness, while Miss Van Vluyck and Laura Glyde seemed to be plumbing the depths of memory, and Mrs Leveret, feeling apprehensively for Appropriate Allusions, was somehow reassured by the uncomfortable pressure of its bulk against her person.

Osric Dane's change of countenance was no less striking than that of her entertainers. She too put down her coffee-cup, but with a look of distinct annoyance; she too wore, for a brief moment, what Mrs Roby afterward described as the look of feeling for something in the back of her head; and before she could dissemble these momentary signs of weakness, Mrs Roby, turning to her with a deferential smile, had said: 'And we've been so hoping that today you would tell us just what you think of it.'

Osric Dane received the homage of the smile as a matter of course; but the accompanying question obviously embarrassed her, and it became clear to her observers that she was not quick at shifting her facial scenery. It was as though her countenance had so long been set in an expression of unchallenged superiority that the muscles had stiffened, and refused to obey her orders.

'Xingu—' she said, as if seeking in her turn to gain time.

Mrs Roby continued to press her. 'Knowing how engrossing the subject is, you will understand how it happens that the club has let everything else go to the wall for the moment. Since we took up Xingu I might almost say – were it not for your books – that nothing else seems to us worth remembering.'

Osric Dane's stern features were darkened rather than lit up by an uneasy smile. 'I am glad to hear that you make one exception,' she gave out between narrowed lips.

'Oh, of course,' Mrs Roby said prettily; 'but as you have shown us that – so very naturally! – you don't care to talk of your own things, we really can't let you off from telling us exactly what you think about Xingu; especially,' she added, with a still more persuasive smile, 'as some people say that one of your last books was saturated with it.'

It was an *it*, then – the assurance sped like fire through the parched minds of the other members. In their eagerness to gain the least little clue to Xingu they almost forgot the joy of assisting at the discomfiture of Mrs Dane.

The latter reddened nervously under her antagonist's challenge. 'May I ask,' she faltered out, 'to which of my books you refer?'

Mrs Roby did not falter. 'That's just what I want you to tell us; because, though I was present, I didn't actually take part.'

'Present at what?' Mrs Dane took her up; and for an instant the trembling members of the Lunch Club thought that the champion Providence had raised up for them had lost a point. But Mrs Roby explained herself gaily: 'At the discussion, of course. And so we're dreadfully anxious to know just how it was that you went into the Xingu.'

There was a portentous pause, a silence so big with incalculable dangers that the members with one accord checked the words on their lips, like soldiers dropping their arms to watch a single combat between their leaders. Then Mrs Dane gave expression to their inmost dread by saying sharply: 'Ah – you say *the* Xingu, do you?'

Mrs Roby smiled undauntedly. 'It *is* a shade pedantic, isn't it? Personally, I always drop the article; but I don't know how the other members feel about it.'

The other members looked as though they would willingly have dispensed with this appeal to their opinion, and Mrs Roby, after a bright glance about the group, went on: 'They probably think, as I do, that nothing really matters except the thing itself – except Xingu.'

No immediate reply seemed to occur to Mrs Dane, and Mrs Ballinger gathered courage to say: 'Surely everyone must feel that about Xingu.'

Mrs Plinth came to her support with a heavy murmur of assent, and Laura Glyde sighed out emotionally: 'I have known cases where it has changed a whole life.'

'It has done me worlds of good,' Mrs Leveret interjected, seeming to herself to remember that she had either taken it or read it the winter before.

'Of course,' Mrs Roby admitted, 'the difficulty is that one must give up so much time to it. It's very long.'

'I can't imagine,' said Miss Van Vluyck, 'grudging the time given to such a subject.'

'And deep in places,' Mrs Roby pursued; (so then it was a book!) 'And it isn't easy to skip.'

'I never skip,' said Mrs Plinth dogmatically.

'Ah, it's dangerous to, in Xingu. Even at the start there are places where one can't. One must just wade through.'

'I should hardly call it *wading*,' said Mrs Ballinger sarcastically.

Mrs Roby sent her a look of interest. 'Ah – you always found it went swimmingly?'

Mrs Ballinger hesitated. 'Of course there are difficult passages,' she conceded.

'Yes; some are not at all clear – even,' Mrs Roby added, 'if one is familiar with the original.'

'As I suppose you are?' Osric Dane interposed, suddenly fixing her with a look of challenge.

Mrs Roby met it by a deprecating gesture. 'Oh, it's really not difficult up to a certain point; though some of the branches are very little known, and it's almost impossible to get at the source.'

'Have you ever tried?' Mrs Plinth inquired, still distrustful of Mrs Roby's thoroughness.

Mrs Roby was silent for a moment; then she replied with lowered lids: 'No – but a friend of mine did; a very brilliant man; and he told me it was best for women – not to. . . .'

A shudder ran around the room. Mrs Leveret coughed so that the parlormaid, who was handing the cigarettes, should not hear; Miss Van Vluyck's face took on a nauseated expression, and Mrs

Plinth looked as if she were passing some one she did not care to bow to. But the most remarkable result of Mrs Roby's words was the effect they produced on the Lunch Club's distinguished guest. Osric Dane's impassive features suddenly softened to an expression of the warmest human sympathy, and edging her chair toward Mrs Roby's she asked: 'Did he really? And – did you find he was right?'

Mrs Ballinger, in whom annoyance at Mrs Roby's unwonted assumption of prominence was beginning to displace gratitude for the aid she had rendered, could not consent to her being allowed, by such dubious means, to monopolize the attention of their guest. If Osric Dane had not enough self-respect to resent Mrs Roby's flippancy, at least the Lunch Club would do so in the person of its President.

Mrs Ballinger laid her hand on Mrs Roby's arm. 'We must not forget,' she said with a frigid amiability, 'that absorbing as Xingu is to *us*, it may be less interesting to—'

'Oh, no, on the contrary, I assure you,' Osric Dane intervened.

'—to others,' Mrs Ballinger finished firmly; 'and we must not allow our little meeting to end without persuading Mrs Dane to say a few words to us on a subject which, today, is much more present in all our thoughts. I refer, of course, to "The Wings of Death."'

The other members, animated by various degrees of the same sentiment, and encouraged by the humanized mien of their redoubtable guest, repeated after Mrs Ballinger: 'Oh, yes, you really *must* talk to us a little about your book.'

Osric Dane's expression became as bored, though not as haughty, as when her work had been previously mentioned. But before she could respond to Mrs Ballinger's request, Mrs Roby had risen from her seat, and was pulling down her veil over her frivolous nose.

'I'm so sorry,' she said, advancing toward her hostess with outstretched hand, 'but before Mrs Dane begins I think I'd better run away. Unluckily, as you know, I haven't read her books, so I should be at a terrible disadvantage among you all, and besides, I've an engagement to play bridge.'

If Mrs Roby had simply pleaded her ignorance of Osric Dane's works as a reason for withdrawing, the Lunch Club, in view of her recent prowess, might have approved such evidence of discretion;

but to couple this excuse with the brazen announcement that she was foregoing the privilege for the purpose of joining a bridge-party was only one more instance of her deplorable lack of discrimination.

The ladies were disposed, however, to feel that her departure – now that she had performed the sole service she was ever likely to render them – would probably make for greater order and dignity in the impending discussion, besides relieving them of the sense of self-distrust which her presence always mysteriously produced. Mrs Ballinger therefore restricted herself to a formal murmur of regret, and the other members were just grouping themselves comfortably about Osric Dane when the latter, to their dismay, started up from the sofa on which she had been seated.

'Oh wait – do wait, and I'll go with you!' she called out to Mrs Roby; and, seizing the hands of the disconcerted members, she administered a series of farewell pressures with the mechanical haste of a railway-conductor punching tickets.

'I'm so sorry – I'd quite forgotten—' she flung back at them from the threshold; and as she joined Mrs Roby, who had turned in surprise at her appeal, the other ladies had the mortification of hearing her say, in a voice which she did not take the pains to lower: 'If you'll let me walk a little way with you, I should so like to ask you a few more questions about Xingu . . .'

3

The incident had been so rapid that the door closed on the departing pair before the other members had time to understand what was happening. Then a sense of the indignity put upon them by Osric Dane's unceremonious desertion began to contend with the confused feeling that they had been cheated out of their due without exactly knowing how or why.

There was a silence, during which Mrs Ballinger, with a perfunctory hand, rearranged the skilfully grouped literature at which her distinguished guest had not so much as glanced; then Miss Van Vluyck tartly pronounced: 'Well, I can't say that I consider Osric Dane's departure a great loss.'

This confession crystallized the resentment of the other members, and Mrs Leveret exclaimed: 'I do believe she came on purpose to be nasty!'

It was Mrs Plinth's private opinion that Osric Dane's attitude toward the Lunch Club might have been very different had it welcomed her in the majestic setting of the Plinth drawing-rooms; but not liking to reflect on the inadequacy of Mrs Ballinger's establishment she sought a roundabout satisfaction in depreciating her lack of foresight.

'I said from the first that we ought to have had a subject ready. It's what always happens when you're unprepared. Now if we'd only got up Xingu—'

The slowness of Mrs Plinth's mental processes was always allowed for by the club; but this instance of it was too much for Mrs Ballinger's equanimity.

'Xingu!' she scoffed. 'Why, it was the fact of our knowing so much more about it than she did – unprepared though we were – that made Osric Dane so furious. I should have thought that was plain enough to everybody!'

This retort impressed even Mrs Plinth, and Laura Glyde, moved by an impulse of generosity, said: 'Yes, we really ought to be grateful to Mrs Roby for introducing the topic. It may have made Osric Dane furious, but at least it made her civil.'

'I am glad we were able to show her,' added Miss Van Vluyck, 'that a broad and up-to-date culture is not confined to the great intellectual centers.'

This increased the satisfaction of the other members, and they began to forget their wrath against Osric Dane in the pleasure of having contributed to her discomfiture.

Miss Van Vluyck thoughtfully rubbed her spectacles. 'What surprised me most,' she continued, 'was that Fanny Roby should be so up on Xingu.'

This remark threw a slight chill on the company, but Mrs Ballinger said with an air of indulgent irony: 'Mrs Roby always has the knack of making a little go a long way; still, we certainly owe her a debt for happening to remember that she'd heard of Xingu.' And this was felt by the other members to be a graceful way of cancelling once for all the club's obligation to Mrs Roby.

Even Mrs Leveret took courage to speed a timid shaft of irony. 'I fancy Osric Dane hardly expected to take a lesson in Xingu at Hillbridge!'

Mrs Ballinger smiled. 'When she asked me what we represented

– do you remember? – I wish I'd simply said we represented Xingu!'

All the ladies laughed appreciatively at this sally, except Mrs Plinth, who said, after a moment's deliberation: 'I'm not sure it would have been wise to do so.'

Mrs Ballinger, who was already beginning to feel as if she had launched at Osric Dane the retort which had just occurred to her, turned ironically on Mrs Plinth. 'May I ask why?' she inquired.

Mrs Plinth looked grave. 'Surely,' she said, 'I understood from Mrs Roby herself that the subject was one it was as well not to go into too deeply?'

Miss Van Vluyck rejoined with precision: 'I think that applied only to an investigation of the origin of the – of the—'; and suddenly she found that her usually accurate memory had failed her. 'It's a part of the subject I never studied myself,' she concluded.

'Nor I,' said Mrs Ballinger.

Laura Glyde bent toward them with widened eyes. 'And yet it seems – doesn't it? – the part that is fullest of an esoteric fascination?'

'I don't know on what you base that,' said Miss Van Vluyck argumentatively.

'Well, didn't you notice how intensely interested Osric Dane became as soon as she heard what the brilliant foreigner – he *was* a foreigner, wasn't he? – had told Mrs Roby about the origin – the origin of the rite – or whatever you call it?'

Mrs Plinth looked disapproving, and Mrs Ballinger visibly wavered. Then she said: 'It may not be desirable to touch on the – on that part of the subject in general conversation; but, from the importance it evidently has to a woman of Osric Dane's distinction, I feel as if we ought not to be afraid to discuss it among ourselves – without gloves – though with closed doors, if necessary.'

'I'm quite of your opinion,' Miss Van Vluyck came briskly to her support; 'on condition, that is, that all grossness of language is avoided.'

'Oh, I'm sure we shall understand without that,' Mrs Leveret tittered; and Laura Glyde added significantly: 'I fancy we can read between the lines,' while Mrs Ballinger rose to assure herself that the doors were really closed.

Mrs Plinth had not yet given her adhesion. 'I hardly see,' she began, 'what benefit is to be derived from investigating such peculiar customs—'

But Mrs Ballinger's patience had reached the extreme limit of tension. 'This at least,' she returned; 'that we shall not be placed again in the humiliating position of finding ourselves less up on our own subjects than Fanny Roby!'

Even to Mrs Plinth this argument was conclusive. She peered furtively about the room and lowered her commanding tones to ask: 'Have you got a copy?'

'A – a copy?' stammered Mrs Ballinger. She was aware that the other members were looking at her expectantly, and that this answer was inadequate, so she supported it by asking another question. 'A copy of what?'

Her companions bent their expectant gaze on Mrs Plinth, who, in turn, appeared less sure of herself than usual. 'Why, of – of – the book,' she explained.

'What book?' snapped Miss Van Vluyck, almost as sharply as Osric Dane.

Mrs Ballinger looked at Laura Glyde, whose eyes were interrogatively fixed on Mrs Leveret. The fact of being deferred to was so new to the latter that it filled her with an insane temerity. 'Why, Xingu, of course!' she exclaimed.

A profound silence followed this challenge to the resources of Mrs Ballinger's library, and the latter, after glancing nervously toward the Books of the Day, returned with dignity: 'It's not a thing one cares to leave about.'

'I should think *not*!' exclaimed Mrs Plinth.

'It *is* a book, then?' said Miss Van Vluyck.

This again threw the company into disarray, and Mrs Ballinger, with an impatient sigh, rejoined: 'Why – there *is* a book – naturally. . . .'

'Then why did Miss Glyde call it a religion?'

Laura Glyde started up. 'A religion? I never—'

'Yes, you did,' Miss Van Vluyck insisted; 'you spoke of rites; and Mrs Plinth said it was a custom.'

Miss Glyde was evidently making a desperate effort to recall her statement; but accuracy of detail was not her strongest point. At length she began in a deep murmur: 'Surely they used to do something of the kind at the Eleusinian mysteries—'

'Oh—' said Miss Van Vluyck, on the verge of disapproval; and Mrs Plinth protested: 'I understood there was to be no indelicacy!'

Mrs Ballinger could not control her irritation. 'Really, it is too bad that we should not be able to talk the matter over quietly among ourselves. Personally, I think that if one goes into Xingu at all—'

'Oh, so do I!' cried Miss Glyde.

'And I don't see how one can avoid doing so, if one wishes to keep up with the Thought of the Day—'

Mrs Leveret uttered an exclamation of relief. 'There – that's it!' she interposed.

'What's it?' the President took her up.

'Why – it's a – a Thought: I mean a philosophy.'

This seemed to bring a certain relief to Mrs Ballinger and Laura Glyde, but Miss Van Vluyck said: 'Excuse me if I tell you that you're all mistaken. Xingu happens to be a language.'

'A language!' the Lunch Club cried.

'Certainly. Don't you remember Fanny Roby's saying that there were several branches, and that some were hard to trace? What could that apply to but dialects?'

Mrs Ballinger could no longer restrain a contemptuous laugh. 'Really, if the Lunch Club has reached such a pass that it has to go to Fanny Roby for instruction on a subject like Xingu, it had almost better cease to exist!'

'It's really her fault for not being clearer,' Laura Glyde put in.

'Oh, clearness and Fanny Roby!' Mrs Ballinger shrugged. 'I daresay we shall find she was mistaken on almost every point.'

'Why not look it up?' said Mrs Plinth.

As a rule this recurrent suggestion of Mrs Plinth's was ignored in the heat of discussion, and only resorted to afterward in the privacy of each member's home. But on the present occasion the desire to ascribe their own confusion of thought to the vague and contradictory nature of Mrs Roby's statements caused the members of the Lunch Club to utter a collective demand for a book of reference.

At this point the production of her treasured volume gave Mrs Leveret, for a moment, the unusual experience of occupying the center front; but she was not able to hold it long, for Appropriate Allusions contained no mention of Xingu.

'Oh, that's not the kind of thing we want!' exclaimed Miss Van

Vluyck. She cast a disparaging glance over Mrs Ballinger's assortment of literature, and added impatiently: 'Haven't you any useful books?'

'Of course I have,' replied Mrs Ballinger indignantly; 'I keep them in my husband's dressing-room.'

From this region, after some difficulty and delay, the parlormaid produced the W–Z volume of an encyclopedia and, in deference to the fact that the demand for it had come from Miss Van Vluyck, laid the ponderous tome before her.

There was a moment of painful suspense while Miss Van Vluyck rubbed her spectacles, adjusted them, and turned to Z; and a murmur of surprise when she said: 'It isn't here.'

'I suppose,' said Mrs Plinth, 'it's not fit to be put in a book of reference.'

'Oh, nonsense!' exclaimed Mrs Ballinger. 'Try X.'

Miss Van Vluyck turned back through the volume, peering short-sightedly up and down the pages, till she came to a stop and remained motionless, like a dog on a point.

'Well, have you found it?' Mrs Ballinger inquired after a considerable delay.

'Yes. I've found it,' said Miss Van Vluyck in a queer voice.

Mrs Plinth hastily interposed: 'I beg you won't read it aloud if there's anything offensive.'

Miss Van Vluyck, without answering, continued her silent scrutiny.

'Well, what *is* it?' exclaimed Laura Glyde excitedly.

'*Do* tell us!' urged Mrs Leveret, feeling that she would have something awful to tell her sister.

Miss Van Vluyck pushed the volume aside and turned slowly toward the expectant group.

'It's a river.'

'A *river*?'

'Yes: in Brazil. Isn't that where she's been living?'

'Who? Fanny Roby? Oh, but you must be mistaken. You've been reading the wrong thing,' Mrs Ballinger exclaimed, leaning over her to seize the volume.

'It's the only *Xingu* in the encyclopedia; and she *has* been living in Brazil,' Miss Van Vluyck persisted.

'Yes: her brother has a consulship there,' Mrs Leveret interposed.

'But it's too ridiculous! I – we – why we *all* remember studying Xingu last year – or the year before last,' Mrs Ballinger stammered.

'I thought I did when *you* said so,' Laura Glyde avowed.

'*I* said so?' cried Mrs Ballinger.

'Yes. You said it had crowded everything else out of your mind.'

'Well *you* said it had changed your whole life!'

'For that matter, Miss Van Vluyck said she had never grudged the time she'd given it.'

Mrs Plinth interposed: 'I made it clear that I knew nothing whatever of the original.'

Mrs Ballinger broke off the dispute with a groan. 'Oh, what does it all matter if she's been making fools of us? I believe Miss Van Vluyck's right – she was talking of the river all the while!'

'How could she? It's too preposterous,' Miss Glyde exclaimed.

'Listen.' Miss Van Vluyck had repossessed herself of the encyclopedia, and restored her spectacles to a nose reddened by excitement. ' "The Xingu, one of the principal rivers of Brazil, rises on the plateau of Mato Grosso, and flows in a northerly direction for a length of no less than one thousand one hundred and eighteen miles, entering the Amazon near the mouth of the latter river. The upper course of the Xingu is auriferous and fed by numerous branches. Its source was first discovered in 1884 by the German explorer von den Steinen, after a difficult and dangerous expedition through a region inhabited by tribes still in the Stone Age of culture." '

The ladies received this communication in a state of stupefied silence from which Mrs Leveret was the first to rally. 'She certainly *did* speak of its having branches.'

The word seemed to snap the last thread of their incredulity. 'And of its great length,' gasped Mrs Ballinger.

'She said it was awfully deep, and you couldn't skip – you just had to wade through,' Miss Glyde added.

The idea worked its way more slowly through Mrs Plinth's compact resistances. 'How could there be anything improper about a river?' she inquired.

'Improper?'

'Why, what she said about the source – that it was corrupt?'

'Not corrupt, but hard to get at,' Laura Clyde corrected. 'Some one who'd been there had told her so. I daresay it was the explorer himself – doesn't it say the expedition was dangerous?'

' "Difficult and dangerous," ' read Miss Van Vluyck.

Mrs Ballinger pressed her hands to her throbbing temples. 'There's nothing she said that wouldn't apply to a river – to this river!' She swung about excitedly to the other members. 'Why, do you remember her telling us that she hadn't read "The Supreme Instant" because she'd taken it on a boating party while she was staying with her brother, and some one had "shied" it overboard – "shied" of course was her own expression.'

The ladies breathlessly signified that the expression had not escaped them.

'Well – and then didn't she tell Osric Dane that one of her books was simply saturated with Xingu? Of course it was, if one of Mrs Roby's rowdy friends had thrown it into the river!'

This surprising reconstruction of the scene in which they had just participated left the members of the Lunch Club inarticulate. At length, Mrs Plinth, after visibly laboring with the problem, said in a heavy tone: 'Osric Dane was taken in too.'

Mrs Leveret took courage at this. 'Perhaps that's what Mrs Roby did it for. She said Osric Dane was a brute, and she may have wanted to give her a lesson.'

Miss Van Vluyck frowned. 'It was hardly worthwhile to do it at our expense.'

'At least,' said Miss Glyde with a touch of bitterness, 'she succeeded in interesting her, which was more than we did.'

'What chance had we?' rejoined Mrs Ballinger. 'Mrs Roby monopolized her from the first. And *that*, I've no doubt, was her purpose – to give Osric Dane a false impression of her own standing in the club. She would hesitate at nothing to attract attention: we all know how she took in poor Professor Foreland.'

'She actually makes him give bridge-teas every Thursday,' Mrs Leveret piped up.

Laura Glyde struck her hands together. 'Why, this is Thursday, and it's *there* she's gone, of course; and taken Osric with her!'

'And they're shrieking over us at this moment,' said Mrs Ballinger between her teeth.

This possibility seemed too preposterous to be admitted. 'She would hardly dare,' said Miss Van Vluyck, 'confess the imposture to Osric Dane.'

'I'm not so sure: I thought I saw her make a sign as she left. If she hadn't made a sign, why should Osric Dane have rushed out after her?'

'Well, you know, we'd all been telling her how wonderful Xingu was, and she said she wanted to find out more about it,' Mrs Leveret said, with a tardy impulse of justice to the absent.

This reminder, far from mitigating the wrath of the other members, gave it a stronger impetus.

'Yes – and that's exactly what they're both laughing over now,' said Laura Glyde ironically.

Mrs Plinth stood up and gathered her expensive furs about her monumental form. 'I have no wish to criticize,' she said; 'but unless the Lunch Club can protect its members against the recurrence of such – such unbecoming scenes, I for one—'

'Oh, so do I!' agreed Miss Glyde, rising also.

Miss Van Vluyck closed the encyclopedia and proceeded to button herself into her jacket. 'My time is really too valuable—' she began.

'I fancy we are all of one mind,' said Mrs Ballinger, looking searchingly at Mrs Leveret, who looked at the others.

'I always deprecate anything like a scandal—' Mrs Plinth continued.

'She has been the cause of one today!' exclaimed Miss Glyde.

Mrs Leveret moaned: 'I don't see how she *could*!' and Miss Van Vluyck said, picking up her note-book: 'Some women stop at nothing.'

'—but if,' Mrs Plinth took up her argument impressively, 'anything of the kind had happened in *my* house' (it never would have, her tone implied), 'I should have felt that I owed it to myself either to ask for Mrs Roby's resignation – or to offer mine.'

'Oh, Mrs Plinth—' gasped the Lunch Club.

'Fortunately for me,' Mrs Plinth continued with an awful magnanimity, 'the matter was taken out of my hands by our President's decision that the right to entertain distinguished guests was a privilege vested in her office; and I think the other members will agree that, as she was alone in this opinion, she ought to be alone in deciding on the best way of effacing its – its really deplorable consequences.'

A deep silence followed this outbreak of Mrs Plinth's long-stored resentment.

'I don't see why *I* should be expected to ask her to resign—' Mrs Ballinger at length began; but Laura Glyde turned back to remind her: 'You know she made you say that you'd got on swimmingly in Xingu.'

An ill-timed giggle escaped from Mrs Leveret, and Mrs Ballinger energetically continued '—but you needn't think for a moment that I'm afraid to!'

The door of the drawing-room closed on the retreating backs of the Lunch Club, and the President of that distinguished association, seating herself at her writing-table, and pushing away a copy of 'The Wings of Death' to make room for her elbow, drew forth a sheet of the club's note-paper, on which she began to write: 'My dear Mrs Roby—'

Bewitched

1

The snow was still falling thickly when Orrin Bosworth, who farmed the land south of Lonetop, drove up in his cutter to Saul Rutledge's gate. He was surprised to see two other cutters ahead of him. From them descended two muffled figures. Bosworth, with increasing surprise, recognized Deacon Hibben, from North Ashmore, and Sylvester Brand, the widower, from the old Bearcliff farm on the way to Lonetop.

It was not often that anybody in Hemlock County entered Saul Rutledge's gate; least of all in the dead of winter, and summoned (as Bosworth, at any rate, had been) by Mrs Rutledge, who passed, even in that unsocial region, for a woman of cold manners and solitary character. The situation was enough to excite the curiosity of a less imaginative man than Orrin Bosworth.

As he drove in between the broken-down white gateposts topped by fluted urns the two men ahead of him were leading their horses to the adjoining shed. Bosworth followed, and hitched his horse to a post. Then the three tossed off the snow from their shoulders, clapped their numb hands together, and greeted each other.

'Hallo, Deacon.'

'Well, well, Orrin—' They shook hands.

' 'Day, Bosworth,' said Sylvester Brand, with a brief nod. He seldom put any cordiality into his manner, and on this occasion he was still busy about his horse's bridle and blanket.

Orrin Bosworth, the youngest and most communicative of the three, turned back to Deacon Hibben, whose long face, queerly blotched and moldy-looking, with blinking peering eyes, was yet less forbidding than Brand's heavily-hewn countenance.

'Queer, our all meeting here this way. Mrs Rutledge sent me a message to come,' Bosworth volunteered.

The Deacon nodded. 'I got a word from her too – Andy Pond come with it yesterday noon. I hope there's no trouble here—'

He glanced through the thickening fall of snow at the desolate front of the Rutledge house, the more melancholy in its present neglected state because, like the gateposts, it kept traces of former elegance. Bosworth had often wondered how such a house had come to be built in that lonely stretch between North Ashmore and Cold Corners. People said there had once been other houses like it, forming a little township called Ashmore, a sort of mountain colony created by the caprice of an English Royalist officer, one Colonel Ashmore, who had been murdered by the Indians, with all his family, long before the Revolution. This tale was confirmed by the fact that the ruined cellars of several smaller houses were still to be discovered under the wild growth of the adjoining slopes, and that the Communion plate of the moribund Episcopal church of Cold Corners was engraved with the name of Colonel Ashmore, who had given it to the church of Ashmore in the year 1723. Of the church itself no traces remained. Doubtless it had been a modest wooden edifice, built on piles, and the conflagration which had burnt the other houses to the ground's edge had reduced it utterly to ashes. The whole place, even in summer, wore a mournful solitary air, and people wondered why Saul Rutledge's father had gone there to settle.

'I never knew a place,' Deacon Hibben said, 'as seemed as far away from humanity. And yet it ain't so in miles.'

'Miles ain't the only distance,' Orrin Bosworth answered; and the two men, followed by Sylvester Brand, walked across the drive to the front door. People in Hemlock County did not usually come and go by their front doors, but all three men seemed to feel that, on an occasion which appeared to be so exceptional, the usual and more familiar approach by the kitchen would not be suitable.

They had judged rightly; the Deacon had hardly lifted the knocker when the door opened and Mrs Rutledge stood before them.

'Walk right in,' she said in her usual dead-level tone; and Bosworth, as he followed the others, thought to himself: 'Whatever's happened, she's not going to let it show in her face.'

It was doubtful, indeed, if anything unwonted could be made to show in Prudence Rutledge's face, so limited was its scope, so fixed were its features. She was dressed for the occasion in a black calico with white spots, a collar of crochet lace fastened by a gold brooch, and a gray woollen shawl, crossed under her arms and tied at the back. In her small narrow head the only marked prominence was that of the brow projecting roundly over pale spectacled eyes. Her dark hair, parted above this prominence, passed tight and flat over the tips of her ears into a small braided coil at the nape; and her contracted head looked still narrower from being perched on a long hollow neck with cord-like throat muscles. Her eyes were of a pale cold gray, her complexion was an even white. Her age might have been anywhere from thirty-five to sixty.

The room into which she led the three men had probably been the dining-room of the Ashmore house. It was now used as a front parlor, and a black stove planted on a sheet of zinc stuck out from the delicately-fluted panels of an old wooden mantel. A newly-lit fire smoldered reluctantly, and the room was at once close and bitterly cold.

'Andy Pond,' Mrs Rutledge cried out to some one at the back of the house, 'Step out and call Mr Rutledge. You'll likely find him in the woodshed, or round the barn somewhere.' She rejoined her visitors. 'Please suit yourselves to seats,' she said.

The three men, with an increasing air of constraint, took the chairs she pointed out, and Mrs Rutledge sat stiffly down upon a fourth, behind a rickety beadwork table. She glanced from one to the other of her visitors.

'I presume you folks are wondering what it is I asked you to come here for,' she said in her dead-level voice. Orrin Bosworth and Deacon Hibben murmured an assent; Sylvester Brand sat silent, his eyes, under their great thicket of eyebrows, fixed on the huge boot tip swinging before him.

'Well, I allow you didn't expect it was for a party,' continued Mrs Rutledge.

No one ventured to respond to this chill pleasantry, and she continued: 'We're in trouble here, and that's the fact. And we need advice – Mr Rutledge and myself do.' She cleared her throat, and added in a lower tone, her pitilessly clear eyes looking straight before her: 'There's a spell been cast over Mr Rutledge.'

The Deacon looked up sharply, an incredulous smile pinching his thin lips. 'A spell?'

'That's what I said: he's bewitched.'

Again the three visitors were silent; then Bosworth, more at ease or less tongue-tied than the others, asked with an attempt at humor: 'Do you use the word in the strict Scripture sense, Mrs Rutledge?'

She glanced at him before replying: 'That's how *he* uses it.'

The Deacon coughed and cleared his long rattling throat. 'Do you care to give us more particulars before your husband joins us?'

Mrs Rutledge looked down at her clasped hands, as if considering the question. Bosworth noticed that the inner fold of her lids was of the same uniform white as the rest of her skin, so that when she drooped them her rather prominent eyes looked like the sightless orbs of a marble statue. The impression was unpleasing, and he glanced away at the text over the mantelpiece, which read:

The Soul That Sinneth It Shall Die.

'No,' she said at length, 'I'll wait.'

At this moment Sylvester Brand suddenly stood up and pushed back his chair. 'I don't know,' he said, in his rough bass voice, 'as I've got any particular lights on Bible mysteries; and this happens to be the day I was to go down to Starkfield to close a deal with a man.'

Mrs Rutledge lifted one of her long thin hands. Withered and wrinkled by hard work and cold, it was nevertheless of the same leaden white as her face. 'You won't be kept long,' she said. 'Won't you be seated?'

Farmer Brand stood irresolute, his purplish underlip twitching. 'The Deacon here – such things is more in his line. . . .'

'I want you should stay,' said Mrs Rutledge quietly; and Brand sat down again.

A silence fell, during which the four persons present seemed all to be listening for the sound of a step; but none was heard, and after a minute or two Mrs Rutledge began to speak again.

'It's down by that old shack on Lamer's pond; that's where they meet,' she said suddenly.

Bosworth, whose eyes were on Sylvester Brand's face, fancied he saw a sort of inner flush darken the farmer's heavy leathern skin. Deacon Hibben leaned forward, a glitter of curiosity in his eyes.

'They – *who*, Mrs Rutledge?'

'My husband, Saul Rutledge . . . and her. . . .'

Sylvester Brand again stirred in his seat. 'Who do you mean by *her?*' he asked abruptly, as if roused out of some far-off musing.

Mrs Rutledge's body did not move; she simply revolved her head on her long neck and looked at him.

'Your daughter, Sylvester Brand.'

The man staggered to his feet with an explosion of inarticulate sounds. 'My – my daughter? What the hell are you talking about? My daughter? It's a damned lie . . . it's . . . it's . . .'

'Your daughter *Ora*, Mr Brand,' said Mrs Rutledge slowly.

Bosworth felt an icy chill down his spine. Instinctively he turned his eyes away from Brand, and they rested on the mildewed countenance of Deacon Hibben. Between the blotches it had become as white as Mrs Rutledge's, and the Deacon's eyes burned in the whiteness like live embers among ashes.

Brand gave a laugh: the rusty creaking laugh of one whose springs of mirth are never moved by gaiety. 'My daughter *Ora?*' he repeated.

'Yes.'

'My *dead* daughter?'

'That's what he says.'

'Your husband?'

'That's what Mr Rutledge says.'

Orrin Bosworth listened with a sense of suffocation; he felt as if he were wrestling with long-armed horrors in a dream. He could no longer resist letting his eyes turn to Sylvester Brand's face. To his surprise it had resumed a natural imperturbable expression. Brand rose to his feet. 'Is that all?' he queried contemptuously.

'All? Ain't it enough? How long is it since you folks seen Saul Rutledge, any of you?' Mrs Rutledge flew out at them.

Bosworth, it appeared, had not seen him for nearly a year; the Deacon had only run across him once, for a minute, at the North Ashmore post office, the previous autumn, and acknowledged that he wasn't looking any too good then. Brand said nothing, but stood irresolute.

'Well, if you wait a minute you'll see with your own eyes; and he'll tell you with his own words. That's what I've got you here for – to see for yourselves what's come over him. Then you'll talk different,' she added, twisting her head abruptly toward Sylvester Brand.

The Deacon raised a lean hand of interrogation.

'Does your husband know we've been sent for on this business, Mrs Rutledge?'

Mrs Rutledge signed assent.

'It was with his consent, then − ?'

She looked coldly at her questioner. 'I guess it had to be,' she said. Again Bosworth felt the chill down his spine. He tried to dissipate the sensation by speaking with an affectation of energy.

'Can you tell us, Mrs Rutledge, how this trouble you speak of shows itself . . . what makes you think . . . ?'

She looked at him for a moment; then she leaned forward across the rickety beadwork table. A thin smile of disdain narrowed her colorless lips. 'I don't think − I know.'

'Well − but how?'

She leaned closer, both elbows on the table, her voice dropping. 'I seen 'em.'

In the ashen light from the veiling of snow beyond the windows the Deacon's little screwed-up eyes seemed to give out red sparks. 'Him and the dead?'

'Him and the dead.'

'Saul Rutledge and − and Ora Brand?'

'That's so.'

Sylvester Brand's chair fell backward with a crash. He was on his feet again, crimson and cursing. 'It's a God-damned fiend-begotten lie. . . .'

'Friend Brand . . . friend Brand . . .' the Deacon protested.

'Here, let me get out of this. I want to see Saul Rutledge himself, and tell him—'

'Well, here he is,' said Mrs Rutledge.

The outer door had opened; they heard the familiar stamping and shaking of a man who rids his garments of their last snowflakes before penetrating to the sacred precincts of the best parlor. Then Saul Rutledge entered.

2

As he came in he faced the light from the north window, and Bosworth's first thought was that he looked like a drowned man fished out from under the ice − 'self-drowned,' he added. But the snow light plays cruel tricks with a man's color, and even with the shape of his features; it must have been partly that, Bosworth reflected, which transformed Saul Rutledge from the straight muscular fellow he had been a year before into the haggard wretch now before them.

The Deacon sought for a word to ease the horror. 'Well, now, Saul – you look's if you'd ought to set right up to the stove. Had a touch of ague, maybe?'

The feeble attempt was unavailing. Rutledge neither moved nor answered. He stood among them silent, incommunicable, like one risen from the dead.

Brand grasped him roughly by the shoulder. 'See here, Saul Rutledge, what's this dirty lie your wife tells us you've been putting about?'

Still Rutledge did not move. 'It's no lie,' he said.

Brand's hand dropped from his shoulder. In spite of the man's rough bullying power he seemed to be undefinably awed by Rutledge's look and tone.

'No lie? You've gone plumb crazy, then, have you?'

Mrs Rutledge spoke. 'My husband's not lying, nor he ain't gone crazy. Don't I tell you I seen 'em?'

Brand laughed again. 'Him and the dead?'

'Yes.'

'Down by the Lamer pond, you say?'

'Yes.'

'And when was that, if I might ask?'

'Day before yesterday.'

A silence fell on the strangely assembled group. The Deacon at length broke it to say to Mr Brand: 'Brand, in my opinion we've got to see this thing through.'

Brand stood for a moment in speechless contemplation: there was something animal and primitive about him, Bosworth thought, as he hung thus, lowering and dumb, a little foam beading the corners of that heavy purplish underlip. He let himself slowly down into his chair. 'I'll see it through.'

The two other men and Mrs Rutledge had remained seated. Saul Rutledge stood before them, like a prisoner at the bar, or rather like a sick man before the physicians who were to heal him. As Bosworth scrutinized that hollow face, so wan under the dark sunburn, so sucked inward and consumed by some hidden fever, there stole over the sound healthy man the thought that perhaps, after all, husband and wife spoke the truth, and that they were all at that moment really standing on the edge of some forbidden mystery. Things that the rational mind would reject without a thought seemed no longer so easy to dispose of as one looked at the actual Saul Rutledge and remembered the man he had been a year before. Yes; as the Deacon said, they would have to see it through. . . .

'Sit down then, Saul; draw up to us, won't you?' the Deacon suggested, trying again for a natural tone.

Mrs Rutledge pushed a chair forward, and her husband sat down on it. He stretched out his arms and grasped his knees in his brown bony fingers; in that attitude he remained, turned neither his head nor his eyes.

'Well, Saul,' the Deacon continued, 'your wife says you thought mebbe we could do something to help you through this trouble, whatever it is.'

Rutledge's gray eyes widened a little. 'No; I didn't think that. It was her idea to try what could be done.'

'I presume, though, since you've agreed to our coming, that you don't object to our putting a few questions?'

Rutledge was silent for a moment; then he said with a visible effort: 'No; I don't object.'

'Well – you've heard what your wife says?'

Rutledge made a slight motion of assent.

'And – what have you got to answer? How do you explain . . . ?'

Mrs Rutledge intervened. 'How can he explain? I seen 'em.'

There was a silence; then Bosworth, trying to speak in an easy reassuring tone, queried: 'That so, Saul?'

'That's so.'

Brand lifted up his brooding head. 'You mean to say you . . . you sit here before us all and say . . .'

The Deacon's hand again checked him. 'Hold on, friend Brand. We're all of us trying for the facts, ain't we?' He turned to Rutledge. 'We've heard what Mrs Rutledge says. What's your answer?'

'I don't know as there's any answer. She found us.'

'And you mean to tell me the person with you was . . . was what you took to be . . .' the Deacon's thin voice grew thinner, 'Ora Brand?'

Saul Rutledge nodded.

'You knew . . . or thought you knew . . . you were meeting with the dead?'

Rutledge bent his head again. The snow continued to fall in a steady unwavering sheet against the window, and Bosworth felt as if a winding sheet were descending from the sky to envelop them all in a common grave.

'Think what you're saying! It's against our religion! Ora . . . poor child! . . . died over a year ago. I saw you at her funeral, Saul. How can you make such a statement?'

'What else can he do?' thrust in Mrs Rutledge.

There was another pause. Bosworth's resources had failed him, and Brand once more sat plunged in dark meditation. The Deacon laid his quivering fingertips together, and moistened his lips.

'Was the day before yesterday the first time?' he asked.

The movement of Rutledge's head was negative.

'Not the first? Then when . . . ?'

'Nigh on a year ago, I reckon.'

'God! And you mean to tell us that ever since – ?'

'Well . . . look at him,' said his wife. The three men lowered their eyes.

After a moment Bosworth, trying to collect himself, glanced at the Deacon. 'Why not ask Saul to make his own statement, if that's what we're here for?'

'That's so,' the Deacon assented. He turned to Rutledge. 'Will you try and give us your idea . . . of . . . of how it began?'

There was another silence. Then Rutledge tightened his grasp on his gaunt knees, and still looking straight ahead, with his curiously clear, unseeing gaze: 'Well,' he said, 'I guess it begun away back, afore even I was married to Mrs Rutledge. . . .' He spoke in a low automatic voice, as if some invisible agent were dictating his words, or even uttering them for him. 'You know,' he added, 'Ora and me was to have been married.'

Sylvester Brand lifted his head. 'Straighten that statement out first, please,' he interjected.

'What I mean is, we kept company. But Ora she was very young. Mr Brand here he sent her away. She was gone nigh to three years, I guess. When she come back I was married.'

'That's right,' Brand said, relapsing once more into his sunken attitude.

'And after she came back did you meet her again?' the Deacon continued.

'Alive?' Rutledge questioned.

A perceptible shudder ran through the room.

'Well – of course,' said the Deacon nervously.

Rutledge seemed to consider. 'Once I did – only once. There was a lot of other people round. At Cold Corners Fair it was.'

'Did you talk with her then?'

'Only a minute.'

'What did she say?'

His voice dropped. 'She said she was sick and knew she was going to die, and when she was dead she'd come back to me.'

'And what did you answer?'

'Nothing.'

'Did you think anything of it at the time?'

'Well, no. Not till I heard she was dead I didn't. After that I thought of it – and I guess she drew me.' He moistened his lips.

'Drew you down to that abandoned house by the pond?'

Rutledge made a faint motion of assent, and the Deacon added: 'How did you know it was there she wanted you to come?'

'She . . . just drew me. . . .'

There was a long pause. Bosworth felt, on himself and the other two men, the oppressive weight of the next question to be asked. Mrs Rutledge opened and closed her narrow lips once or twice, like some beached shellfish gasping for the tide. Rutledge waited.

'Well, now, Saul, won't you go on with what you was telling us?' the Deacon at length suggested.

'That's all. There's nothing else.'

The Deacon lowered his voice. 'She just draws you?'

'Yes.'

'Often?'

'That's as it happens. . . .'

'But if it's always there she draws you, man, haven't you the strength to keep away from the place?'

For the first time, Rutledge wearily turned his head toward his questioner. A spectral smile narrowed his colorless lips. 'Ain't any use. She follers after me. . . .'

There was another silence. What more could they ask, then and there? Mrs Rutledge's presence checked the next question. The Deacon seemed hopelessly to revolve the matter. At length he spoke in a more authoritative tone. 'These are forbidden things. You know that, Saul. Have you tried prayer?'

Rutledge shook his head.

'Will you pray with us now?'

Rutledge cast a glance of freezing indifference on his spiritual adviser. 'If you folks want to pray, I'm agreeable,' he said. But Mrs Rutledge intervened.

'Prayer ain't any good. In this kind of thing it ain't no manner of use; you know it ain't. I called you here, Deacon, because you remember the last case in this parish. Thirty years ago it was, I guess; but you remember. Lefferts Nash – did praying help *him*? I was a little girl then, but I used to hear my folks talk of it winter nights. Lefferts Nash and Hannah Cory. They drove a stake through her breast. That's what cured him.'

'Oh—' Orrin Bosworth exclaimed.

Sylvester Brand raised his head. 'You're speaking of that old story as if this was the same sort of thing?'

'Ain't it? Ain't my husband pining away the same as Lefferts Nash did? The Deacon here knows—'

The Deacon stirred anxiously in his chair. 'These are forbidden things,' he repeated. 'Supposing your husband is quite sincere in thinking himself haunted, as you might say. Well, even then, what proof have we that the . . . the dead woman . . . is the specter of that poor girl?'

'Proof? Don't he say so? Didn't she tell him? Ain't I seen 'em?' Mrs Rutledge almost screamed.

The three men sat silent, and suddenly the wife burst out: 'A stake through the breast! That's the old way; and it's the only way. The Deacon knows it!'

'It's against our religion to disturb the dead.'

'Ain't it against your religion to let the living perish as my husband is perishing?' She sprang up with one of her abrupt movements and took the family Bible from the whatnot in a corner of the parlor. Putting the book on the table, and moistening a livid fingertip, she turned the pages rapidly, till she came to one on which she laid her hand like a stony paperweight. 'See here,' she said, and read out in her level chanting voice:

' "*Thou shalt not suffer a witch to live.*" '

'That's in Exodus, that's where it is,' she added, leaving the book open as if to confirm the statement.

Bosworth continued to glance anxiously from one to the other of
the four people about the table. He was younger than any of
them, and had had more contact with the modern world; down in
Starkfield, in the bar of the Fielding House, he could hear himself
laughing with the rest of the men at such old wives' tales. But it
was not for nothing that he had been born under the icy shadow
of Lonetop, and had shivered and hungered as a lad through the
bitter Hemlock County winters. After his parents died, and he had
taken hold of the farm himself, he had got more out of it by using
improved methods, and by supplying the increasing throng of
summer boarders over Stotesbury way with milk and vegetables.
He had been made a Selectman of North Ashmore; for so young a
man he had a standing in the county. But the roots of the old life
were still in him. He could remember, as a little boy, going twice a
year with his mother to that bleak hill farm out beyond Sylvester
Brand's, where Mrs Bosworth's aunt, Cressidora Cheney, had
been shut up for years in a cold clean room with iron bars to the
windows. When little Orrin first saw Aunt Cressidora she was a
small white old woman, whom her sisters use to 'make decent' for
visitors the day that Orrin and his mother were expected. The
child wondered why there were bars on the window. 'Like a
canary bird,' he said to his mother. The phrase made Mrs
Bosworth reflect. 'I do believe they keep Aunt Cressidora too lonesome,' she said; and the next time she went up the mountain with
the little boy he carried to his great-aunt a canary in a little wooden
cage. It was a great excitement; he knew it would make her happy.

The old woman's motionless face lit up when she saw the bird,
and her eyes began to glitter. 'It belongs to me,' she said instantly,
stretching her soft bony hand over the cage.

'Of course it does, Aunt Cressy,' said Mrs Bosworth, her eyes
filling.

But the bird, startled by the shadow of the old woman's hand,
began to flutter and beat its wings distractedly. At the sight, Aunt
Cressidora's calm face suddenly became a coil of twitching
features. 'You she-devil, you!' she cried in a high, squealing voice;
and thrusting her hand into the cage she dragged out the terrified
bird and wrung its neck. She was plucking the hot body, and
squealing 'she-devil, she-devil!' as they drew little Orrin from the
room. On the way down the mountain his mother wept a great
deal, and said: 'You must never tell anybody that poor Auntie's

crazy, or the men would come and take her down to the asylum at Starkfield, and the shame of it would kill us all. Now promise.' The child promised.

He remembered the scene now, with its deep fringe of mystery, secrecy and rumor. It seemed related to a great many other things below the surface of his thoughts, things which stole up anew, making him feel that all the old people he had known, and who 'believed in these things,' might after all be right. Hadn't a witch been burned at North Ashmore? Didn't the summer folk still drive over in jolly buckboard loads to see the meetinghouse where the trial had been held, the pond where they had ducked her and she had floated? . . . Deacon Hibben believed; Bosworth was sure of it. If he didn't, why did people from all over the place come to him when their animals had queer sicknesses, or when there was a child in the family that had to be kept shut up because it fell down flat and foamed? Yes, in spite of his religion, Deacon Hibben *knew*. . . .

And Brand? Well, it came to Bosworth in a flash: that North Ashmore woman who was burned had the name of Brand. The same stock, no doubt; there had been Brands in Hemlock County ever since the white men had come there. And Orrin, when he was a child, remembered hearing his parents say that Sylvester Brand hadn't ever oughter married his own cousin, because of the blood. Yet the couple had had two healthy girls, and when Mrs Brand pined away and died nobody suggested that anything had been wrong with her mind. And Vanessa and Ora were the handsomest girls anywhere round. Brand knew it, and scrimped and saved all he could to send Ora, the eldest, down to Starkfield to learn bookkeeping. 'When she's married I'll send you,' he used to say to little Venny, who was his favorite. But Ora never married. She was away three years, during which Venny ran wild on the slopes of Lonetop; and when Ora came back she sickened and died – poor girl! Since then Brand had grown more savage and morose. He was a hard-working farmer, but there wasn't much to be got out of those barren Bearcliff acres. He was said to have taken to drink since his wife's death; now and then men ran across him in the 'dives' of Stotesbury. But not often. And between times he labored hard on his stony acres and did his best for his daughters. In the neglected graveyard of Cold Corners there was a slanting headstone marked with his wife's name; near it, a year since, he had laid his eldest daughter. And sometimes, at dusk, in the autumn, the village people saw him walk slowly by, turn in between the graves, and stand looking down on the two stones. But he never brought a flower there, or planted a bush; nor Venny either. She was too wild and ignorant. . . .

Mrs Rutledge repeated: 'That's in Exodus.'

The three visitors remained silent, turning about their hats in reluctant hands. Rutledge faced them, still with that empty pellucid gaze which frightened Bosworth. What was he seeing?

'Ain't any of you folks got the grit – ?' his wife burst out again, half hysterically.

Deacon Hibben held up his hand. 'That's no way, Mrs Rutledge. This ain't a question of having grit. What we want first of all is . . . proof . . .'

'That's so,' said Bosworth, with an explosion of relief, as if the words had lifted something black and crouching from his breast. Involuntarily the eyes of both men had turned to Brand. He stood there smiling grimly, but did not speak.

'Ain't it so, Brand?' the Deacon prompted him.

'Proof that spooks walk?' the other sneered.

'Well – I presume you want this business settled too?'

The old farmer squared his shoulders. 'Yes – I do. But I ain't a sperritualist. How the hell are you going to settle it?'

Deacon Hibben hesitated; then he said, in a low incisive tone: 'I don't see but one way – Mrs Rutledge's.'

There was a silence.

'What?' Brand sneered again. 'Spying?'

The Deacon's voice sank lower. 'If the poor girl *does* walk . . . her that's your child . . . wouldn't you be the first to want her laid quiet? We all know there've been such cases . . . mysterious visitations. . . . Can any one of us here deny it?'

'I seen 'em,' Mrs Rutledge interjected.

There was another heavy pause. Suddenly Brand fixed his gaze on Rutledge. 'See here, Saul Rutledge, you've got to clear up this damned calumny, or I'll know why. You say my dead girl comes to you.' He labored with his breath, and then jerked out: 'When? You tell me that, and I'll be there.'

Rutledge's head drooped a little, and his eyes wandered to the window. 'Round about sunset, mostly.'

'You know beforehand?'

Rutledge made a sign of assent.

'Well, then – tomorrow, will it be?'

Rutledge made the same sign.

Brand turned to the door. 'I'll be there.' That was all he said. He strode out between them without another glance or word. Deacon Hibben looked at Mrs Rutledge. 'We'll be there too,' he said, as if she had asked him; but she had not spoken, and Bosworth saw that her thin body was trembling all over. He was glad when he and Hibben were out again in the snow.

3

They thought that Brand wanted to be left to himself, and to give him time to unhitch his horse they made a pretense of hanging about in the doorway while Bosworth searched his pockets for a pipe he had no mind to light.

But Brand turned back to them as they lingered. 'You'll meet me down by Lamer's pond tomorrow?' he suggested. 'I want witnesses. Round about sunset.'

They nodded their acquiescence, and he got into his sleigh, gave the horse a cut across the flanks, and drove off under the snow-smothered hemlocks. The other two men went to the shed.

'What do you make of this business, Deacon?' Bosworth asked, to break the silence.

The Deacon shook his head. 'The man's a sick man – that's sure. Something's sucking the life clean out of him.'

But already, in the biting outer air, Bosworth was getting himself under better control. 'Looks to me like a bad case of the ague, as you said.'

'Well – ague of the mind, then. It's his brain that's sick.'

Bosworth shrugged. 'He ain't the first in Hemlock County.'

'That's so,' the Deacon agreed. 'It's a worm in the brain, solitude is.'

'Well, we'll know this time tomorrow, maybe,' said Bosworth. He scrambled into his sleigh, and was driving off in his turn when he heard his companion calling after him. The Deacon explained that his horse had cast a shoe; would Bosworth drive him down to the forge near North Ashmore, if it wasn't too much out of his way? He didn't want the mare slipping about on the freezing snow, and he could probably get the blacksmith to drive him back and shoe her in Rutledge's shed. Bosworth made room for him under the bearskin, and the two men drove off, pursued by a puzzled whinny from the Deacon's old mare.

The road they took was not the one that Bosworth would have followed to reach his own home. But he did not mind that. The shortest way to the forge passed close by Lamer's pond, and Bosworth, since he was in for the business, was not sorry to look the ground over. They drove on in silence.

The snow had ceased, and a green sunset was spreading upward into the crystal sky. A stinging wind barbed with ice flakes caught them in the face on the open ridges, but when they dropped down into the hollow by Lamer's pond the air was as soundless and empty as an unswung bell. They jogged along slowly, each thinking his own thoughts.

'That's the house . . . that tumble-down shack over there, I suppose?' the Deacon said, as the road drew near the edge of the frozen pond.

'Yes: that's the house. A queer hermit fellow built it years ago, my father used to tell me. Since then I don't believe it's ever been used but by the gypsies.'

Bosworth had reined in his horse, and sat looking through pine trunks purpled by the sunset at the crumbling structure. Twilight already lay under the trees, though day lingered in the open. Between two sharply-patterned pine boughs he saw the evening star, like a white boat in a sea of green.

His gaze dropped from that fathomless sky and followed the blue-white undulations of the snow. It gave him a curious agitated feeling to think that here, in this icy solitude, in the tumble-down house he had so often passed without heeding it, a dark mystery, too deep for thought, was being enacted. Down that very slope, coming from the graveyard at Cold Corners, the being they called 'Ora' must pass toward the pond. His heart began to beat stiflingly. Suddenly he gave an exclamation: 'Look!'

He had jumped out of the cutter and was stumbling up the bank toward the slope of snow. On it, turned in the direction of the house by the pond, he had detected a woman's footprints; two; then three; then more. The Deacon scrambled out after him, and they stood and stared.

'God – barefoot!' Hibben gasped. 'Then it *is* . . . the dead. . . .'

Bosworth said nothing. But he knew that no live woman would travel with naked feet across that freezing wilderness. Here, then, was the proof the Deacon had asked for – they held it. What should they do with it?

'Supposing we was to drive up nearer – round the turn of the pond, till we get close to the house,' the Deacon proposed in a colorless voice. 'Mebbe then. . . .'

Postponement was a relief. They got into the sleigh and drove on. Two or three hundred yards farther the road, a mere lane under steep bushy banks, turned sharply to the right, following the bend of the pond. As they rounded the turn they saw Brand's cutter ahead of them. It was empty, the horse tied to a treetrunk. The two men looked at each other again. This was not Brand's nearest way home.

Evidently he had been actuated by the same impulse which had made them rein in their horse by the pondside, and then hasten on to the deserted hovel. Had he too discovered those spectral footprints? Perhaps it was for that very reason that he had left his cutter and vanished in the direction of the house. Bosworth found himself shivering all over under his bearskin. 'I wish to God the dark wasn't coming on,' he muttered. He tethered his own horse near Brand's, and without a word he and the Deacon ploughed through the snow, in the track of Brand's huge feet. They had only a few yards to walk to overtake him. He did not hear them following him, and when Bosworth spoke his name, and he stopped short and turned, his heavy face was dim and confused, like a darker blot on the dusk. He looked at them dully, but without surprise.

'I wanted to see the place,' he merely said.

The Deacon cleared his throat. 'Just take a look . . . yes . . . we thought so. . . . But I guess there won't be anything to *see*. . . .' He attempted a chuckle.

The other did not seem to hear him, but labored on ahead through the pines. The three men came out together in the cleared space before the house. As they emerged from beneath the trees they seemed to have left night behind. The evening star shed a luster on the speckless snow, and Brand, in that lucid circle, stopped with a jerk, and pointed to the same light footprints turned toward the house – the track of a woman in the snow. He stood still, his face working. 'Bare feet. . . .' he said.

The Deacon piped up in a quavering voice: 'The feet of the dead.'

Brand remained motionless. 'The feet of the dead,' he echoed.

Deacon Hibben laid a frightened hand on his arm. 'Come away now, Brand; for the love of God come away.'

The father hung there, gazing down at those light tracks on the snow – light as fox or squirrel trails they seemed, on the white immensity. Bosworth thought to himself: 'The living couldn't walk so light – not even Ora Brand couldn't have, when she lived. . . .' The cold seemed to have entered into his very marrow. His teeth were chattering.

Brand swung about on them abruptly. '*Now!*' he said, moving on as if to an assault, his head bowed forward on his bull neck.

'Now – now? Not in there?' gasped the Deacon. 'What's the use? It was tomorrow he said—' He shook like a leaf.

'It's now,' said Brand. He went up to the door of the crazy house, pushed it inward, and meeting with an unexpected resistance, thrust his heavy shoulder against the panel. The door collapsed like a playing card, and Brand stumbled after it into the darkness of the hut. The others, after a moment's hesitation, followed.

Bosworth was never quite sure in what order the events that succeeded took place. Coming in out of the snow dazzle, he seemed to be plunging into total blackness. He groped his way across the threshold, caught a sharp splinter of the fallen door in his palm, seemed to see something white and wraithlike surge up out of the darkest corner of the hut, and then heard a revolver shot at his elbow, and a cry—

Brand had turned back, and was staggering past him out into the lingering daylight. The sunset, suddenly flushing through the trees, crimsoned his face like blood. He held a revolver in his hand and looked about him in his stupid way.

'They *do* walk, then,' he said and began to laugh. He bent his head to examine his weapon. 'Better here than in the churchyard. They shan't dig her up *now*,' he shouted out. The two men caught him by the arms, and Bosworth got the revolver away from him.

4

The next day Bosworth's sister Loretta, who kept house for him, asked him, when he came in for his midday dinner, if he had heard the news.

Bosworth had been sawing wood all the morning, and in spite of the cold and the driving snow, which had begun again in the night, he was covered with an icy sweat, like a man getting over a fever.

'What news?'

'Venny Brand's down sick with pneumonia. The Deacon's been there. I guess she's dying.'

Bosworth looked at her with listless eyes. She seemed far off from him, miles away. 'Venny Brand?' he echoed.

'You never liked her, Orrin.'

'She's a child. I never knew much about her.'

'Well,' repeated his sister, with the guileless relish of the unimaginative for bad news, 'I guess she's dying.' After a pause she added: 'It'll kill Sylvester Brand, all alone up there.'

Bosworth got up and said: 'I've got to see to poulticing the gray's fetlock.' He walked out into the steadily falling snow.

Venny Brand was buried three days later. The Deacon read the service; Bosworth was one of the pallbearers. The whole countryside turned out, for the snow had stopped falling, and at any season a funeral offered an opportunity for an outing that was not to be missed. Besides, Venny Brand was young and handsome – at least some people thought her handsome, though she was so swarthy – and her dying like that, so suddenly, had the fascination of tragedy.

'They say her lungs filled right up. . . . Seems she'd had bronchial troubles before. . . . I always said both them girls was frail. . . . Look at Ora, how she took and wasted away! And it's colder'n all outdoors up there to Brand's. . . . Their mother, too, *she* pined away just the same. They don't ever make old bones on the mother's side of the family. . . . There's that young Bedlow over there; they say Venny was engaged to him. . . . Oh, Mrs Rutledge, excuse *me*. . . . Step right into the pew; there's a seat for you alongside of grandma. . . .'

Mrs Rutledge was advancing with deliberate step down the narrow aisle of the bleak wooden church. She had on her best bonnet, a monumental structure which no one had seen out of her trunk since old Mrs Silsee's funeral, three years before. All the women remembered it. Under its perpendicular pile her narrow face, swaying on the long thin neck, seemed whiter than ever; but her air of fretfulness had been composed into a suitable expression of mournful immobility.

'Looks as if the stonemason had carved her to put atop of Venny's grave,' Bosworth thought as she glided past him; and then shivered at his own sepulchral fancy. When she bent over her hymn book her lowered lids reminded him again of marble eyeballs; the bony hands clasping the book were bloodless. Bosworth had never seen such hands since he had seen old Aunt Cressidora Cheney strangle the canary bird because it fluttered.

The service was over, the coffin of Venny Brand had been lowered into her sister's grave, and the neighbors were slowly dispersing. Bosworth, as pallbearer, felt obliged to linger and say a word to the stricken father. He waited till Brand had turned from the grave with the Deacon at his side. The three men stood together for a moment; but not one of them spoke. Brand's face was the closed door of a vault, barred with wrinkles like bands of iron.

Finally the Deacon took his hand and said: 'The Lord gave—'

Brand nodded and turned away toward the shed where the horses were hitched. Bosworth followed him. 'Let me drive along home with you,' he suggested.

Brand did not so much as turn his head. 'Home? What home?' he said; and the other fell back.

Loretta Bosworth was talking with the other women while the men unblanketed their horses and backed the cutters out into the heavy snow. As Bosworth waited for her, a few feet off, he saw Mrs Rutledge's tall bonnet lording it above the group. Andy Pond, the Rutledge farm hand, was backing out the sleigh.

'Saul ain't here today, Mrs Rutledge, is he?' one of the village elders piped, turning a benevolent old tortoise head about on a loose neck, and blinking up into Mrs Rutledge's marble face.

Bosworth heard her measure out her answer in slow incisive words. 'No. Mr Rutledge he ain't here. He would 'a' come for certain, but his aunt Minorca Cummins is being buried down to Stotesbury this very day and he had to go down there. Don't it sometimes seem zif we was all walking right in the Shadow of Death?'

As she walked toward the cutter, in which Andy Pond was already seated, the Deacon went up to her with visible hesitation. Involuntarily Bosworth also moved nearer. He heard the Deacon say: 'I'm glad to hear that Saul is able to be up and around.'

She turned her small head on her rigid neck, and lifted the lids of marble.

'Yes, I guess he'll sleep quieter now. And *her* too, maybe, now she don't lay there alone any longer,' she added in a low voice, with a sudden twist of her chin toward the fresh black stain in the graveyard snow. She got into the cutter, and said in a clear tone to Andy Pond: ' 'S long as we're down here I don't know but what I'll just call round and get a box of soap at Hiram Pringle's.'

Roman Fever

1

From the table at which they had been lunching two American ladies of ripe but well-cared-for middle age moved across the lofty terrace of the Roman restaurant and, leaning on its parapet, looked first at each other, and then down on the outspread glories of the Palatine and the Forum, with the same expression of vague but benevolent approval.

As they leaned there a girlish voice echoed up gaily from the stairs leading to the court below. 'Well, come along, then,' it cried, not to them but to an invisible companion, 'and let's leave the young things to their knitting'; and a voice as fresh laughed back: 'Oh, look here, Babs, not actually knitting—' 'Well, I mean figuratively,' rejoined the first. 'After all, we haven't left our poor parents much else to do . . .' and at that point the turn of the stairs engulfed the dialogue.

The two ladies looked at each other again, this time with a tinge of smiling embarrassment, and the smaller and paler one shook her head and colored slightly.

'Barbara!' she murmured, sending an unheard rebuke after the mocking voice in the stairway.

The other lady, who was fuller, and higher in color, with a small determined nose supported by vigorous black eyebrows, gave a good-humored laugh. 'That's what our daughters think of us!'

Her companion replied by a deprecating gesture. 'Not of us individually. We must remember that. It's just the collective modern idea of Mothers. And you see—' Half guiltily she drew from her handsomely mounted black hand-bag a twist of crimson silk run through by two fine knitting needles. 'One never knows,' she murmured. 'The new system has certainly given us a good deal of time to kill; and sometimes I get tired just looking – even at this.' Her gesture was now addressed to the stupendous scene at their feet.

The dark lady laughed again, and they both relapsed upon the view, contemplating it in silence, with a sort of diffused serenity which might have been borrowed from the spring effulgence of the Roman skies. The luncheon-hour was long past, and the two had their end of the vast terrace to themselves. At its opposite extremity a few groups, detained by a lingering look at the outspread city, were gathering up guide-books and fumbling for tips. The last of them scattered, and the two ladies were alone on the air-washed height.

'Well, I don't see why we shouldn't just stay here,' said Mrs Slade, the lady of the high color and energetic brows. Two derelict basketchairs stood near, and she pushed them into the angle of the parapet, and settled herself in one, her gaze upon the Palatine. 'After all, it's still the most beautiful view in the world.'

'It always will be, to me,' assented her friend Mrs Ansley, with so slight a stress on the 'me' that Mrs Slade, though she noticed it, wondered if it were not merely accidental, like the random underlinings of old-fashioned letter-writers.

'Grace Ansley was always old-fashioned,' she thought; and added aloud, with a retrospective smile: 'It's a view we've both been familiar with for a good many years. When we first met here we were younger than our girls are now. You remember?'

'Oh, yes, I remember,' murmured Mrs Ansley, with the same undefinable stress. – 'There's that head-waiter wondering,' she interpolated. She was evidently far less sure than her companion of herself and of her rights in the world.

'I'll cure him of wondering,' said Mrs Slade, stretching her hand toward a bag as discreetly opulent-looking as Mrs Ansley's. Signing to the head-waiter, she explained that she and her friend were old lovers of Rome, and would like to spend the end of the afternoon looking down on the view – that is, if it did not disturb the service? The head-waiter, bowing over her gratuity, assured her that the ladies were most welcome, and would be still more so if they would condescend to remain for dinner. A full moon night, they would remember . . .

Mrs Slade's black brows drew together, as though references to the moon were out-of-place and even unwelcome. But she smiled away her frown as the head-waiter retreated. 'Well, why not? We might do worse. There's no knowing, I suppose, when the girls will be back. Do you even know back from *where*? I don't!'

Mrs Ansley colored slightly. 'I think those young Italian aviators we met at the Embassy invited them to fly to Tarquinia for tea. I suppose they'll want to wait and fly back by moonlight.'

'Moonlight – moonlight! What a part it still plays. Do you suppose they're as sentimental as we were?'

'I've come to the conclusion that I don't in the least know what they are,' said Mrs Ansley. 'And perhaps we didn't know much more about each other.'

'No; perhaps we didn't.'

Her friend gave her a shy glance. 'I never should have supposed you were sentimental, Alida.'

'Well, perhaps I wasn't.' Mrs Slade drew her lids together in retrospect; and for a few moments the two ladies, who had been intimate since childhood, reflected how little they knew each other. Each one, of course, had a label ready to attach to the other's name; Mrs Delphin Slade, for instance, would have told herself, or any one who asked her, that Mrs Horace Ansley, twenty-five years ago, had been exquisitely lovely – no, you wouldn't believe it, would you? . . . though, of course, still charming, distinguished . . . Well, as a girl she had been exquisite; far more beautiful than her daughter Barbara, though certainly Babs, according to the new standards at any rate, was more effective – had more *edge*, as they say. Funny where she got it, with those two nullities as parents. Yes; Horace Ansley was – well, just the duplicate of his wife. Museum specimens of old New York. Good-looking, irreproachable, exemplary. Mrs Slade and Mrs Ansley had lived opposite each other – actually as well as figuratively – for years. When the drawing-room curtains in No. 20 East 73rd Street were renewed, No. 23, across the way, was always aware of it. And of all the movings, buyings, travels, anniversaries, illnesses – the tame chronicle of an estimable pair. Little of it escaped Mrs Slade. But she had grown bored with it by the time her husband made his big *coup* in Wall Street, and when they bought in upper Park Avenue had already begun to think: 'I'd rather live opposite a speak-easy for a change; at least one might see it raided.' The idea of seeing Grace raided was so amusing that (before the move) she launched it at a woman's lunch. It made a hit, and went the rounds – she sometimes wondered if it had crossed the street, and reached Mrs Ansley. She hoped not, but didn't much mind. Those were the days when respectability was at a discount, and it did the irreproachable no harm to laugh at them a little.

A few years later, and not many months apart, both ladies lost their husbands. There was an appropriate exchange of wreaths and condolences, and a brief renewal of intimacy in the half-shadow of their mourning; and now, after another interval, they had run across each other in Rome, at the same hotel, each of them the modest appendage of a salient daughter. The similarity of their lot had again drawn them together, lending itself to mild jokes, and the mutual confession that, if in old days it must have been tiring to 'keep up' with daughters, it was now, at times, a little dull not to.

No doubt, Mrs Slade reflected, she felt her unemployment more than poor Grace ever would. It was a big drop from being the wife of Delphin Slade to being his widow. She had always regarded herself (with a certain conjugal pride) as his equal in social gifts, as contributing her full share to the making of the exceptional couple they were: but the difference after his death was irremediable. As the wife of the famous corporation lawyer, always with an international case or two on hand, every day brought its exciting and unexpected obligation: the impromptu entertaining of eminent colleagues from abroad, the hurried dashes on legal business to London, Paris or Rome, where the entertaining was so handsomely reciprocated; the amusement of hearing in her wake: 'What, that handsome woman with the good clothes and the eyes is Mrs Slade – *the* Slade's wife? Really? Generally the wives of celebrities are such frumps.'

Yes; being *the* Slade's widow was a dullish business after that. In living up to such a husband all her faculties had been engaged; now she had only her daughter to live up to, for the son who seemed to have inherited his father's gifts had died suddenly in boyhood. She had fought through that agony because her husband was there, to be helped and to help; now, after the father's death, the thought of the boy had become unbearable. There was nothing left but to mother her daughter; and dear Jenny was such a perfect daughter that she needed no excessive mothering. 'Now with Babs Ansley I don't know that I *should* be so quiet,' Mrs Slade sometimes half-enviously reflected; but Jenny, who was younger than her brilliant friend, was that rare accident, an extremely pretty girl who somehow made youth and prettiness

seem as safe as their absence. It was all perplexing – and to Mrs
Slade a little boring. She wished that Jenny would fall in love –
with the wrong man, even; that she might have to be watched,
out-maneuvered, rescued. And instead, it was Jenny who
watched her mother, kept her out of draughts, made sure that
she had taken her tonic . . .

Mrs Ansley was much less articulate than her friend, and her
mental portrait of Mrs Slade was slighter, and drawn with fainter
touches. 'Alida Slade's awfully brilliant; but not as brilliant as she
thinks,' would have summed it up; though she would have added,
for the enlightenment of strangers, that Mrs Slade had been an
extremely dashing girl; much more so than her daughter, who
was pretty, of course, and clever in a way, but had none of her
mother's – well, 'vividness,' some one had once called it. Mrs
Ansley would take up current words like this, and cite them in
quotation marks, as unheard-of audacities. No; Jenny was not like
her mother. Sometimes Mrs Ansley thought Alida Slade was
disappointed; on the whole she had had a sad life. Full of failures
and mistakes; Mrs Ansley had always been rather sorry for
her . . .

So these two ladies visualized each other, each through the
wrong end of her little telescope.

2

For a long time they continued to sit side by side without
speaking. It seemed as though, to both, there was a relief in
laying down their somewhat futile activities in the presence of the
vast Memento Mori which faced them. Mrs Slade sat quite still,
her eyes fixed on the golden slope of the Palace of the Caesars, and
after a while Mrs Ansley ceased to fidget with her bag, and she too
sank into meditation. Like many intimate friends, the two ladies
had never before had occasion to be silent together, and Mrs
Ansley was slightly embarrassed by what seemed, after so many
years, a new stage in their intimacy, and one with which she did
not yet know how to deal.

Suddenly the air was full of that deep clangor of bells which
periodically covers Rome with a roof of silver. Mrs Slade glanced
at her wrist-watch. 'Five o'clock already,' she said, as though
surprised.

Mrs Ansley suggested interrogatively: 'There's bridge at the Embassy at five.' For a long time Mrs Slade did not answer. She appeared to be lost in contemplation, and Mrs Ansley thought the remark had escaped her. But after a while she said, as if speaking out of a dream: 'Bridge, did you say? Not unless you want to . . . But I don't think I will, you know.'

'Oh, no,' Mrs Ansley hastened to assure her. 'I don't care to at all. It's so lovely here; and so full of old memories, as you say.' She settled herself in her chair, and almost furtively drew forth her knitting. Mrs Slade took sideway note of this activity, but her own beautifully cared-for hands remained motionless on her knee.

'I was just thinking,' she said slowly, 'what different things Rome stands for to each generation of travellers. To our grand-mothers, Roman fever; to our mothers, sentimental dangers – how we used to be guarded! – to our daughters, no more dangers than the middle of Main Street. They don't know it – but how much they're missing!'

The long golden light was beginning to pale, and Mrs Ansley lifted her knitting a little closer to her eyes. 'Yes; how we were guarded!'

'I always used to think,' Mrs Slade continued, 'that our mothers had a much more difficult job than our grandmothers. When Roman fever stalked the streets it must have been comparatively easy to gather in the girls at the danger hour; but when you and I were young, with such beauty calling us, and the spice of disobedience thrown in, and no worse risk than catching cold during the cool hour after sunset, the mothers used to be put to it to keep us in – didn't they?'

She turned again toward Mrs Ansley, but the latter had reached a delicate point in her knitting. 'One, two, three – slip two; yes, they must have been,' she assented, without looking up.

Mrs Slade's eyes rested on her with a deepened attention. 'She can knit – in the face of *this*! How like her . . .'

Mrs Slade leaned back, brooding, her eyes ranging from the ruins which faced her to the long green hollow of the Forum, the fading glow of the church fronts beyond it, and the outlying immensity of the Colosseum. Suddenly she thought: 'It's all very well to say that our girls have done away with sentiment and moonlight. But if Babs Ansley isn't out to catch that young

aviator – the one who's a Marchese – then I don't know anything.
And Jenny has no chance beside her. I know that too. I wonder if
that's why Grace Ansley likes the two girls to go everywhere
together? My poor Jenny as a foil – !' Mrs Slade gave a hardly
audible laugh, and at the sound Mrs Ansley dropped her knitting.

'Yes – ?'

'I – oh, nothing. I was only thinking how your Babs carries
everything before her. That Campolieri boy is one of the best
matches in Rome. Don't look so innocent, my dear – you know he
is. And I was wondering, ever so respectfully, you understand . . .
wondering how two such exemplary characters as you and
Horace had managed to produce anything quite so dynamic.'
Mrs Slade laughed again, with a touch of asperity.

Mrs Ansley's hands lay inert across her needles. She looked
straight out at the great accumulated wreckage of passion and
splendor at her feet. But her small profile was almost expression-
less. At length she said: 'I think you overrate Babs, my dear.'

Mrs Slade's tone grew easier. 'No; I don't. I appreciate her. And
perhaps envy you. Oh, my girl's perfect; if I were a chronic invalid
I'd – well, I think I'd rather be in Jenny's hands. There must be
times . . . but there! I always wanted a brilliant daughter . . . and
never quite understood why I got an angel instead.'

Mrs Ansley echoed her laugh in a faint murmur. 'Babs is an
angel too.'

'Of course – of course! But she's got rainbow wings. Well,
they're wandering by the sea with their young men; and here we
sit . . . and it all brings back the past a little too acutely.'

Mrs Ansley had resumed her knitting. One might almost have
imagined (if one had known her less well, Mrs Slade reflected)
that, for her also, too many memories rose from the lengthening
shadows of those august ruins. But no; she was simply absorbed
in her work. What was there for her to worry about? She knew
that Babs would almost certainly come back engaged to the
extremely eligible Campolieri. 'And she'll sell the New York house,
and settle down near them in Rome, and never be in their
way . . . she's much too tactful. But she'll have an excellent cook,
and just the right people in for bridge and cocktails . . . and a
perfectly peaceful old age among her grandchildren.'

Mrs Slade broke off this prophetic flight with a recoil of self-
disgust. There was no one of whom she had less right to think

unkindly than of Grace Ansley. Would she never cure herself of
envying her? Perhaps she had begun too long ago.

She stood up and leaned against the parapet, filling her
troubled eyes with the tranquillizing magic of the hour. But
instead of tranquillizing her the sight seemed to increase her
exasperation. Her gaze turned toward the Colosseum. Already its
golden flank was drowned in purple shadow, and above it the sky
curved crystal clear, without light or color. It was the moment
when afternoon and evening hang balanced in mid-heaven.

Mrs Slade turned back and laid her hand on her friend's arm.
The gesture was so abrupt that Mrs Ansley looked up, startled.

'The sun's set. You're not afraid, my dear?'

'Afraid—'

'Of Roman fever or pneumonia? I remember how ill you were
that winter. As a girl you had a very delicate throat, hadn't you?'

'Oh, we're all right up here. Down below, in the Forum, it does
get deathly cold, all of a sudden . . . but not here.'

'Ah, of course you know because you had to be so careful.' Mrs
Slade turned back to the parapet. She thought: 'I must make one
more effort not to hate her.' Aloud she said: 'Whenever I look at
the Forum from up here, I remember that story about a great-
aunt of yours, wasn't she? A dreadfully wicked great-aunt?'

'Oh, yes; Great-aunt Harriet. The one who was supposed to
have sent her young sister out to the Forum after sunset to gather
a night-blooming flower for her album. All our great-aunts and
grandmothers used to have albums of dried flowers.'

Mrs Slade nodded. 'But she really sent her because they were in
love with the same man—'

'Well, that was the family tradition. They said Aunt Harriet
confessed it years afterward. At any rate, the poor little sister
caught the fever and died. Mother used to frighten us with the
story when we were children.'

'And you frightened *me* with it, that winter when you and I
were here as girls. The winter I was engaged to Delphin.'

Mrs Ansley gave a faint laugh. 'Oh, did I? Really frightened
you? I don't believe you're easily frightened.'

'Not often; but I was then. I was easily frightened because I was
too happy. I wonder if you know what that means?'

'I – yes . . .' Mrs Ansley faltered.

'Well, I suppose that was why the story of your wicked aunt

made such an impression on me. And I thought: "There's no more Roman fever, but the Forum is deathly cold after sunset – especially after a hot day. And the Colosseum's even colder and damper." '

'The Colosseum – ?'

'Yes. It wasn't easy to get in, after the gates were locked for the night. Far from easy. Still, in those days it could be managed; it *was* managed, often. Lovers met there who couldn't meet elsewhere. You knew that?'

'I – I daresay. I don't remember.'

'You don't remember? You don't remember going to visit some ruins or other one evening, just after dark, and catching a bad chill? You were supposed to have gone to see the moon rise. People always said that expedition was what caused your illness.'

There was a moment's silence; then Mrs Ansley rejoined: 'Did they? It was all so long ago.'

'Yes. And you got well again – so it didn't matter. But I suppose it struck your friends – the reason given for your illness, I mean – because everybody knew you were so prudent on account of your throat, and your mother took such care of you . . . You *had* been out late sight-seeing, hadn't you, that night?'

'Perhaps I had. The most prudent girls aren't always prudent. What made you think of it now?'

Mrs Slade seemed to have no answer ready. But after a moment she broke out: 'Because I simply can't bear it any longer – !'

Mrs Ansley lifted her head quickly. Her eyes were wide and very pale. 'Can't bear what?'

'Why – your not knowing that I've always known why you went.'

'Why I went – ?'

'Yes. You think I'm bluffing, don't you? Well, you went to meet the man I was engaged to – and I can repeat every word of the letter that took you there.'

While Mrs Slade spoke Mrs Ansley had risen unsteadily to her feet. Her bag, her knitting and gloves, slid in a panic-stricken heap to the ground. She looked at Mrs Slade as though she were looking at a ghost.

'No, no – don't,' she faltered out.

'Why not? Listen, if you don't believe me. "My one darling, things can't go on like this. I must see you alone. Come to the

Colosseum immediately after dark tomorrow. There will be somebody to let you in. No one whom you need fear will suspect" – but
perhaps you've forgotten what the letter said?'

Mrs Ansley met the challenge with an unexpected composure.
Steadying herself against the chair she looked at her friend, and
replied: 'No; I know it by heart too.'

'And the signature? "Only *your* D.S." Was that it? I'm right,
am I? That was the letter that took you out that evening after
dark?'

Mrs Ansley was still looking at her. It seemed to Mrs Slade that
a slow struggle was going on behind the voluntarily controlled
mask of her small quiet face. 'I shouldn't have thought she had
herself so well in hand,' Mrs Slade reflected, almost resentfully.
But at this moment Mrs Ansley spoke. 'I don't know how you
knew. I burnt that letter at once.'

'Yes; you would, naturally – you're so prudent!' The sneer was
open now. 'And if you burnt the letter you're wondering how on
earth I know what was in it. That's it, isn't it?'

Mrs Slade waited, but Mrs Ansley did not speak.

'Well, my dear, I know what was in that letter because I wrote
it!'

'You wrote it?'

'Yes.'

The two women stood for a minute staring at each other in the
last golden light. Then Mrs Ansley dropped back into her chair.
'Oh,' she murmured, and covered her face with her hands.

Mrs Slade waited nervously for another word or movement.
None came, and at length she broke out: 'I horrify you.'

Mrs Ansley's hands dropped to her knee. The face they
uncovered was streaked with tears. 'I wasn't thinking of you. I
was thinking – it was the only letter I ever had from him!'

'And I wrote it. Yes; I wrote it! But I was the girl he was
engaged to. Did you happen to remember that?'

Mrs Ansley's head drooped again. 'I'm not trying to excuse
myself . . . I remembered . . .'

'And still you went?'

'Still I went.'

Mrs Slade stood looking down on the small bowed figure at her
side. The flame of her wrath had already sunk, and she wondered
why she had ever thought there would be any satisfaction in

inflicting so purposeless a wound on her friend. But she had to justify herself.

'You do understand? I'd found out – and I hated you, hated you. I knew you were in love with Delphin – and I was afraid; afraid of you, of your quiet ways, your sweetness . . . your . . . well, I wanted you out of the way, that's all. Just for a few weeks; just till I was sure of him. So in a blind fury I wrote that letter . . . I don't know why I'm telling you now.'

'I suppose,' said Mrs Ansley slowly, 'it's because you've always gone on hating me.'

'Perhaps. Or because I wanted to get the whole thing off my mind.' She paused. 'I'm glad you destroyed the letter. Of course I never thought you'd die.'

Mrs Ansley relapsed into silence, and Mrs Slade, leaning above her, was conscious of a strange sense of isolation, of being cut off from the warm current of human communion. 'You think me a monster!'

'I don't know . . . It was the only letter I had, and you say he didn't write it?'

'Ah, how you care for him still!'

'I cared for that memory,' said Mrs Ansley.

Mrs Slade continued to look down on her. She seemed physically reduced by the blow – as if, when she got up, the wind might scatter her like a puff of dust. Mrs Slade's jealousy suddenly leapt up again at the sight. All these years the woman had been living on that letter. How she must have loved him, to treasure the mere memory of its ashes! The letter of the man her friend was engaged to. Wasn't it she who was the monster?

'You tried your best to get him away from me, didn't you? But you failed; and I kept him. That's all.'

'Yes. That's all.'

'I wish now I hadn't told you. I'd no idea you'd feel about it as you do; I thought you'd be amused. It all happened so long ago, as you say; and you must do me the justice to remember that I had no reason to think you'd ever taken it seriously. How could I, when you were married to Horace Ansley two months afterward? As soon as you could get out of bed your mother rushed you off to Florence and married you. People were rather surprised – they wondered at its being done so quickly; but I thought I knew. I had an idea you did it out of *pique* – to be able to say you'd got ahead of

Delphin and me. Girls have such silly reasons for doing the most serious things. And your marrying so soon convinced me that you'd never really cared.'

'Yes. I suppose it would,' Mrs Ansley assented.

The clear heaven overhead was emptied of all its gold. Dusk spread over it, abruptly darkening the Seven Hills. Here and there lights began to twinkle through the foliage at their feet. Steps were coming and going on the deserted terrace – waiters looking out of the doorway at the head of the stairs, then reappearing with trays and napkins and flasks of wine. Tables were moved, chairs straightened. A feeble string of electric lights flickered out. Some vases of faded flowers were carried away, and brought back replenished. A stout lady in a dust-coat suddenly appeared, asking in broken Italian if any one had seen the elastic band which held together her tattered Baedeker. She poked with her stick under the table at which she had lunched, the waiters assisting.

The corner where Mrs Slade and Mrs Ansley sat was still shadowy and deserted. For a long time neither of them spoke. At length Mrs Slade began again: 'I suppose I did it as a sort of joke—'

'A joke?'

'Well, girls are ferocious sometimes, you know. Girls in love especially. And I remember laughing to myself all that evening at the idea that you were waiting around there in the dark, dodging out of sight, listening for every sound, trying to get in—. Of course I was upset when I heard you were so ill afterward.'

Mrs Ansley had not moved for a long time. But now she turned slowly toward her companion. 'But I didn't wait. He'd arranged everything. He was there. We were let in at once,' she said.

Mrs Slade sprang up from her leaning position. 'Delphin there? They let you in? – Ah, now you're lying!' she burst out with violence.

Mrs Ansley's voice grew clearer, and full of surprise. 'But of course he was there. Naturally he came—'

'Came? How did he know he'd find you there? You must be raving!'

Mrs Ansley hesitated, as though reflecting. 'But I answered the letter. I told him I'd be there. So he came.'

Mrs Slade flung her hands up to her face. 'Oh, God – you answered! I never thought of your answering . . .'

'It's odd you never thought of it, if you wrote the letter.'

'Yes. I was blind with rage.'

Mrs Ansley rose, and drew her fur scarf about her. 'It is cold here. We'd better go . . . I'm sorry for you,' she said, as she clasped the fur about her throat.

The unexpected words sent a pang through Mrs Slade. 'Yes; we'd better go.' She gathered up her bag and cloak. 'I don't know why you should be sorry for me,' she muttered.

Mrs Ansley stood looking away from her toward the dusky secret mass of the Colosseum. 'Well – because I didn't have to wait that night.'

Mrs Slade gave an unquiet laugh. 'Yes; I was beaten there. But I oughtn't to begrudge it to you, I suppose. At the end of all these years. After all, I had everything; I had him for twenty-five years. And you had nothing but that one letter that he didn't write.'

Mrs Ansley was again silent. At length she turned toward the door of the terrace. She took a step, and turned back, facing her companion.

'I had Barbara,' she said, and began to move ahead of Mrs Slade toward the stairway.

Diagnosis

'Nothing to worry about – absolutely nothing. Of course not . . .
just what they all say!' Paul Dorrance walked away from his
writing-table to the window of his high-perched flat. The window
looked south, over the crowded towering New York below Wall
Street which was the visible center and symbol of his life's work.
He drew a great breath of relief – for under his surface incredulity
a secret reassurance was slowly beginning to unfold. The two
eminent physicians he had just seen had told him he would be all
right again in a few months; that his dark fears were delusions;
that all he needed was to get away from work till he had recovered
his balance of body and brain. Dorrance had smiled acquiescence
and muttered inwardly: 'Infernal humbugs; as if I didn't know
how I felt!'; yet hardly a quarter of an hour later their words had
woven magic passes about him, and with a timid avidity he had
surrendered to the sense of returning life. 'By George, I *do* feel
better,' he muttered, and swung about to his desk, remembering
he had not breakfasted. The first time in months that he had
remembered that! He touched the bell at his elbow, and with a
half-apologetic smile told his servant that . . . well, yes . . . the
doctors said he ought to eat more. . . . Perhaps he'd have an egg
or two with his coffee . . . yes, with bacon. . . . He chafed with
impatience till the tray was brought.
Breakfast over, he glanced through the papers with the
leisurely eye of a man before whom the human comedy is likely
to go on unrolling itself for many years. 'Nothing to be in a hurry
about, after all,' was his half-conscious thought. That line which
had so haunted him lately, about 'Time's wingèd chariot,'
relapsed into the region of pure aesthetics, now that in his case
the wings were apparently to be refurled. 'No reason whatever
why you shouldn't live to be an old man.' That was pleasant
hearing, at forty-nine. What did they call an old man, nowadays?
He had always imagined that he shouldn't care to live to be an old

man; now he began by asking himself what he understood by the
term 'old.' Nothing that applied to himself, certainly; even if he
were to be mysteriously metamorphosed into an old man at some
far distant day – what then? It was too far off to visualize, it did not
affect his imagination. Why, old age no longer began short of
seventy; almost every day the papers told of hearty old folk
celebrating their hundredth birthdays – sometimes by remarriage.
Dorrance lost himself in pleasant musings over the increased
longevity of the race, evoking visions of contemporaries of his
grandparents, infirm and toothless at an age which found their
descendants still carnivorous and alert.

The papers read, his mind drifted agreeably among the rich
possibilities of travel. A busy man ordered to interrupt his work
could not possibly stay in New York. Names suggestive of idleness
and summer clothes floated before him: the West Indies, the
Canaries, Morocco – why not Morocco, where he had never been?
And from there he could work his way up through Spain. He rose
to reach for a volume from the shelves where his travel books
were ranged – but as he stood fluttering its pages, in a state of
almost thoughtless beatitude, something twitched him out of his
dream. 'I suppose I ought to tell her—' he said aloud.

Certainly he ought to tell her, but the mere thought let loose a
landslide of complications, obligations, explanations . . . their
suffocating descent made him gasp for breath. He leaned against
the desk, closing his eyes.

But of course she would understand. The doctors said he was
going to be all right – that would be enough for her. She would see
the necessity of his going away for some months; a year perhaps.
She couldn't go with him; that was certain! So what was there to
make a fuss about? Gradually, insidiously, there stole into his
mind the thought – at first a mere thread of a suggestion – that
this might be the moment to let her see, oh, ever so gently, that
things couldn't go on forever – nothing did – and that, at his age,
and with this new prospect of restored health, a man might
reasonably be supposed to have his own views, his own plans;
might think of marriage; marriage with a young girl; children; a
place in the country . . . his mind wandered into that dream as it
had into the dream of travel. . . .

Well, meanwhile he must let her know what the diagnosis
was. She had been awfully worried about him, he knew, though

all along she had kept up so bravely. (Should he, in the independence of his recovered health, confess under his breath that her celebrated 'braveness' sometimes got a little on his nerves?) Yes, it had been hard for her; harder than for anyone; he owed it to her to tell her at once that everything was all right; all right as far as *he* was concerned. And in her beautiful unselfishness nothing else would matter to her – at first. Poor child! He could hear her happy voice! 'Really – really and truly? They both said so? You're *sure?* Oh, of course I've always known . . . haven't I always told you?' Bless her, yes; but he'd known all along what she was thinking. . . . He turned to the desk, and took up the telephone.

As he did so, his glance lit on a sheet of paper on the rug at his feet. He had keen eyes: he saw at once that the letterhead bore the name of the eminent consultant whom his own physician had brought in that morning. Perhaps the paper was one of the three or four prescriptions they had left with him; a chance gust from door or window might have snatched it from the table where the others lay. He stooped and picked it up—

That was the truth, then. That paper on the floor held his fate. The two doctors had written out their diagnosis, and forgotten to pocket it when they left. There were their two signatures; and the date. There was no mistake. . . . Paul Dorrance sat for a long time with the paper on the desk before him. He propped his chin on his locked hands, shut his eyes, and tried to grope his way through the illimitable darkness. . . .

Anything, anything but the sights and sounds of the world outside! If he had had the energy to move he would have jumped up, drawn the curtains shut, and cowered in his armchair in absolute blackness till he could come to some sort of terms with this new reality – for him henceforth the sole reality. For what did anything matter now except that he was doomed – was dying? That these two scoundrels had known it, and had lied to him? And that, having lied to him, in their callous professional haste, they had tossed his death sentence down before him, forgotten to carry it away, left it there staring up at him from the floor?

Yes; it would be easier to bear in a pitch-black room, a room from which all sights and sounds, all suggestions of life, were excluded. But the effort of getting up to draw the curtains was too great. It was easier to go on sitting there, in the darkness created

by pressing his fists against his lids. 'Now, then, my good fellow –
this is what it'll be like in the grave. . . .'

Yes; but if he had known the grave was *there*, so close, so all-
including, so infinitely more important and real than any of the
trash one had tossed the years away for; if somebody had told
him . . . he might have done a good many things differently, put
matters in a truer perspective, discriminated, selected,
weighed. . . . Or, no! A thousand times no! Be beaten like that?
Go slinking off to his grave before it was dug for him? His folly had
been that he had not packed enough into life; that he had always
been sorting, discriminating, trying for a perspective, choosing,
weighing – God! When there was barely time to seize life before
the cup that held it was cracked, and gulp it down while you had
a throat that could swallow!

Ah, well – no use in retrospection. What was done was done:
what undone must remain so to all eternity. Eternity – what did
the word mean? How could the least fringe of its meaning be
grasped by ephemeral creatures groping blindly through a few
short years to the grave? Ah, the pity of it – pity, pity! That was
the feeling that rose to the surface of his thoughts. Pity for all the
millions of blind gropers like himself, the millions and millions
who thought themselves alive, as he had, and suddenly found
themselves dead: as he had! Poor mortals all, with that seed of
annihilation that made them brothers – how he longed to help
them, how he winced at the thought that he must so often have
hurt them, brushing by in his fatuous vitality! How many other
lives had he used up in his short span of living? Not consciously, of
course – that was the worst of it! The old nurse who had slaved for
him when he was a child, and then vanished from his life, to be
found again, years after, poor, neglected, dying – well, for her he
had done what he could. And that thin young man in his office,
with the irritating cough, who might perhaps have been saved if
he had been got away sooner? Stuck on to the end because there
was a family to support – of course! And the old bookkeeper
whom Dorrance had inherited from his father, who was deaf and
half blind, and wouldn't go either till he had to be gently told – ?
All that had been, as it were, the stuff out of which he, Paul
Dorrance, had built up his easy, affluent, successful life. But, no,
what nonsense! He had been fair enough, kind enough, whenever
he found out what was wrong; only he hadn't really pitied them,

had considered his debt discharged when he had drawn a check or rung up a Home for Incurables. Whereas pity, he now saw – oh, curse it, he was talking like a Russian novel! Nonsense . . . nonsense . . . everybody's turn came sooner or later. The only way to reform the world was to reform Death out of it. And instead of that, Death was always there, was there now, at the door, in the room, at his elbow . . . *his* Death, his own private and particular end-of-everything. *Now!* He snatched his hands away from his face. They were wet.

A bell rang hesitatingly and the door opened behind him. He heard the servant say: 'Mrs Welwood.' He stood up, blinking at the harsh impact of light and life. 'Mrs Welwood.' Everything was going on again, going on again . . . people were behaving exactly as if he were not doomed . . . the door shut.

'Eleanor!'

She came up to him quickly. How close, alive, oppressive everyone seemed! She seldom came to his flat – he wondered dully why she had come today.

She stammered: 'What has happened? You promised to telephone at ten. I've been ringing and ringing. They said nobody answered. . . .'

Ah, yes; he remembered now. He looked at the receiver. It lay on the desk, where he had dropped it when his eye had lit on that paper. All that had happened in his other life – before. . . . Well, here she was. How pale she looked, her eyelids a little swollen. And yet how strong, how healthy – how obviously undiseased. Queer! She'd been crying too! Instinctively he turned, and put himself between her and the light.

'What's all the fuss about, dear?' he began jauntily.

She colored a little, hesitating as if he had caught her at fault. 'Why, it's nearly one o'clock; and you told me the consultation was to be at nine. And you promised. . . .'

Oh, yes; of course. He had promised. . . . With the hard morning light on her pale face and thin lips, she looked twenty years older. Older than what? After all, she was well over forty, and had never been beautiful. Had he ever thought her beautiful? Poor Eleanor – oh, poor Eleanor!

'Well, yes; it's my fault,' he conceded. 'I suppose I telephoned to somebody' (this fib to gain time) 'and forgot to hang up the

receiver. There it lies; I'm convicted!' He took both her hands –
how they trembled! – and drew her to him.

This was Eleanor Welwood, for fifteen years past the heaviest
burden on his conscience. As he stood there, holding her hands,
he tried to recover a glimpse of the beginnings, and of his own
state of mind at the time. He had been captivated; but never to the
point of wishing she were free to marry him. Her husband was a
pleasant enough fellow; they all belonged to the same little social
group; it was a delightful relation, just as it was. And Dorrance
had the pretext of his old mother, alone and infirm, who lived
with him and whom he could not leave. It was tacitly understood
that old Mrs Dorrance's habits must not be disturbed by any
change in the household. So love, on his part, imperceptibly
cooled (or should he say ripened?) into friendship; and when his
mother's death left him free, there still remained the convenient
obstacle of Horace Welwood. Horace Welwood did not die; but
one day, as the phrase is, he 'allowed' his wife to divorce him. The
news had cost Dorrance a sleepless night or two. The divorce was
obtained by Mrs Welwood, discreetly, in a distant and accommodating state; but it was really Welwood who had repudiated
his wife, and because of Paul Dorrance. Dorrance knew this, and
was aware that Mrs Welwood knew he knew it. But he had kept
his head, she had silenced her heart; and life went on as before,
except that since the divorce it was easier to see her, and he could
telephone to her house whenever he chose. And they continued
to be the dearest of friends.

He had often gone over all this in his mind, with an increasing
satisfaction in his own shrewdness. He had kept his freedom, kept
his old love's devotion – or as much of it as he wanted – and
proved to himself that life was not half bad if you knew how to
manage it. That was what he used to think – and then, suddenly,
two or three hours ago, he had begun to think differently about
everything, and what had seemed shrewdness now unmasked
itself as a pitiless egotism.

He continued to look at Mrs Welwood, as if searching her face
for something it was essential he should find there. He saw her lips
begin to tremble, the tears still on her lashes, her features
gradually dissolving in a blur of apprehension and incredulity.
'Ah – this is beyond her! She won't be "brave" now,' he thought
with an uncontrollable satisfaction. It seemed necessary, at the

moment, that someone should feel the shock of his doom as he was feeling it – should *die with him*, at least morally, since he had to die. And the strange insight which had come to him – this queer 'behind-the-veil' penetration he was suddenly conscious of – had already told him that most of the people he knew, however sorry they might think they were, would really not be in the least affected by his fate, would remain as inwardly unmoved as he had been when, in the plenitude of his vigor, someone had said before him: 'Ah, poor so-and-so – didn't you know? The doctors say it's all up with him.'

With Eleanor it was different. As he held her there under his eyes he could almost trace the course of his own agony in her paling dissolving face, could almost see her as she might one day look if she were his widow – *his widow!* Poor thing. At least if she were that she could proclaim her love and her anguish, could abandon herself to open mourning on his grave. Perhaps that was the only comfort it was still in his power to give her . . . or in hers to give him. For the grave might be less cold if watered by her warm tears. The thought made his own well up, and he pressed her closer. At that moment his first wish was to see how she would look if she were really happy. His friend – his only friend! How he would make up to her now for his past callousness!

'Eleanor—'

'Oh, won't you tell me?' she entreated.

'Yes. Of course. Only I want you to promise me something first—'

'Yes. . . .'

'To do what I want you to – whatever I want you to.'

She could not still the trembling of her hands, though he pressed them so close. She could scarcely articulate: 'Haven't I, always – ?'

Slowly he pronounced: 'I want you to marry me.'

Her trembling grew more violent, and then subsided. The shadow of her terrible fear seemed to fall from her, as the shadow of living falls from the face of the newly dead. Her face looked young and transparent; he watched the blood rise to her lips and cheeks.

'Oh, Paul, Paul – then the news is *good?*'

He felt a slight shrinking at her obtuseness. After all, she was alive (it wasn't her fault), she was merely alive, like all the rest. . . . Magnanimously he rejoined: 'Never mind about the news now.' But to himself he muttered: '*Sancta Simplicitas!*'

She had thought he had asked her to marry him because the news was good!

2

They were married almost immediately, and with as little circumstance as possible. Dorrance's ill-health, already vaguely known of in his immediate group of friends, was a sufficient pretext for hastening and simplifying the ceremony; and the next day the couple sailed for France.

Dorrance had not seen again the two doctors who had pronounced his doom. He had forbidden Mrs Welwood to speak of the diagnosis, to him or to anyone else. 'For God's sake, don't let's dramatize the thing,' he commanded her; and she acquiesced.

He had shown her the paper as soon as she had promised to marry him; and had hastened, as she read it, to inform her that of course he had no intention of holding her to her promise. 'I only wanted to hear you say "yes," ' he explained, on a note of emotion so genuine that it deceived himself as completely as it did her. He was sure she would not accept his offer to release her; if he had not been sure he might not have dared to make it. For he understood now that he must marry her; he simply could not live out these last months alone. For a moment his thoughts had played sentimentally with the idea that he was marrying her to acquit an old debt, to make her happy before it was too late; but that delusion had been swept away like a straw on the torrent of his secret fears. A new form of egotism, fiercer and more impatient than the other, was dictating his words and gestures – and he knew it. He was marrying simply to put a sentinel between himself and the presence lurking on his threshold – with the same blind instinct of self-preservation which had made men, in old days, propitiate death by the lavish sacrifice of life. And, confident as he was, he had felt an obscure dread of her failing him till his ring was actually on her finger; and a great ecstasy of reassurance and gratitude as he walked out into the street with that captive hand on his arm. Could it be that together they would be able to cheat death after all?

They landed at Genoa, and travelled by slow stages toward the Austrian Alps. The journey seemed to do Dorrance good; he was bearing the fatigue better than he had expected; and he was conscious that his attentive companion noted the improvement, though she forbore to emphasize it. 'Above all, don't be too cheerful,' he had warned her, half smilingly, on the day when he had told her of his doom. 'Marry me if you think you can stand it; but don't try to make me think I'm going to get well.'

She had obeyed him to the letter, watching over his comfort, sparing him all needless fatigue and agitation, carefully serving up to him, on the bright surface of her vigilance, the flowers of travel stripped of their thorns. The very qualities which had made her a perfect mistress – self-effacement, opportuneness, the art of being present and visible only when he required her to be – made her (he had to own it) a perfect wife for a man cut off from everything but the contemplation of his own end.

They were bound for Vienna, where a celebrated specialist was said to have found new ways of relieving the suffering caused by such cases as Dorrance's – sometimes even (though Dorrance and his wife took care not to mention this to each other) of checking the disease, even holding it for years in abeyance. 'I owe it to the poor child to give the thing a trial,' the invalid speciously argued, disguising his own passionate impatience to put himself in the great man's hands. 'If she *wants* to drag out her life with a half-dead man, why should I prevent her?' he thought, trying to sum up all the hopeful possibilities on which the new diagnostician might base his verdict. . . . 'Certainly,' Dorrance thought, 'I have had less pain recently. . . .'

It had been agreed that he should go to the specialist's alone; his wife was to wait for him at their hotel. 'But you'll come straight back afterward? You'll take a taxi – you won't walk?' she had pleaded, for the first time betraying her impatience. 'She knows the hours are numbered, and she can't bear to lose one,' he thought, a choking in his throat; and as he bent to kiss her he had a vision of what it would have been, after the interview that lay ahead of him, the verdict he had already discounted, to walk back to an hotel in which no one awaited him, climb to an empty room and sit down alone with his doom. 'Bless you, child, of course I'll take a taxi. . . .'

Now the consultation was over, and he had descended from the specialist's door, and stood alone in the summer twilight, watching the trees darken against the illumination of the street lamps. What a divine thing a summer evening was, even in a crowded city street! He wondered that he had never before felt its peculiar loveliness. Through the trees the sky was deepening from pearl gray to blue as the stars came out. He stood there, unconscious of the hour, gazing at the people hurrying to and fro on the pavement, the traffic flowing by in an unbroken stream, all the ceaseless tides of the city's life which had seemed to him, half an hour ago, forever suspended. . . .

'No, it's too lovely; I'll walk,' he said, rousing himself, and took a direction opposite to that in which his hotel lay. 'After all,' he thought, 'there's no hurry. . . . What a charming town Vienna is – I think I should like to live here,' he mused as he wandered on under the trees. . . .

When at last he reached his hotel he stopped short on the threshold and asked himself: 'How am I going to tell her?' He realized that during his two hours' perambulations since he had left the doctor's office he had thought out nothing, planned nothing, not even let his imagination glance at the future, but simply allowed himself to be absorbed into the softly palpitating life about him, like a tired traveller sinking, at his journey's end, into a warm bath. Only now, at the foot of the stairs, did he see the future facing him, and understand that he knew no more how to prepare for the return to life than he had for the leaving it. . . . 'If only she takes it quietly – without too much fuss,' he thought, shrinking in advance from any disturbance of those still waters into which it was so beatific to subside.

'That New York diagnosis was a mistake – an utter mistake,' he began vehemently, and then paused, arrested, silenced, by something in his wife's face which seemed to oppose an invisible resistance to what he was in the act of saying. He had hoped she would not be too emotional – and now: what was it? Did he really resent the mask of composure she had no doubt struggled to adjust during her long hours of waiting? He stood and stared at her. 'I suppose you don't believe it?' he broke off, with an aimless irritated laugh.

She came to him eagerly. 'But of course I do, of course!' She seemed to hesitate for a second. 'What I never did believe,' she said abruptly, 'was the other – the New York diagnosis.'

He continued to stare, vaguely resentful of this new attitude, and of the hint of secret criticism it conveyed. He felt himself suddenly diminished in her eyes, as though she were retrospectively stripping him of some prerogative. If she had not believed in the New York diagnosis, what must her secret view of him have been all the while? 'Oh, you never believed in it? And may I ask why?' He heard the edge of sarcasm in his voice.

She gave a little laugh that sounded almost as aimless as his. 'I – I don't know. I suppose I couldn't *bear* to, simply; I couldn't believe fate could be so cruel.'

Still with a tinge of sarcasm he rejoined: 'I'm glad you had your incredulity to sustain you.' Inwardly he was saying: 'Not a tear . . . not an outbreak of emotion . . .' and his heart, dilated by the immense inrush of returning life, now contracted as if an invisible plug had been removed from it, and its fullness were slowly ebbing. 'It's a queer business, anyhow,' he mumbled.

'What is, dear?'

'This being alive again. I'm not sure I know yet what it consists in.'

She came up and put her arms about him, almost shyly. 'We'll try to find out, love – together.'

3

This magnificent gift of life, which the Viennese doctor had restored to him as lightly as his New York colleagues had withdrawn it, lay before Paul Dorrance like something external, outside of himself, an honor, an official rank, unexpectedly thrust on him: he did not discover till then how completely he had dissociated himself from the whole business of living. It was as if life were a growth which the surgeon's knife had already extirpated, leaving him, disembodied, on the pale verge of nonentity. All the while that he had kept saying to himself: 'In a few weeks more I shall be dead,' had he not really known that he was dead already?

'But what are we to do, then, dearest?' he heard his wife asking. 'What do you want? Would you like to go home at once? Do you want me to cable to have the flat got ready?'

He looked at her in astonishment, wounded by such unperceiv-
ingness. Go home – to New York? To his old life there? Did she
really think of it as something possible, even simple and natural?
Why, the small space he had occupied there had closed up
already; he felt himself as completely excluded from that other
life as if his absence had lasted for years. And what did she mean
by 'going home'? The old Paul Dorrance who had made his will,
wound up his affairs, resigned from his clubs and directorships,
pensioned off his old servants and married his old mistress – that
Dorrance was as dead as if he had taken that final step for which
all those others were but the hasty preparation. He *was* dead; this
new man, to whom the doctor had said: 'Cancer? Nothing of the
sort – not a trace of it. Go home and tell your wife that in a few
months you'll be as sound as any man of fifty I ever met—' this
new Dorrance, with his new health, his new leisure and his new
wife, was an intruder for whom a whole new existence would
have to be planned out. And how could anything be decided until
one got to know the new Paul Dorrance a little better?

Conscious that his wife was waiting for his answer, he said:
'Oh, this fellow here may be all wrong. Anyhow, he wants me to
take a cure somewhere first – I've got the name written down.
After that we'll see. . . . But wouldn't you rather travel for a year
or so? How about South Africa or India next winter?' he ventured
at random, after trying to think of some point of the globe even
more remote from New York.

4

The cure was successful, the Viennese specialist's diagnosis
proved to be correct; and the Paul Dorrances celebrated the event
by two years of foreign travel. But Dorrance never felt again the
unconditioned ecstasy he had tasted as he walked out from
the doctor's door into the lamplit summer streets. After that, at
the very moment of re-entering his hotel, the effort of readjustment had begun; and ever since it had gone on.

For a few months the wanderers, weary of change, had settled
in Florence, captivated by an arcaded villa on a cypress-walled
hill, and the new Paul Dorrance, whom it was now the other's
incessant task to study and placate, had toyed with the idea of a
middle life of cultivated leisure. But he soon grew tired of his

opportunities, and found it necessary to move on, and forget in strenuous travel his incapacity for assimilation and reflection. And before the two years were over the old Paul Dorrance, who had constituted himself the other's courier and prime minister, discovered that the old and the new were one, and that the original Paul Dorrance was there, unchanged, unchangeable, and impatient to get back to his old niche because it was too late to adapt himself to any other. So the flat was reopened and the Dorrances returned to New York.

The completeness of his identity with the old Paul Dorrance was indelibly impressed on the new one on the first evening of his return home. There he was, the same man in the same setting as when, two years earlier, he had glanced down from the same armchair and seen the diagnosis of the consulting physicians at his feet. The hour was late, the room profoundly still; no touch of outward reality intervened between him and that hallucinating vision. He almost saw the paper on the floor, and with the same gesture as before he covered his eyes to shut it out. Two years ago – and nothing was changed, after so many changes, except that he should not hear the hesitating ring at the door, should not again see Eleanor Welwood, pale and questioning, on the threshold. Eleanor Welwood did not ring his doorbell now; she had her own latchkey; she was no longer Eleanor Welwood but Eleanor Dorrance, and asleep at this moment in the bedroom which had been Dorrance's, and was now encumbered with feminine properties, while his own were uncomfortably wedged into the cramped guest room of the flat.

Yes – that was the only change in his life; and how aptly the change in the rooms symbolized it! During their travels, even after Dorrance's return to health, his wife's presence had been like a soft accompaniment of music, a painted background to the idle episodes of convalescence; now that he was about to fit himself into the familiar furrow of old habits and relations he felt as if she were already expanding and crowding him into a corner. He did not mind about the room – so he assured himself, though with a twinge of regret for the slant of winter sun which never reached the guest room; what he minded was what he now recognized as the huge practical joke that fate had played on him. He had never meant, he the healthy, vigorous, middle-aged Paul Dorrance, to marry this faded woman for whom he had so long ceased to feel anything but a friendly tenderness. It was the bogey of death, starting out from the warm folds of his closely-curtained life, that had tricked him into the marriage, and then left him to expiate his folly.

Poor Eleanor! It was not her fault if he had imagined, in a moment of morbid retrospection, that happiness would transform and enlarge her. Under the surface changes she was still the same: a perfect companion while he was ill and lonely, an unwitting encumbrance now that (unchanged also) he was restored to the life from which his instinct of self-preservation had so long excluded her. Why had he not trusted to that instinct, which had warned him she was the woman for a sentimental parenthesis, not for the pitiless continuity of marriage? Why, even her face declared it. A lovely profile, yes; but somehow the full face was inadequate. . . .

Dorrance suddenly remembered another face; that of a girl they had met in Cairo the previous winter. He felt the shock of her young fairness, saw the fruity bloom of her cheeks, the light animal vigor of every movement, he heard her rich beckoning laugh, and met the eyes questioning his under the queer slant of her lids. Someone had said: 'She's had an offer from a man who can give her everything a woman wants; but she's refused, and no one can make out why. . . .' Dorrance knew. . . . She had written to him since, and he had not answered her letters. And now here he was, installed once more in the old routine he could not live without, yet from which all the old savor was gone. 'I wonder why I was so scared of dying,' he thought; then the truth flashed on him. 'Why, you fool, you've been dead all the time. That first diagnosis was the true one. Only they put it on the physical plane by mistake. . . .' The next day he began to insert himself painfully into his furrow.

5

One evening some two years later, as Paul Dorrance put his latchkey into his door, he said to himself reluctantly: 'Perhaps I really ought to take her away for a change.'

There was nothing nowadays that he dreaded as much as change. He had had his fill of the unexpected, and it had not agreed with him. Now that he had fitted himself once more into his furrow all he asked was to stay there. It had even become an effort, when summer came, to put off his New York habits and go with his wife to their little place in the country. And the idea that he might have to go away with her in mid-February was positively disturbing.

For the past ten days she had been fighting a bad bronchitis, following on influenza. But 'fighting' was hardly the right word. She, usually so elastic, so indomitable, had not shown her usual resiliency, and Dorrance, from the vantage ground of his recovered health, wondered a little at her lack of spirit. She mustn't let herself go, he warned her gently. 'I was in a good deal tighter place myself not so many years ago – and look at me now. Don't you let the doctors scare you.' She had promised him again that morning that she wouldn't, and he had gone off to his office without waiting for the physician's visit. But during the day he began in an odd way to feel his wife's nearness. It was as though she needed him, as though there were something she wanted to say; and he concluded that she probably knew she ought to go south, and had been afraid to tell him so. 'Poor child – of course I'll take her if the doctor says it's really necessary.' Hadn't he always done everything he could for her? It seemed to him that they had been married for years and years, and that as a husband he had behind him a long and irreproachable record. Why, he hadn't even answered that girl's letters. . . .

As he opened the door of the flat a strange woman in a nurse's dress crossed the hall. Instantly Dorrance felt the alien atmosphere of the place, the sense of something absorbing and exclusive which ignores and averts itself from the common doings of men. He had felt that same atmosphere, in all its somber implications, the day he had picked up the cancer diagnosis from the floor.

The nurse stopped to say 'Pneumonia,' and hurried down the passage to his wife's room. The doctor was coming back at nine o'clock; he had left a note in the library, the butler said. Dorrance knew what was in the note before he opened it. Precipitately, with the vertical drop of a bird of prey, death was descending on his house again. And this time there was no mistake in the diagnosis.

The nurse said he could come in for a minute; but he wasn't to stay long, for she didn't like the way the temperature was rising . . . and there, between the chalk-white pillows, in the green-shaded light, he saw his wife's face. What struck him first was the way it had shrunk and narrowed after a few hours of fever; then, that though it wore a just-perceptible smile of welcome, there was no sign of the tremor of illumination which usually greeted his appearance. He remembered how once, encountering that light, he had grumbled inwardly: 'I wish to God she wouldn't always unroll a red carpet when I come in—' and then been ashamed of his thought. She never embarrassed him by any public show of feeling; that subtle play of light remained invisible to others, and his irritation was caused simply by knowing it was there. 'I don't want to be anybody's sun and moon,' he concluded. But now she was looking at him with a new, an almost critical equality of expression. His first thought was: 'Is it possible she doesn't know me?' But her eyes met his with a glance of recognition, and he understood that the change was simply due to her being enclosed in a world of her own, complete, and independent of his.

'Please, now—' the nurse reminded him; and obediently he stole out of the room.

The next day there was a slight improvement; the doctors were encouraged; the day nurse said: 'If only it goes on like this—'; and as Dorrance opened the door of his wife's room he thought: 'If only she looks more like her own self – !'

But she did not. She was still in that new and self-contained world which he had immediately identified as the one he had lived in during the months when he had thought he was to die. 'After all, I didn't die,' he reminded himself; but the reminder brought no solace, for he knew exactly what his wife was feeling, he had tested the impenetrability of the barrier which shut her off from the living. 'The truth is, one doesn't only die once,' he mused, aware that he had died already; and the memory of the process, now being re-enacted before him, laid a chill on his heart. If only he could have helped her, made her understand! But the barrier was there, the transparent barrier through which everything on the hither side looked so different. And today it was he who was on the hither side.

Then he remembered how, in his loneliness, he had yearned for the beings already so remote, the beings on the living side; and he felt for his wife the same rush of pity as when he had thought himself dying, and known what agony his death would cost her.

That day he was allowed to stay five minutes; the next day ten; she continued to improve, and the doctors would have been perfectly satisfied if her heart had not shown signs of weakness. Hearts, however, medically speaking, are relatively easy to deal with; and to Dorrance she seemed much stronger.

Soon the improvement became so marked that the doctor made no objection to his sitting with her for an hour or two; the nurse was sent for a walk, and Dorrance was allowed to read the morning paper to the invalid. But when he took it up his wife stretched out her hand. 'No – I want to talk to you.'

He smiled, and met her smile. It was as if she had found a slit in the barrier and were reaching out to him. 'Dear – but won't talking tire you?'

'I don't know. Perhaps.' She waited. 'You see, I'm talking to you all the time, while I lie here. . . .'

He knew – he knew! How her pangs went through him! 'But you see, dear, raising your voice. . . .'

She smiled incredulously, that remote behind-the-barrier smile he had felt so often on his own lips. Though she could reach through to him the dividing line was still there, and her eyes met his with a look of weary omniscience.

'But there's no hurry,' he argued. 'Why not wait a day or two? Try to lie there and not even think.'

'Not think!' She raised herself on a weak elbow. 'I want to think every minute – every second. I want to relive everything, day by day, to the last atom of time. . . .'

'Time? But there'll be plenty of time!'

She continued to lean on her elbow, fixing her illumined eyes on him. She did not seem to hear what he said; her attention was concentrated on some secret vision of which he felt himself the mere transparent mask.

'Well,' she exclaimed, with a sudden passionate energy, 'it was worth it! I always knew—'

Dorrance bent toward her. 'What was worth – ?' But she had sunk back with closed eyes, and lay there reabsorbed into the cleft of the pillows, merged in the inanimate, a mere part of the furniture of the sick-room. Dorrance waited for a moment, hardly understanding the change; then he started up, rang, called, and in a few moments the professionals were in possession, the air was full of ether and camphor, the telephone ringing, the disarray of death in the room. Dorrance knew that he would never know what she had found worth it. . . .

6

He sat in his library, waiting. Waiting for what? Life was over for him now that she was dead. Until after the funeral a sort of factitious excitement had kept him on his feet. Now there was nothing left but to go over and over those last days. Every detail of them stood out before him in unbearable relief; and one of the most salient had been the unexpected appearance in the sick-room of Dorrance's former doctor – the very doctor who, with the cancer specialist, had signed the diagnosis of Dorrance's case. Dorrance, since that day, had naturally never consulted him professionally; and it chanced that they had never met. But Eleanor's physician, summoned at the moment of her last heart attack, without even stopping to notify Dorrance, had called in his colleague. The latter had a high standing as a consultant (the idea made Dorrance smile); and besides, what did it matter? By that time they all knew – nurses, doctors, and most of all Dorrance himself – that nothing was possible but to ease the pangs of Eleanor's last hours. And Dorrance had met his former doctor without resentment; hardly even with surprise.

But the doctor had not forgotten that he and his former patient had been old friends; and the day after the funeral, late in the evening, had thought it proper to ring the widower's doorbell and present his condolences. Dorrance, at his entrance, looked up in surprise, at first resenting the intrusion, then secretly relieved at the momentary release from the fiery wheel of his own thoughts. 'The man is a fool – but perhaps,' Dorrance reflected, 'he'll give me something that will make me sleep. . . .'

The two men sat down, and the doctor began to talk gently of Eleanor. He had known her for many years, though not professionally. He spoke of her goodness, her charity, the many instances he had come across among his poor patients of her discreet and untiring ministrations. Dorrance, who had dreaded hearing her spoken of, and by this man above all others, found himself listening with a curious avidity to these reminiscences. He needed no one to tell him of Eleanor's kindness, her devotion – yet at the moment such praise was sweet to him. And he took up the theme; but not without a secret stir of vindictiveness, a vague desire to make the doctor suffer for the results of his now-distant blunder. 'She always gave too much of herself – that was the trouble. No one knows that better than I do. She was never really the same after those months of incessant anxiety about me that you doctors made her undergo.' He had not intended to say anything of the sort; but as he spoke the resentment he had thought extinct was fanned into flame by his words. He had forgiven the two doctors for himself, but he suddenly found he could not forgive them for Eleanor, and he had an angry wish to let them know it. 'That diagnosis of yours nearly killed her, though it didn't kill *me*,' he concluded sardonically.

The doctor had followed this outburst with a look of visible perplexity. In the crowded life of a fashionable physician, what room was there to remember a mistaken diagnosis? The sight of his forgetfulness made Dorrance continue with rising irritation: 'The shock of it *did* kill her – I see that now.'

'Diagnosis – what diagnosis?' echoed the doctor blankly.

'I see you don't remember,' said Dorrance.

'Well, no; I don't, for the moment.'

'I'll remind you, then. When you came to see me with that cancer specialist four or five years ago, one of you dropped your diagnosis by mistake in going out. . . .'

'Oh, *that*?' The doctor's face lit up with sudden recollection. 'Of course! The diagnosis of the other poor fellow we'd been to see before coming to you. I remember it all now. Your wife – Mrs Welwood then, wasn't she? – brought the paper back to me a few hours later – before I'd even missed it. I think she said you'd picked it up after we left, and thought it was meant for *you*.' The doctor gave an easy retrospective laugh. 'Luckily I was able to reassure her at once.' He leaned back comfortably in his armchair and shifted his voice to the pitch of condolence. 'A beautiful life, your wife's was. I only wish it had been in our power to prolong it. But these cases of heart failure . . . you must tell yourself that at least you had a few happy years; and so many of us haven't even that.' The doctor stood up and held out his hand.

'Wait a moment, please,' Dorrance said hurriedly. 'There's something I want to ask you.' His brain was whirling so that he could not remember what he had started to say. 'I can't sleep. . . .' he began.

'Yes?' said the doctor, assuming a professional look, but with a furtive glance at his wrist-watch.

Dorrance's throat felt dry and his head empty. He struggled with the difficulty of ordering his thoughts, and fitting rational words to them.

'Yes – but no matter about my sleeping. What I meant was: do I understand you to say that the diagnosis you dropped in leaving was not intended for me?'

The doctor stared. 'Good Lord, no – of course it wasn't. You never had a symptom. Didn't we both tell you so at the time?'

'Yes,' Dorrance slowly acquiesced.

'Well, if you didn't believe us, your scare was a short one, anyhow,' the doctor continued with a mild jocularity; and he put his hand out again.

'Oh, wait,' Dorrance repeated. 'What I really wanted to ask was what day you said my wife returned the diagnosis to you? But I suppose you don't remember.'

The doctor reflected. 'Yes, I do; it all comes back to me now. It was the very same day. We called on you in the morning, didn't we?'

'Yes; at nine o'clock,' said Dorrance, the dryness returning to his throat.

'Well, Mrs Welwood brought the diagnosis back to me directly afterward.'

'You think it was the very same day?' (Dorrance wondered to himself why he continued to insist on this particular point.)

The doctor took another stolen glance at his watch. 'I'm sure it was. I remember now that it was my consultation day, and that she caught me at two o'clock, before I saw my first patient. We had a good laugh over the scare you'd had.'

'I see,' said Dorrance.

'Your wife had one of the sweetest laughs I ever heard,' continued the doctor, with an expression of melancholy reminiscence.

There was a silence, and Dorrance was conscious that his visitor was looking at him with growing perplexity. He too gave a slight laugh. 'I thought perhaps it was the day after,' he mumbled vaguely. 'Anyhow, you did give me a good scare.'

'Yes,' said the doctor. 'But it didn't last long, did it? I asked your wife to make my peace with you. You know such things will happen to hurried doctors. I hope she persuaded you to forgive me?'

'Oh, yes,' said Dorrance, as he followed the doctor to the door to let him out.

'Well, now about that sleeping—' the doctor checked himself on the threshold to ask.

'Sleeping?' Dorrance stared. 'Oh, I shall sleep all right tonight,' he said with sudden decision, as he closed the door on his visitor.

The Day of the Funeral

His wife had said: 'If you don't give her up I'll throw myself from the roof.' He had not given her up, and his wife had thrown herself from the roof.

Nothing of this had of course come out in the inquest. Luckily Mrs Trenham had left no letters or diary – no papers of any sort, in fact; not even a little mound of ashes on the hearth. She was the kind of woman who never seemed to have many material appurtenances or encumbrances. And Dr Lanscomb, who had attended her ever since her husband had been called to his professorship at Kingsborough, testified that she had always been excessively emotional and high-strung, and never 'quite right' since her only child had died. The doctor's evidence closed the inquiry; the whole business had not lasted more than ten minutes.

Then, after another endless interval of forty-eight hours, came the funeral. Ambrose Trenham could never afterward recall what he did during those forty-eight hours. His wife's relations lived at the other end of the continent, in California; he himself had no immediate family; and the house – suddenly become strange and unfamiliar, a house that seemed never to have been his – had been given over to benevolent neighbors, soft-stepping motherly women, and to glib, subservient men who looked like a cross between book agents and revivalists. These men took measures, discussed technical questions in undertones with the motherly women, and presently came back with a coffin with plated handles. Someone asked Trenham what was to be engraved on the plate on the lid, and he said: 'Nothing.' He understood afterward that the answer had not been what was expected; but at the time everyone evidently ascribed it to his being incapacitated by grief.

Before the funeral one horrible moment stood out from the others, though all were horrible. It was when Mrs Cossett, the wife of the professor of English Literature, came to him and said: 'Do you want to see her?'

'See her – ?' Trenham gasped, not understanding.

Mrs Cossett looked surprised, and a little shocked. 'The time has come – they must close the coffin. . . .'

'Oh, let them close it,' was on the tip of the widower's tongue; but he saw from Mrs Cossett's expression that something very different was expected of him. He got up and followed her out of the room and up the stairs. . . . He looked at his wife. Her face had been spared. . . .

That too was over now, and the funeral as well. Somehow, after all, the time had worn on. At the funeral, Trenham had discovered in himself – he, the absent-minded, the unobservant – an uncanny faculty for singling out everyone whom he knew in the crowded church. It was incredible; sitting in the front pew, his head bowed forward on his hands, he seemed suddenly gifted with the power of knowing who was behind him and on either side. And when the service was over, and to the sound of 'O Paradise' he turned to walk down the nave behind the coffin, though his head was still bowed, and he was not conscious of looking to the right or the left, face after face thrust itself forward into his field of vision – and among them, yes: of a sudden, Barbara Wake's!

The shock was terrible; Trenham had been so sure she would not come. Afterward he understood that she had had to – for the sake of appearances. 'Appearances' still ruled at Kingsborough – where didn't they, in the university world, and more especially in New England? But at the moment, and for a long time, Trenham had felt horrified, and outraged in what now seemed his holiest feelings. What right had she? How dared she? It was indecent. . . . In the reaction produced by the shock of seeing her, his remorse for what had happened hardened into icy hate of the woman who had been the cause of the tragedy. The sole cause – for in a flash Trenham had thrown off his own share in the disaster. 'The woman tempted me—' Yes, she had! It was what his poor wronged Milly had always said: 'You're so weak: and she's always tempting you—'

He used to laugh at the idea of Barbara Wake as a temptress; one of poor Milly's delusions! It seemed to him, then, that he was always pursuing, the girl evading; but now he saw her as his wife had seen her, and despised her accordingly. The indecency of her

coming to the funeral! To have another look at him, he
supposed . . . she was insatiable . . . it was as if she could never
fill her eyes with him. But, if he could help it, they should never be
laid on him again. . . .

2

His indignation grew; it filled the remaining hours of the endless
day, the empty hours after the funeral was over; it occupied and
sustained him. The President of the University, an old friend, had
driven him back to his lonely house, had wanted to get out and
come in with him. But Trenham had refused, had shaken hands
at the gate, and walked alone up the path to his front door. A cold
lunch was waiting on the dining-room table. He left it untouched,
poured out some whisky and water, carried the glass into his
study, lit his pipe and sat down in his armchair to think, not of
his wife, with whom the inquest seemed somehow to have settled
his account, but of Barbara Wake. With her he must settle his
account himself. And he had known at once how he would do it;
simply by tying up all her letters, and the little photograph he
always carried in his note-case (the only likeness he had of her),
and sending them back without a word.

A word! What word indeed could equal the emphasis of that
silence? Barbara Wake had all the feminine passion for going over
and over things; talking them inside out; in that respect she was
as bad as poor Milly had been, and nothing would humiliate and
exasperate her as much as an uncommented gesture of dismissal.
It was so fortifying to visualize that scene – the scene of her
opening the packet alone in her room – that Trenham's sense of
weariness disappeared, his pulses began to drum excitedly, and he
was torn by a pang of hunger, the first he had felt in days. Was the
cold meat still on the table, he wondered? Shamefacedly he stole
back to the dining-room. But the table had been cleared, of course
– just today! On ordinary days the maid would leave the empty
dishes for hours unremoved; it was one of poor Milly's household
grievances. How often he had said to her, impatiently: 'Good Lord,
what does it matter?' and she had answered: 'But, Ambrose, the
flies!' . . . And now, of all days, the fool of a maid had cleared
away everything. He went back to his study, sat down again, and
suddenly felt too hungry to think of anything but his hunger.

Even his vengeance no longer nourished him; he felt as if nothing would replace that slice of pressed beef, with potato salad and pickles, of which his eyes had rejected the disgusted glimpse an hour or two earlier.

He fought his hunger for a while longer; then he got up and rang. Promptly, attentively, Jane, the middle-aged disapproving maid, appeared – usually one had to rip out the bell before she disturbed herself. Trenham felt sheepish at having to confess his hunger to her, as if it made him appear unfeeling, unheroic; but he could not help himself. He stammered out that he supposed he ought to eat something . . . and Jane, at once, was all tearful sympathy. 'That's right, sir; you must *try* . . . you must force yourself. . . .' Yes, he said; he realized that. He would force himself. 'We were saying in the kitchen, Katy and me, that you couldn't go on any longer this way. . . .' He could hardly wait till she had used up her phrases and got back to the pantry. . . . Through the half-open dining-room door he listened avidly to her steps coming and going, to the clatter of china, the rattle of the knife basket. He met her at the door when she returned to tell him that his lunch was ready . . . and that Katy had scrambled some eggs for him the way he liked them.

At the dining-room table, when the door had closed on her, he squared his elbows, bent his head over his plate, and emptied every dish. Had he ever before known the complex exquisiteness of a slice of pressed beef? He filled his glass again, leaned luxuriously, waited without hurry for the cheese and biscuits, the black coffee, and a slice of apple pie apologetically added from the maids' dinner – and then – oh, resurrection! – felt for his cigar case, and calmly, carelessly almost, under Jane's moist and thankful eyes, cut his Corona and lit it.

'Now he's saved,' her devout look seemed to say.

3

The letters must be returned at once. But to whom could he entrust them? Certainly not to either one of the maidservants. And there was no one else but the slow-witted man who looked after the garden and the furnace, and who would have been too much dazed by such a commission to execute it without first receiving the most elaborate and reiterated explanations, and then would probably have delivered the packet to Professor Wake, or posted it – the latter a possibility to be at all costs avoided, since Trenham's writing might have been recognized by someone at the post office, one of the chief centers of gossip at Kingsborough. How it complicated everything to live in a small, prying community! He had no reason to suppose that anyone divined the cause of his wife's death, yet he was aware that people had seen him more than once in out-of-the-way places, and at queer hours, with Barbara Wake; and if his wife knew, why should not others suspect? For a while, at any rate, it behoved him to avoid all appearance of wishing to communicate with the girl. Returning a packet to her on the very day of the funeral would seem particularly suspicious. . . .

Thus, after coffee and cigar, and a nip of old Cognac, argued the normal sensible man that Trenham had become again. But if his nerves had been steadied by food his will had been strengthened by it, and instead of a weak, vacillating wish to let Barbara Wake feel the weight of his scorn he was now animated by the furious resolution to crush her with it, and at once. That packet should be returned to her before night.

He shut the study door, drew out his keys, and unlocked the cabinet in which he kept the letters. He had no need now to listen for his wife's step, or to place himself between the cabinet and the door of the study, as he used to when he thought he heard her coming. Now, had he chosen, he could have spread the letters out all over the table. Jane and Katy were busy in the kitchen, and the rest of the house was his to do what he liked in. He could have sat down and read the serried pages one by one, lingeringly, gloatingly, as he had so often longed to do when the risk was too great – and now they were but so much noisome rubbish to him, to be crammed into a big envelope, and sealed up out of sight. He began to hunt for an envelope. . . .

God! What dozens and dozens of letters there were! And all written within eighteen months. No wonder poor Milly . . . but what a blind reckless fool he had been! The reason of their abundance was, of course, the difficulty of meeting. . . . So often he and Barbara had had to write because they couldn't contrive to see each other . . . but still, this bombardment of letters was monstrous, inexcusable. . . . He hunted for a long time for an envelope big enough to contain them; finally found one, a huge linen-lined envelope meant for college documents, and jammed the letters into it with averted head. But what, he thought suddenly, if she mistook his silence, imagined he had sent her the letters simply as a measure of prudence? No – that was hardly likely, now that all need of prudence was over; but she might affect to think so, use the idea as a pretext to write and ask what he meant, what she was to understand by his returning her letters without a word. It might give her an opening, which was probably what she was hoping for, and certainly what he was most determined she should not have.

He found a sheet of note-paper, shook his fountain pen, wrote a few words (hardly looking at the page as he did so), and thrust the note in among the letters. His hands turned clammy as he touched them; he felt cold and sick . . . and the cursed flap of the envelope wouldn't stick – those linen envelopes were always so stiff. And where the devil was the sealing wax? He rummaged frantically among the odds and ends on his desk. A provision of sealing wax used always to be kept in the lower left-hand drawer. He groped about in it and found only some yellowing newspaper clippings. Milly used to be so careful about seeing that his writing-table was properly supplied; but lately – ah, his poor poor Milly! If she could only know how he was suffering and atoning already. . . . Some string, then. . . . He fished some string out of another drawer. He would have to make it do instead of sealing wax; he would have to try to tie a double knot. But his fingers, always clumsy, were twitching like a drug fiend's; the letters seemed to burn them through the envelope. With a shaking hand he addressed the packet, and sat there, his eyes turned from it, while he tried again to think out some safe means of having it delivered. . . .

4

He dined hungrily, as he had lunched; and after dinner he took his hat from its peg in the hall, and said to Jane: 'I think I'll smoke my cigar in the campus.'

That was a good idea; he saw at once that she thought it a hopeful sign, his wanting to take the air after being mewed up in the house for so long. The night was cold and moonless, and the college grounds, at that hour, would be a desert . . . after all, delivering the letters himself was the safest way: openly, at the girl's own door, without any mystery. . . . If Malvina, the Wakes' old maid, should chance to open the door, he'd pull the packet out and say at once: 'Oh, Malvina, I've found some books that Miss Barbara lent me last year, and as I'm going away—' He had gradually learned that there was nothing as safe as simplicity.

He was reassured by the fact that the night was so dark. It felt queer, unnatural somehow, to be walking abroad again like the Ambrose Trenham he used to be; he was glad there were so few people about, and that the Kingsborough suburbs were so scantily lit. He walked on, his elbow hitting now and then against the bundle, which bulged out of his pocket. Every time he felt it a sort of nausea rose in him. Professor Wake's house stood half-way down one of the quietest of Kingsborough's outlying streets. It was withdrawn from the road under the hanging boughs of old elms; he could just catch a glint of light from one or two windows. And suddenly, as he was almost abreast of the gate, Barbara Wake came out of it.

For a moment she stood glancing about her, then she turned in the direction of the narrow lane bounding the farther side of the property. What took her there, Trenham wondered? His first impulse had been to draw back, and let her go her way; then he saw how providential the encounter was. The lane was dark, deserted – a mere passage between widely scattered houses, all asleep in their gardens. The chilly night had sent people home early; there was not a soul in sight. In another moment the packet would be in her hands, and he would have left her, just silently raising his hat.

He remembered now where she was going. The garage, built in the far corner of the garden, opened into the lane. The Wakes had no chauffeur, and Barbara, who drove the car, was sole mistress of the garage and of its keys. Trenham and she had met there sometimes; a desolate trysting place! But what could they do, in a town like Kingsborough? At one time she had talked of setting up a studio – she dabbled in painting; but the suggestion had alarmed him (he knew the talk it would create), and he had discouraged her. Most often they took the train and went to Ditson, a manufacturing town an hour away, where no one knew them . . . but what could she be going to the garage for at this hour?

The thought of his wife rushed into Trenham's mind. The discovery that she had lived there beside him, knowing all, and that suddenly, when she found she could not regain his affection, life had seemed worthless, and without a moment's hesitation she had left it. . . . Why, if he had known the quiet woman at his side had such springs of passion in her, how differently he would have regarded her, how little this girl's insipid endearments would have mattered to him! He was a man who could not live without tenderness, without demonstrative tenderness; his own shyness and reticence had to be perpetually broken down, laughingly scattered to the winds. His wife, he now saw, had been too much like him, had secretly suffered from the same inhibitions. She had always seemed ashamed, and frightened by her feeling for him, and half repelled, half fascinated by his response. At times he imagined that she found him physically distasteful, and wondered how, that being the case, she could be so fiercely jealous of him. Now he understood that her cold reluctant surrender concealed a passion so violent that it humiliated her, and so incomprehensible that she had never mastered its language. She reminded him of a clumsy little girl he had once known at a dancing class he had been sent to as a boy – a little girl who had a feverish passion for dancing, but could never learn the steps. And because he too had felt the irresistible need to join in the immemorial love dance he had ended by choosing a partner more skilled in its intricacies. . . .

These thoughts wandered through his mind as he stood watching Barbara Wake. Slowly he took a few steps down the lane; then he halted again. He had not yet made up his mind what to do. If she were going to the garage to get something she had forgotten (as was most probable, at that hour) she would no doubt be coming back in a few moments, and he could meet her and hand her the letters. Above all, he wanted to avoid going into the garage. To do so at that moment would have been a profanation of Milly's memory. He would have liked to efface from his own all recollection of the furtive hours spent there; but the vision returned with intolerable acuity as the girl's slim figure, receding from him, reached the door. How often he had stood at that corner, under those heavy trees, watching for her to appear and slip in ahead of him – so that they should not be seen entering together. The elaborate precautions with which their meetings had been surrounded – how pitiably futile they now seemed! They had not even achieved their purpose, but had only belittled his love and robbed it of its spontaneity. Real passion ought to be free, reckless, audacious, unhampered by the fear of a wife's feelings, of the university's regulations, the president's friendship, the deadly risk of losing one's job and wrecking one's career. It seemed to him now that the love he had given to Barbara Wake was almost as niggardly as that which he had doled out to his wife. . . .

He walked down the lane and saw that Barbara was going into the garage. It was so dark that he could hardly make out her movements; but as he reached the door she drew out her electric lamp (that recalled memories too), and by its flash he saw her slim gloveless hand put the key into the lock. The key turned, the door creaked, and all was darkness. . . .

The glimpse of her hand reminded him of the first time he had dared to hold it in his and press a kiss on the palm. They had met accidentally in the train, both of them on their way home from Boston, and he had proposed that they should get off at the last station before Kingsborough, and walk back by a short cut he knew, through the woods and along the King river. It was a shining summer day, and the girl had been amused at the idea and had accepted. . . . He could see now every line, every curve of her hand, a quick strong young hand, with long fingers, slightly blunt at the tips, and a sensuous elastic palm. It would be queer to have to carry on life without ever again knowing the feel of that hand. . . .

Of course he would go away; he would have to. If possible he would leave the following week. Perhaps the faculty would let him advance his sabbatical year. If not, they would probably let him off for the winter term, and perhaps after that he might make up his mind to resign, and look for a professorship elsewhere – in the South, or in California – as far away from that girl as possible. Meanwhile what he wanted was to get away to some hot climate, steamy, tropical, where one could lie out all night on a white beach and hear the palms chatter to the waves, and the trade winds blow from God knew where . . . one of those fiery flowery islands where marriage and love were not regarded so solemnly, and a man could follow his instinct without calling down a catastrophe, or feeling himself morally degraded. . . . Above all, he never wanted to see again a woman who argued and worried and reproached, and dramatized things that ought to be as simple as eating and drinking. . . .

Barbara, he had to admit, had never been frightened or worried, had never reproached him. The girl had the true sporting instinct; he never remembered her being afraid of risks, or nervous about 'appearances.' Once or twice, at moments when detection seemed imminent, she had half frightened him by her cool resourcefulness. He sneered at the remembrance. 'An old hand, no doubt!' But the sneer did not help him. Whose fault was it if the girl had had to master the arts of dissimulation? Whose but his? He alone (he saw in sudden terror) was responsible for what he supposed would be called her downfall. Poor child – poor Barbara! Was it possible that he, the seducer, the corrupter, had presumed to judge her? The thought was monstrous. . . . His resentment had already vanished like a puff of mist. The feeling of his responsibility, which had seemed so abhorrent, was now almost sweet to him. He was responsible – he owed her something! Thank heaven for that! For now he could raise his passion into a duty, and thus disguised and moralized, could once more – oh, could he, dared he? – admit it openly into his life. The mere possibility made him suddenly feel less cold and desolate. That the something-not-himself that made for righteousness should take on the tender lineaments, the human warmth of love, should come to sit by his hearth in the shape of Barbara – how warm, how happy and reassured it made him! He had a swift vision of her, actually sitting there in the shabby old leather chair (he would have it re-covered), her slim feet on the faded Turkey rug (he would have it replaced). It was almost a pity – he thought madly – that they would probably not be able to stay on at Kingsborough, there, in that very house where for so long he had not even dared to look at her letters. . . . Of course, if they did decide to, he would have it all done over for her.

5

The garage door creaked and again he saw the flash of the electric lamp on her bare hand as she turned the key; then she moved toward him in the darkness.

'Barbara!'

She stopped short at his whisper. They drew closer to each

other. 'You wanted to see me?' she whispered back. Her voice flowed over him like summer air.

'Can we go in there – ?' he gestured.

'Into the garage? Yes – I suppose so.'

They turned and walked in silence through the obscurity. The comfort of her nearness was indescribable.

She unlocked the door again, and he followed her in. 'Take care; I left the wheel jack somewhere,' she warned him. Automatically he produced a match, and she lit the candle in an old broken-paned lantern that hung on a nail against the wall. How familiar it all was – how often he had brought out his matchbox and she had lit that candle! In the little pool of yellowish light they stood and looked at each other.

'You didn't expect me?' he stammered.

'I'm not sure I didn't,' she returned softly, and he just caught her smile in the half-light. The divineness of it!

'I didn't suppose I should see you. I just wandered out. . . .' He suddenly felt the difficulty of accounting for himself.

'My poor Ambrose!' She laid her hand on his arm. 'How I've ached for you—'

Yes; that was right; the tender sympathizing friend . . . anything else, at that moment, would have been unthinkable. He drew a breath of relief and self-satisfaction. Her pity made him feel almost heroic – had he not lost sight of his own sufferings in the thought of hers? 'It's been awful—' he muttered.

'Yes; I know.'

She sat down on the step of the old Packard, and he found a wooden stool and dragged it into the candle ray.

'I'm glad you came,' she began, still in the same soft healing voice, 'because I'm going away tomorrow early, and—'

He started to his feet, upsetting the stool with a crash. 'Going away? Early tomorrow?' Why hadn't he known of this? He felt weak and injured. Where could she be going in this sudden way? If they hadn't happened to meet, would he have known nothing of it till she was gone? His heart grew small and cold.

She was saying quietly: 'You must see – it's better. I'm going out to the Jim Southwicks, in California. They're always asking me. Mother and father think it's on account of my colds . . . the winter climate here . . . they think I'm right.' She paused, but he could find nothing to say. The future had become a featureless desert. 'I wanted to see you before going,' she continued, 'and I didn't exactly know . . . I hoped you'd come—'

'When are you coming back?' he interrupted desperately.

'Oh, I don't know; they want me for the winter, of course. There's a crazy plan about Hawaii and Samoa . . . sounds lovely, doesn't it? And from there on. . . . But I don't know. . . .'

He felt a suffocation in his throat. If he didn't cry out, do something at once to stop her, he would choke. 'You can't go – you can't leave me like this!' It seemed to him that his voice had risen to a shout.

'Ambrose—' she murmured, subdued, half warning.

'You can't. How can you? It's madness. You don't understand. You say you ought to go – it's better you should go. What do you mean – why better? Are you afraid of what people might say? Is that it? How can they say anything when they know we're going to be married? Don't you know we're going to be married?' he burst out weakly, his words stumbling over each other in the effort to make her understand.

She hesitated a moment, and he stood waiting in an agony of suspense. How women loved to make men suffer! At last she said in a constrained voice: 'I don't think we ought to talk of all this yet—'

Rebuking him – she was actually rebuking him for his magnanimity! But couldn't she see – couldn't she understand? Or was it that she really enjoyed torturing him? 'How can I help talking of it, when you tell me you're going away tomorrow morning? Did you really mean to go without even telling me?'

'If I hadn't seen you I should have written,' she faltered.

'Well, now I'm here you needn't write. All you've got to do is to answer me,' he retorted almost angrily. The calm way in which she dealt with the situation was enough to madden a man – actually as if she hadn't made up her mind, good God! 'What are you afraid of?' he burst out harshly.

'I'm not afraid – only I didn't expect . . . I thought we'd talk of all this later . . . if you feel the same when I come back – if we both do.'

'If we both do!' Ah, there was the sting – the devil's claw! What was it? Was she being superhumanly magnanimous – or proud, oversensitive, afraid that he might be making the proposal out of pity? Poor girl – poor child! That must be it. He loved her all the more for it, bless her! Or was it (ah, now again the claw tightened), was it that she really didn't want to commit herself, wanted to reserve her freedom for this crazy expedition, to see whether she couldn't do better by looking about out there – she, so young, so fresh and radiant – than by binding herself in advance to an elderly professor at Kingsborough? Hawaii – Samoa – swarming with rich idle yachtsmen and young naval officers (he had an excruciating vision of a throng of *Madame Butterfly* tenors in immaculate white duck and gold braid) – cocktails, fox-trot, moonlight in the tropics . . . he felt suddenly middle-aged, round shouldered, shabby, with thinning graying hair. . . . Of course what she wanted was to look round and see what her chances were! He retrieved the fallen stool, set it up again, and sat down on it.

'I suppose you're not sure you'll feel the same when you get back? Is that it?' he suggested bitterly.

Again she hesitated. 'I don't think we ought to decide now – tonight. . . .'

His anger blazed. 'Why oughtn't we? Tell me that! I've decided. Why shouldn't you?'

'You haven't really decided either,' she returned gently.

'I haven't – haven't I? Now what do you mean by that?' He forced a laugh that was meant to be playful but sounded defiant. He was aware that his voice and words were getting out of hand – but what business had she to keep him on the stretch like this?

'I mean, after what you've been through. . . .'

'After what I've been through? But don't you see that's the very reason? I'm at the breaking point – I can't bear any more.'

'I know; I know.' She got up and came close, laying a quiet hand on his shoulder. 'I've suffered for you too. The shock it must have been. That's the reason why I don't want to say anything now that you might—'

He shook off her hand, and sprang up. 'What hypocrisy!' He heard himself beginning to shout again. 'I suppose what you mean is that you want to be free to marry out there if you see anybody you like better. Then why not admit it at once?'

'Because it's not what I mean. I don't want to marry anyone else, Ambrose.'

Oh, the melting music of it! He lifted his hands and hid his burning eyes in them. The sound of her voice wove magic passes above his forehead. Was it possible that such bliss could come out of such anguish? He forgot the place – forgot the day – and abruptly, blindly, caught her by the arm, and flung his own about her.

'Oh, Ambrose—' he heard her, reproachful, panting. He struggled with her, feverish for her lips.

In the semiobscurity there was the sound of something crashing to the floor between them. They drew apart, and she looked at him, bewildered. 'What was that?'

What was it? He knew well enough; a shiver of cold ran over him. The letters, of course – her letters! The bulging clumsily-tied envelope had dropped out of his pocket onto the floor of the garage; in the fall the string had come undone, and the mass of papers had tumbled out, scattering themselves like a pack of cards at Barbara's feet. She picked up her electric lamp, and bending over shot its sharp ray on them.

'Why, they're letters! Ambrose – are they my letters?' She waited; but silence lay on him like lead. 'Was that what you came for?' she exclaimed.

If there was an answer to that he couldn't find it, and stupidly, without knowing what he was doing, he bent down and began to gather up the letters.

For a while he was aware of her standing there motionless, watching him; then she too bent over, and took up the gaping linen envelope. '"Miss Barbara Wake,"' she read out; and suddenly she began to laugh. 'Why,' she said, 'there's something left in it! A letter for *me*? Is that it?'

He put his hand out. 'Barbara – don't! Barbara – I implore you!'

She turned the electric ray on the sheet of paper, which detached itself from the shadows with the solidity of a graven tablet. Slowly she read out, in a cool measured voice, almost as though she were parodying his poor phrases: '"November tenth. . . . You will probably feel as I do" (no – don't snatch! Ambrose, I forbid you!) "You will probably feel, as I do, that after what has happened you and I can never"—' She broke off and raised her eyes to Trenham's. '"After what has happened"? I don't understand. What do you mean? What *has* happened, Ambrose – between you and me?'

He had retreated a few steps, and stood leaning against the side of the motor. 'I didn't say "Between you and me."'

'What did you say?' She turned the light once more on the fatal page. ' "You and I can never wish to meet again." ' Her hand sank, and she stood facing him in silence.

Feeling her gaze fixed on him, he muttered miserably: 'I asked you not to read the thing.'

'But if it was meant for me why do you want me not to read it?'

'Can't you see? It doesn't mean anything. I was raving mad when I wrote it. . . .'

'But you wrote it only a few hours ago. It's dated today. How can you have changed so in a few hours? And you say: "After what has happened." That must mean something. What does it mean? What *has* happened?'

He thought he would go mad indeed if she repeated the word again. 'Oh, don't – !' he exclaimed.

'Don't what?'

'Say it over and over – "what has happened?" Can't you understand that just at first—'

He broke off, and she prompted him: 'Just at first – ?'

'I couldn't bear the horror alone. Like a miserable coward I let myself think you were partly responsible – I wanted to think so, you understand. . . .'

Her face seemed to grow white and wavering in the shadows. 'What do you mean? Responsible for what?'

He straightened his shoulders and said slowly: 'Responsible for her death. I was too weak to carry it alone.'

'Her death?' There was a silence that seemed to make the shadowy place darker. He could hardly see her face now, she was so far off. 'How could I be responsible?' she broke off, and then began again: 'Are you – trying to tell me – that it wasn't an accident?'

'No – it wasn't an accident.'

'She—'

'Well, can't you guess?' he stammered, panting.

'You mean – she killed herself?'

'Yes.'

'Because of us?'

He could not speak, and after a moment she hurried on: 'But what makes you think so? What proof have you? Did she tell anyone? Did she leave a message – a letter?'

He summoned his voice to his dry throat. 'No; nothing.'

'Well, then – ?'

'She'd told me beforehand; she'd warned me—'

'Warned you?'

'That if I went on seeing you . . . and I did go on seeing you . . . she warned me again and again. Do you understand now?' he exclaimed, twisting round on her fiercely, like an animal turning on its torturer.

There was an interval of silence – endless it seemed to him. She did not speak or move; but suddenly he heard a low sobbing sound. She was weeping, weeping like a frightened child. . . . Well, of all the unexpected turns of fate! A moment ago he had seemed to feel her strength flowing into his cold veins, had thought to himself: 'I shall never again be alone with my horror—' and now the horror had spread from him to her, and he felt her inwardly recoiling as though she shuddered away from the contagion.

'Oh, how dreadful, how dreadful—' She began to cry again, like a child swept by a fresh gust of misery as the last subsides.

'Why dreadful?' he burst out, unnerved by the continuance of her soft unremitting sobs. 'You must have known she didn't like it – didn't you?'

Through her lament a whisper issued: 'I never dreamed she knew.'

'You mean to say you thought we'd deceived her? All those months? In a one-horse place where everybody is on the watch to see what everybody else is doing? Likely, isn't it? My God—'

'I never dreamed . . . I never dreamed. . . .' she reiterated.

His exasperation broke out again. 'Well, now you begin to see what I've suffered—'

'Suffered? *You* suffered?' She uttered a low sound of derision. 'I see what she must have suffered – what we both of us must have made her suffer.'

'Ah, at least you say "both of us"!'

She made no answer, and through her silence he felt again that she was inwardly shrinking, averting herself from him. What! His accomplice deserting him? She acknowledged that she was his accomplice – she said 'both of us' – and yet she was drawing back from him, flying from him, leaving him alone! Ah, no – she shouldn't escape as easily as that, she shouldn't leave him; he couldn't face that sense of being alone again. 'Barbara!' he cried out, as if the actual distance between them had already doubled.

She still remained silent, and he hurried on, almost cringingly: 'Don't think I blame you, child – don't think. . . .'

'Oh, what does it matter, when I blame myself?' she wailed out, her face in her hands.

'Blame yourself? What folly! When you say you didn't know—'

'Of course I didn't know! How can you imagine – ?' But this dreadful thing has happened; and *you* knew it might happen . . . you knew it all along . . . all the while it was in the back of your mind . . . the days when we used to meet here . . . and the days when we went to Ditson . . . oh, that horrible room at Ditson! All that time she was sitting at home alone, knowing everything, and hating me as if I'd been her murderess. . . .'

'Good God, Barbara! Don't you suppose I blame myself?'

'But if you blamed yourself how could you go on, how could you let me think she didn't care?'

'I didn't suppose she did,' he muttered sullenly.

'But you say she told you – she warned you! Over and over again she warned you.'

'Well, I didn't want to believe her – and so I didn't. When a man's infatuated. . . . Don't you see it's hard enough to bear without all this? Haven't you any pity for me, Barbara?'

'Pity?' she repeated slowly. 'The only pity I feel is for *her* – for what she must have gone through, day after day, week after week, sitting there all alone and knowing . . . imagining exactly what you were saying to me . . . the way you kissed me . . . and watching the clock, and counting the hours . . . and then having you come back, and explain, and pretend – I suppose you *did* pretend? . . . and all the while secretly knowing you were lying, and yet longing to believe you . . . and having warned you, and seeing that her warnings made no difference . . . that you didn't care if she died or not . . . that you were doing all you could to kill her . . . that you were probably counting the days till she was dead!' Her passionate apostrophe broke down in a sob, and again she stood weeping like an inconsolable child.

Trenham was struck silent. It was true. He had never been really able to enter into poor Milly's imaginings, the matter of her lonely musings; and here was this girl to whom, in a flash, that solitary mind lay bare. Yes; that must have been the way Milly felt – he knew it now – and the way poor Barbara herself would feel if he ever betrayed her. Ah, but he was never going to betray her –

the thought was monstrous! Never for a moment would he cease to love her. This catastrophe had bound them together as a happy wooing could never have done. It was her love for him, her fear for their future, that was shaking her to the soul, giving her this unnatural power to enter into Milly's mind. If only he could find words to reassure her, now, at once. But he could not think of any.

'Barbara – Barbara,' he kept on repeating, as if her name were a sort of incantation.

'Oh, think of it – those lonely endless hours! I wonder if you ever did think of them before? When you used to go home after one of our meetings, did you remember each time what she'd told you, and begin to wonder, as you got near the house, if she'd done it *that day?*'

'Barbara—'

'Perhaps you did – perhaps you were even vexed with her for being so slow about it. Were you?'

'Oh, Barbara – Barbara. . . .'

'And when the day came at last, were you surprised? Had you got so impatient waiting that you'd begun to believe she'd never do it? Were there days when you went almost mad at having to wait so long for your freedom? It was the way I used to feel when I was rushing for the train to Ditson, and father would call me at the last minute to write letters for him, or mother to replace her on some charity committee; there were days when I could have *killed* them, almost, for interfering with me, making me miss one of our precious hours together. *Killed them*, I say! Don't you suppose I know how murderers feel? How *you* feel – for you're a murderer, you know! And now you come here, when the earth's hardly covered her, and try to kiss me, and ask me to marry you – and think, I suppose, that by doing so you're covering up her memory more securely, you're pounding down the earth on her a little harder. . . .'

She broke off, as if her own words terrified her, and hid her eyes from the vision they called up.

Trenham stood without moving. He had gathered up the letters, and they lay in a neat pile on the floor between himself and her, because there seemed no other place to put them. He said to himself (reflecting how many million men must have said the same thing at such moments): 'After this she'll calm down, and by tomorrow she'll be telling me how sorry she is. . . .' But the reflection did not seem to help him. She might forget – but he would not. He had forgotten too easily before; he had an idea that his future would be burdened with long arrears of remembrance. Just as the girl described Milly, so he would see her in the years to come. He would have to pay the interest on his oblivion; and it would not help much to have Barbara pay it with him. The job was probably one that would have to be accomplished alone. At last words shaped themselves without his knowing it. 'I'd better go,' he said.

Unconsciously he had expected an answer; an appeal; a protest, perhaps. But none came. He moved away a few steps in the direction of the door. As he did so he heard Barbara break into a laugh, and the sound, so unnatural in that place, and at that moment, brought him abruptly to a halt.

'Yes – ?' he said, half turning, as though she had called him.

'And I sent a wreath – I sent her a wreath! It's on her grave now – it hasn't even had time to fade!'

'Oh—' he gasped, as if she had struck him across the face. They stood forlornly confronting each other. Her last words seemed to have created an icy void between them. Within himself a voice whispered: 'She can't find anything worse than that.' But he saw by the faint twitch of her lips that she was groping, groping—

'And the worst of it is,' she broke out, 'that if I didn't go away, and we were to drag on here together, after a time I might even drift into forgiving you.'

Yes; she was right; that was certainly the worst of it. Human imagination could not go beyond that, he thought. He moved away again stiffly.

'Well, you *are* going away, aren't you?' he said.

'Yes; I'm going.'

He walked back slowly through the dark deserted streets. His brain, reeling with the shock of the encounter, gradually cleared, and looked about on the new world within itself. At first the inside of his head was like a deserted house out of which all the furniture had been moved, down to the last familiar encumbrances. It was empty, absolutely empty. But gradually a small speck of consciousness appeared in the dreary void, like a mouse scurrying across bare floors. He stopped on a street corner to say to himself:

'But after all nothing is changed – absolutely nothing. I went there to tell her that we should probably never want to see each other again; and she agreed with me. She agreed with me – that's all.'

It was a relief, almost, to have even that little thought stirring about in the resonant void of his brain. He walked on more quickly, reflecting, as he reached his own corner: 'In a minute it's going to rain.' He smiled a little at his unconscious precaution in hurrying home to escape the rain. 'Jane will begin to fret – she'll be sure to notice that I didn't take my umbrella.' And his cold heart felt a faint warmth at the thought that someone in the huge hostile world would really care whether he had taken his umbrella or not. 'But probably she's in bed and asleep,' he mused, despondently.

On his doorstep he paused and began to grope for his latchkey. He felt impatiently in one pocket after another – but the key was not to be found. He had an idea that he had left it lying on his study table when he came in after – after what? Why, that very morning, after the funeral! He had flung the key down among his papers – and Jane would never notice that it was there. She would never think of looking; she had been bidden often enough on no account to meddle with the things on his desk. And besides she would take for granted that he had the key in his pocket. And here he stood, in the middle of the night, locked out of his own house—

A sudden exasperation possessed him. He was aware that he must have lost all sense of proportion, all perspective, for he felt as baffled and as angry as when Barbara's furious words had beaten down on him. Yes; it made him just as unhappy to find himself locked out of his house – he could have sat down on the doorstep and cried. And here was the rain beginning. . . .

He put his hand to the bell; but did the front doorbell ring in the far-off attic where the maids were lodged? And was there the least chance of the faint tinkle from the pantry mounting two flights, and penetrating to their sleep-muffled ears? Utterly improbable, he knew. And if he couldn't make them hear he would have to spend the night at a hotel – the night of his wife's funeral! And the next morning all Kingsborough would know of it, from the President of the University to the boy who delivered the milk. . . .

But his hand had hardly touched the bell when he felt a vibration of life in the house. First there was a faint flash of light through the transom above the front door; then, scarcely distinguishable from the noises of the night, a step sounded far off; it grew louder on the hall floor, and after an interval that seemed endless the door was flung open by a Jane still irreproachably capped and aproned.

'Why, Jane – I didn't think you'd be awake! I forgot my key. . . .'

'I know, sir. I found it. I was waiting.' She took his wet coat from him. 'Dear, dear! And you hadn't your umbrella.'

He stepped into his own hall, and heard her close and bar the door behind him. He liked to listen to that familiar slipping of the bolts and clink of the chain. He liked to think that she minded about his not having his umbrella. It was his own house, after all – and this friendly hand was shutting him safely into it. The dreadful sense of loneliness melted a little at the old reassuring touch of habit.

'Thank you, Jane; sorry I kept you up,' he muttered, nodding to her as he went upstairs.

All Souls'

Queer and inexplicable as the business was, on the surface it appeared fairly simple – at the time, at least; but with the passing of years, and owing to there not having been a single witness of what happened except Sara Clayburn herself, the stories about it have become so exaggerated, and often so ridiculously inaccurate, that it seems necessary that someone connected with the affair, though not actually present – I repeat that when it happened my cousin was (or thought she was) quite alone in her house – should record the few facts actually known.

In those days I was often at Whitegates (as the place had always been called) – I was there, in fact, not long before, and almost immediately after, the strange happenings of those thirty-six hours. Jim Clayburn and his widow were both my cousins, and because of that, and of my intimacy with them, both families think I am more likely than anybody else to be able to get at the facts, as far as they can be called facts, and as anybody can get at them. So I have written down, as clearly as I could, the gist of the various talks I had with cousin Sara, when she could be got to talk – it wasn't often – about what occurred during that mysterious weekend.

I read the other day in a book by a fashionable essayist that ghosts went out when electric light came in. What nonsense! The writer, though he is fond of dabbling, in a literary way, in the supernatural, hasn't even reached the threshold of his subject. As between turreted castles patrolled by headless victims with clanking chains, and the comfortable suburban house with a refrigerator and central heating where you feel, as soon as you're in it, *that there's something wrong*, give me the latter for sending a chill down the spine! And, by the way, haven't you noticed that it's generally not the high-strung and imaginative who see ghosts, but the calm matter-of-fact people who don't believe in them, and are sure they wouldn't mind if they did see one? Well, that was the case with Sara Clayburn and her house. The house, in spite of its age – it was built, I believe, about 1780 – was open, airy, high-ceilinged, with electricity, central heating and all the modern appliances: and its mistress was – well, very much like her house. And, anyhow, this isn't exactly a ghost story and I've dragged in the analogy only as a way of showing you what kind of woman my cousin was, and how unlikely it would have seemed that what happened at Whitegates should have happened just there – or to her.

When Jim Clayburn died the family all thought that, as the couple had no children, his widow would give up Whitegates and move either to New York or Boston – for being of good Colonial stock, with many relatives and friends, she would have found a place ready for her in either. But Sara Clayburn seldom did what other people expected, and in this case she did exactly the contrary; she stayed at Whitegates.

'What, turn my back on the old house – tear up all the family roots, and go and hang myself up in a bird-cage flat in one of those new sky-scrapers in Lexington Avenue, with a bunch of chick-weed and a cuttlefish to replace my good Connecticut mutton? No, thank you. Here I belong, and here I stay till my executors hand the place over to Jim's next-of-kin – that stupid fat Presley boy. . . . Well, don't let's talk about him. But I tell you what – I'll keep him out of here as long as I can.' And she did – for being still in the early fifties when her husband died, and a muscular, resolute figure of a woman, she was more than a match for the fat Presley boy, and attended his funeral a few years ago, in correct mourning, with a faint smile under her veil.

Whitegates was a pleasant hospitable-looking house, on a height overlooking the stately windings of the Connecticut River; but it was five or six miles from Norrington, the nearest town, and its situation would certainly have seemed remote and lonely to modern servants. Luckily, however, Sara Clayburn had inherited from her mother-in-law two or three old stand-bys who seemed as much a part of the family tradition as the roof they lived under; and I never heard of her having any trouble in her domestic arrangements.

The house, in Colonial days, had been foursquare, with four spacious rooms on the ground floor, an oak-floored hall dividing them, the usual kitchen extension at the back, and a good attic under the roof. But Jim's grandparents, when interest in the

'Colonial' began to revive, in the early eighties, had added two wings, at right angles to the south front, so that the old 'circle' before the front door became a grassy court, enclosed on three sides, with a big elm in the middle. Thus the house was turned into a roomy dwelling, in which the last three generations of Clayburns had exercised a large hospitality; but the architect had respected the character of the old house, and the enlargement made it more comfortable without lessening its simplicity. There was a lot of land about it, and Jim Clayburn, like his fathers before him, farmed it, not without profit, and played a considerable and respected part in state politics. The Clayburns were always spoken of as a 'good influence' in the county, and the townspeople were glad when they learned that Sara did not mean to desert the place – 'though it must be lonesome, winters, living all alone up there atop of that hill' – they remarked as the days shortened, and the first snow began to pile up under the quadruple row of elms along the common.

Well, if I've given you a sufficiently clear idea of Whitegates and the Clayburns – who shared with their old house a sort of reassuring orderliness and dignity – I'll efface myself, and tell the tale, not in my cousin's words, for they were too confused and fragmentary, but as I built it up gradually out of her half-avowals and nervous reticences. If the thing happened at all – and I must leave you to judge of that – I think it must have happened in this way. . . .

1

The morning had been bitter, with a driving sleet – though it was only the last day of October – but after lunch a watery sun showed for a while through banked-up woolly clouds, and tempted Sara Clayburn out. She was an energetic walker, and given, at that season, to tramping three or four miles along the valley road, and coming back by way of Shaker's wood. She had made her usual round, and was following the main drive to the house when she overtook a plainly-dressed woman walking in the same direction. If the scene had not been so lonely – the way to Whitegates at the end of an autumn day was not a frequented one – Mrs Clayburn might not have paid any attention to the woman, for she was in no way noticeable; but when she caught up with the intruder my cousin was surprised to find that she was a stranger – for the mistress of Whitegates prided herself on knowing, at least by sight, most of her country neighbors. It was almost dark, and the woman's face was hardly visible, but Mrs Clayburn told me she recalled her as middle-aged, plain and rather pale.

Mrs Clayburn greeted her, and then added: 'You're going to the house?'

'Yes, ma'am,' the woman answered, in a voice that the Connecticut Valley in old days would have called 'foreign,' but that would have been unnoticed by ears used to the modern multiplicity of tongues. 'No, I couldn't say where she came from,' Sara always said. 'What struck me as queer was that I didn't know her.'

She asked the woman, politely, what she wanted, and the woman answered: 'Only to see one of the girls.' The answer was natural enough, and Mrs Clayburn nodded and turned off from the drive to the lower part of the gardens, so that she saw no more of the visitor then or afterward. And, in fact, a half hour later something happened which put the stranger entirely out of her mind. The brisk and light-footed Mrs Clayburn, as she approached the house, slipped on a frozen puddle, turned her ankle and lay suddenly helpless.

Price, the butler, and Agnes, the dour old Scottish maid whom Sara had inherited from her mother-in-law, of course knew exactly what to do. In no time they had their mistress stretched out on a lounge, and Dr Selgrove had been called up from Norrington. When he arrived, he ordered Mrs Clayburn to bed, did the necessary examining and bandaging, and shook his head over her ankle, which he feared was fractured. He thought, however, that if she would swear not to get up, or even shift the position of her leg, he could spare her the discomfort of putting it in plaster. Mrs Clayburn agreed, the more promptly as the doctor warned her that any rash movement would prolong her immobility. Her quick imperious nature made the prospect trying, and she was annoyed with herself for having been so clumsy. But the mischief was done, and she immediately thought what an opportunity she would have for going over her accounts and catching up with her correspondence. So she settled down resignedly in her bed.

'And you won't miss much, you know, if you have to stay there a few days. It's beginning to snow, and it looks as if we are in for a good spell of it,' the doctor remarked, glancing through the window as he gathered up his implements. 'Well, we don't often get snow here as early as this; but winter's got to begin sometime,' he concluded philosophically. At the door he stopped to add: 'You don't want me to send up a nurse from Norrington? Not to nurse you, you know; there's nothing much to do till I see you again. But this is a pretty lonely place when the snow begins, and I thought maybe—'

Sara Clayburn laughed. 'Lonely? With my old servants? You forget how many winters I've spent here alone with them. Two of them were with me in my mother-in-law's time.'

'That's so,' Dr Selgrove agreed. 'You're a good deal luckier than most people, that way. Well, let me see; this is Saturday. We'll have to let the inflammation go down before we can X-ray you. Monday morning, first thing, I'll be here with the X-ray man. If you want me sooner, call me up.' And he was gone.

2

The foot, at first, had not been very painful; but toward the small hours Mrs Clayburn began to suffer. She was a bad patient, like most healthy and active people. Not being used to pain she did not know how to bear it, and the hours of wakefulness and immobility seemed endless. Agnes, before leaving her, had made everything as comfortable as possible. She had put a jug of lemonade within reach, and had even (Mrs Clayburn thought it odd afterward) insisted on bringing in a tray with sandwiches and a thermos of tea. 'In case you're hungry in the night, madam.'

'Thank you; but I'm never hungry in the night. And I certainly shan't be tonight – only thirsty. I think I'm feverish.'

'Well, there's the lemonade, madam.'

'That will do. Take the other things away, please.' (Sara had always hated the sight of unwanted food 'messing about' in her room.)

'Very well, madam. Only you might—'

'Please take it away,' Mrs Clayburn repeated irritably.

'Very good, madam.' But as Agnes went out, her mistress heard her set the tray down softly on a table behind the screen which shut off the door.

'Obstinate old goose!' she thought, rather touched by the old woman's insistence.

Sleep, once it had gone, would not return, and the long black hours moved more and more slowly. How late the dawn came in November! 'If only I could move my leg,' she grumbled.

She lay still and strained her ears for the first steps of the servants. Whitegates was an early house, its mistress setting the example; it would surely not be long now before one of the women came. She was tempted to ring for Agnes, but refrained. The woman had been up late, and this was Sunday morning, when the household was always allowed a little extra time. Mrs Clayburn reflected restlessly: 'I was a fool not to let her leave the tea beside the bed, as she wanted to. I wonder if I could get up and get it?' But she remembered the doctor's warning, and dared not move. Anything rather than risk prolonging her imprisonment. . . .

Ah, there was the stable clock striking. How loud it sounded in the snowy stillness! One – two – three – four – five. . . .

What? Only five? Three hours and a quarter more before she could hope to hear the door handle turned. . . . After a while she dozed off again, uncomfortably.

Another sound aroused her. Again the stable clock. She listened. But the room was still in deep darkness, and only six strokes fell. . . . She thought of reciting something to put her to sleep; but she seldom read poetry, and being naturally a good sleeper, she could not remember any of the usual devices against insomnia. The whole of her leg felt like lead now. The bandages had grown terribly tight – her ankle must have swollen. . . . She lay staring at the dark windows, watching for the first glimmer of dawn. At last she saw a pale filter of daylight through the shutters. One by one the objects between the bed and the window recovered first their outline, then their bulk, and seemed to be stealthily regrouping themselves, after goodness knows what secret displacements during the night. Who that has lived in an old house could possibly believe that the furniture in it stays still all night? Mrs Clayburn almost fancied she saw one little slender-legged table slipping hastily back into its place.

'It knows Agnes is coming, and it's afraid,' she thought

whimsically. Her bad night must have made her imaginative for such nonsense as that about the furniture had never occurred to her before. . . .

At length, after hours more, as it seemed, the stable clock struck eight. Only another quarter of an hour. She watched the hand moving slowly across the face of the little clock beside her bed . . . ten minutes . . . five . . . only five! Agnes was as punctual as destiny . . . in two minutes now she would come. The two minutes passed, and she did not come. Poor Agnes – she had looked pale and tired the night before. She had overslept herself, no doubt – or perhaps she felt ill, and would send the housemaid to replace her. Mrs Clayburn waited.

She waited half an hour; then she reached up to the bell at the head of the bed. Poor old Agnes – her mistress felt guilty about waking her. But Agnes did not appear – and after a considerable interval Mrs Clayburn, now with a certain impatience, rang again. She rang once; twice; three times – but still no one came.

Once more she waited; then she said to herself: 'There must be something wrong with the electricity.' Well – she could find out by switching on the bed lamp at her elbow (how admirably the room was equipped with every practical appliance!). She switched it on – but no light came. Electric current cut off; and it was Sunday, and nothing could be done about it till the next morning. Unless it turned out to be just a burnt-out fuse, which Price could remedy. Well, in a moment now someone would surely come to her door.

It was nine o'clock before she admitted to herself that something uncommonly strange must have happened in the house. She began to feel a nervous apprehension; but she was not the woman to encourage it. If only she had had the telephone put in her room, instead of out on the landing! She measured mentally the distance to be travelled, remembered Dr Selgrove's admonition, and wondered if her broken ankle would carry her there. She dreaded the prospect of being put in plaster, but she had to get to the telephone, whatever happened.

She wrapped herself in her dressing gown, found a walking stick, and, resting heavily on it, dragged herself to the door. In her bedroom the careful Agnes had closed and fastened the shutters, so that it was not much lighter there than at dawn; but outside in the corridor the cold whiteness of the snowy morning seemed almost reassuring. Mysterious things – dreadful things – were associated with darkness; and here was the wholesome prosaic daylight come again to banish them. Mrs Clayburn looked about her and listened. Silence. A deep nocturnal silence in that day-lit house, in which five people were presumably coming and going about their work. It was certainly strange. . . . She looked out of the window, hoping to see someone crossing the court or coming along the drive. But no one was in sight, and the snow seemed to have the place to itself: a quiet steady snow. It was still falling, with a business-like regularity, muffling the outer world in layers on layers of thick white velvet, and intensifying the silence within. A noiseless world – were people so sure that absence of noise was what they wanted? Let them first try a lonely country house in a November snowstorm!

She dragged herself along the passage to the telephone. When she unhooked the receiver she noticed that her hand trembled.

She rang up the pantry – no answer. She rang again. Silence – more silence! It seemed to be piling itself up like the snow on the roof and in the gutters. Silence. How many people that she knew had any idea what silence was – and how loud it sounded when you really listened to it?

Again she waited: then she rang up 'Central.' No answer. She tried three times. After that she tried the pantry again. . . . The telephone was cut off, then; like the electric current. Who was at work downstairs, isolating her thus from the world? Her heart began to hammer. Luckily there was a chair near the telephone, and she sat down to recover her strength – or was it her courage?

Agnes and the housemaid slept in the nearest wing. She would certainly get as far as that when she had pulled herself together. Had she the courage – ? Yes, of course she had. She had always been regarded as a plucky woman; and had so regarded herself. But this silence—

It occurred to her that by looking from the window of a neighboring bathroom she could see the kitchen chimney. There ought to be smoke coming from it at that hour; and if there were she thought she would be less afraid to go on. She got as far as the bathroom and looking through the window saw that no smoke came from the chimney. Her sense of loneliness grew more acute. Whatever had happened belowstairs must have happened before the morning's work had begun. The cook had not had time to light the fire, the other servants had not yet begun their round. She sank down on the nearest chair, struggling against her fears. What next would she discover if she carried on her investigations?

The pain in her ankle made progress difficult; but she was aware of it now only as an obstacle to haste. No matter what it cost her in physical suffering, she must find out what was happening belowstairs – or had happened. But first she would go to the maid's room. And if that were empty – well, somehow she would have to get herself downstairs.

She limped along the passage, and on the way steadied herself by resting her hand on a radiator. It was stone-cold. Yet in that well-ordered house in winter the central heating, though damped down at night, was never allowed to go out, and by eight in the morning a mellow warmth pervaded the rooms. The icy chill of the pipes startled her. It was the chauffeur who looked after the heating – so he too was involved in the mystery, whatever it was, as well as the house servants. But this only deepened the problem.

3

At Agnes's door Mrs Clayburn paused and knocked. She expected no answer, and there was none. She opened the door and went in. The room was dark and very cold. She went to the window and flung back the shutters; then she looked slowly around, vaguely apprehensive of what she might see. The room was empty but what frightened her was not so much its emptiness as its air of scrupulous and undisturbed order. There was no sign of anyone having lately dressed in it – or undressed the night before. And the bed had not been slept in.

Mrs Clayburn leaned against the wall for a moment; then she crossed the floor and opened the cupboard. That was where Agnes kept her dresses; and the dresses were there, neatly hanging in a row. On the shelf above were Agnes's few and unfashionable hats, rearrangements of her mistress's old ones. Mrs Clayburn, who knew them all, looked at the shelf, and saw that one was missing. And so was also the warm winter coat she had given to Agnes the previous winter.

The woman was out, then; had gone out, no doubt, the night before, since the bed was unslept in, the dressing and washing appliances untouched. Agnes, who never set foot out of the house after dark, who despised the movies as much as she did the wireless, and could never be persuaded that a little innocent amusement was a necessary element in life, had deserted the house on a snowy winter night, while her mistress lay upstairs, suffering and helpless! Why had she gone, and where had she gone? When she was undressing Mrs Clayburn the night before, taking her orders, trying to make her more comfortable, was she already planning this mysterious nocturnal escape? Or had something – the mysterious and dreadful Something for the clue of which Mrs Clayburn was still groping – occurred later in the evening, sending the maid downstairs and out of doors into the bitter night? Perhaps one of the men at the garage – where the chauffeur and gardener lived – had been suddenly taken ill, and someone had run up to the house for Agnes. Yes – that must be the explanation. . . . Yet how much it left unexplained.

Next to Agnes's room was the linen room; beyond that was the housemaid's door. Mrs Clayburn went to it and knocked. 'Mary!' No one answered, and she went in. The room was in the same immaculate order as her maid's, and here too the bed was unslept in, and there were no signs of dressing or undressing. The two women had no doubt gone out together – gone where?

More and more the cold unanswering silence of the house weighed down on Mrs Clayburn. She had never thought of it as a big house, but now, in this snowy winter light, it seemed immense, and full of ominous corners around which one dared not look.

Beyond the housemaid's room were the back stairs. It was the nearest way down, and every step that Mrs Clayburn took was increasingly painful; but she decided to walk slowly back, the whole length of the passage, and go down by the front stairs. She did not know why she did this; but she felt that at the moment she was past reasoning, and had better obey her instinct.

More than once she had explored the ground floor alone in the small hours, in search of unwonted midnight noises; but now it was not the idea of noises that frightened her, but that inexorable and hostile silence, the sense that the house had retained in full daylight its nocturnal mystery, and was watching her as she was watching it; that in entering those empty orderly rooms she might be disturbing some unseen confabulation on which beings of flesh-and-blood had better not intrude.

The broad oak stairs were beautifully polished, and so slippery that she had to cling to the rail and let herself down tread by tread. And as she descended, the silence descended with her – heavier, denser, more absolute. She seemed to feel its steps just behind her, softly keeping time with hers. It had a quality she had never been aware of in any other silence, as though it were not merely an absence of sound, a thin barrier between the ear and the surging murmur of life just beyond, but an impenetrable substance made out of the worldwide cessation of all life and all movement.

Yes, that was what laid a chill on her: the feeling that there was no limit to this silence, no outer margin, nothing beyond it. By this time she had reached the foot of the stairs and was limping across the hall to the drawing-room. Whatever she found there, she was sure, would be mute and lifeless; but what would it be? The bodies of her dead servants, mown down by some homicidal maniac? And what if it were her turn next – if he were waiting for her behind the heavy curtains of the room she was about to enter? Well, she must find out – she must face whatever lay in wait. Not impelled by bravery – the last drop of courage had oozed out of her – but because anything, anything was better than to remain shut up in that snowbound house without knowing whether she was alone in it or not. 'I must find that out, I must find that out,' she repeated to herself in a sort of meaningless sing-song.

The cold outer light flooded the drawing-room. The shutters had not been closed, nor the curtains drawn. She looked about her. The room was empty, and every chair in its usual place. Her armchair was pushed up by the chimney, and the cold hearth was piled with the ashes of the fire at which she had warmed herself before starting on her ill-fated walk. Even her empty coffee-cup stood on a table near the armchair. It was evident that the servants had not been in the room since she had left it the day before after luncheon. And suddenly the conviction entered into her that, as she found the drawing-room, so she would find the rest of the house; cold, orderly – and empty. She would find nothing, she would find no one. She no longer felt any dread of ordinary human dangers lurking in those dumb spaces ahead of her. She knew she was utterly alone under her own roof. She sat down to rest her aching ankle, and looked slowly about her.

There were the other rooms to be visited, and she was

determined to go through them all – but she knew in advance that they would give no answer to her question. She knew it, seemingly, from the quality of the silence which enveloped her. There was no break, no thinnest crack in it anywhere. It had the cold continuity of the snow which was still falling steadily outside.

She had no idea how long she waited before nerving herself to continue her inspection. She no longer felt the pain in her ankle, but was only conscious that she must not bear her weight on it, and therefore moved very slowly, supporting herself on each piece of furniture in her path. On the ground floor no shutter had been closed, no curtain drawn, and she progressed without difficulty from room to room: the library, her morning-room, the dining-room. In each of them, every piece of furniture was in its usual place. In the dining-room, the table had been laid for her dinner of the previous evening, and the candelabra, with candles unlit, stood reflected in the dark mahogany. She was not the kind of woman to nibble a poached egg on a tray when she was alone, but always came down to the dining-room, and had what she called a civilized meal.

The back premises remained to be visited. From the dining-room she entered the pantry, and there too everything was in irreproachable order. She opened the door and looked down the back passage with its neat linoleum floor covering. The deep silence accompanied her; she still felt it moving watchfully at her side, as though she were its prisoner and it might throw itself upon her if she attempted to escape. She limped on toward the kitchen. That of course would be empty too, and immaculate. But she must see it.

She leaned a minute in the embrasure of a window in the passage. 'It's like the "Mary Celeste" – a "Mary Celeste" on *terra firma*,' she thought, recalling the unsolved sea mystery of her childhood. 'No one ever knew what happened on board the "Mary Celeste." And perhaps no one will ever know what has happened here. Even I shan't know.'

At the thought her latent fear seemed to take on a new quality. It was like an icy liquid running through every vein, and lying in a pool about her heart. She understood now that she had never before known what fear was, and that most of the people she had met had probably never known either. For this sensation was something quite different. . . .

It absorbed her so completely that she was not aware how long she remained leaning there. But suddenly a new impulse pushed her forward, and she walked on toward the scullery. She went there first because there was a service slide in the wall, through which she might peep into the kitchen without being seen; and some indefinable instinct told her that the kitchen held the clue to the mystery. She still felt strongly that whatever had happened in the house must have its source and center in the kitchen.

In the scullery, as she had expected, everything was clean and tidy. Whatever had happened, no one in the house appeared to have been taken by surprise; there was nowhere any sign of confusion or disorder. 'It looks as if they'd known beforehand, and put everything straight,' she thought. She glanced at the wall facing the door, and saw that the slide was open. And then, as she was approaching it, the silence was broken. A voice was speaking in the kitchen – a man's voice, low but emphatic, and which she had never heard before.

She stood still, cold with fear. But this fear was again a different one. Her previous terrors had been speculative, conjectural, a ghostly emanation of the surrounding silence. This was a plain everyday dread of evildoers. Oh, God, why had she not remembered her husband's revolver, which ever since his death had lain in a drawer in her room?

She turned to retreat across the smooth slippery floor but half-way her stick slipped from her, and crashed down on the tiles. The noise seemed to echo on and on through the emptiness, and she stood still, aghast. Now that she had betrayed her presence, flight was useless. Whoever was beyond the kitchen door would be upon her in a second. . . .

But to her astonishment the voice went on speaking. It was as though neither the speaker nor his listeners had heard her. The invisible stranger spoke so low that she could not make out what he was saying, but the tone was passionately earnest, almost threatening. The next moment she realized that he was speaking in a foreign language, a language unknown to her. Once more her terror was surmounted by the urgent desire to know what was going on, so close to her yet unseen. She crept to the slide, peered cautiously through into the kitchen, and saw that it was as orderly and empty as the other rooms. But in the middle of the carefully scoured table stood a portable wireless, and the voice she heard came out of it. . . .

She must have fainted then, she supposed; at any rate she felt so weak and dizzy that her memory of what next happened remained indistinct. But in the course of time she groped her way back to the pantry, and there found a bottle of spirits – brandy or whisky, she could not remember which. She found a glass, poured herself a stiff drink, and while it was flushing through her veins, managed, she never knew with how many shuddering delays, to drag herself through the deserted ground floor, up the stairs, and down the corridor to her own room. There, apparently, she fell across the threshold, again unconscious. . . .

When she came to, she remembered, her first care had been to lock herself in; then to recover her husband's revolver. It was not loaded, but she found some cartridges, and succeeded in loading it. Then she remembered that Agnes, on leaving her the evening before, had refused to carry away the tray with the tea and sandwiches, and she fell on them with a sudden hunger. She recalled also noticing that a flask of brandy had been put beside the thermos, and being vaguely surprised. Agnes's departure, then, had been deliberately planned, and she had known that her mistress, who never touched spirits, might have need of a stimulant before she returned. Mrs Clayburn poured some of the brandy into her tea, and swallowed it greedily.

After that (she told me later) she remembered that she had managed to start a fire in her grate, and after warming herself, had got back into her bed, piling on it all the coverings she could find. The afternoon passed in a haze of pain, out of which there emerged now and then a dim shape of fear – the fear that she might lie there alone and untended till she died of cold, and of the terror of her solitude. For she was sure by this time that the house was empty – completely empty, from garret to cellar. She knew it was so, she could not tell why; but again she felt that it must be because of the peculiar quality of the silence – the silence which had dogged her steps wherever she went, and was now folded down on her like a pall. She was sure that the nearness of any other human being, however dumb and secret, would have made a faint crack in the texture of that silence, flawed it as a sheet of glass is flawed by a pebble thrown against it. . . .

4

'Is that easier?' the doctor asked, lifting himself from bending over her ankle. He shook his head disapprovingly. 'Looks to me as if you'd disobeyed orders – eh? Been moving about, haven't you? And I guess Dr Selgrove told you to keep quiet till he saw you again, didn't he?'

The speaker was a stranger, whom Mrs Clayburn knew only by name. Her own doctor had been called away that morning to the bedside of an old patient in Baltimore, and had asked this young man, who was beginning to be known at Norrington, to replace him. The newcomer was shy, and somewhat familiar, as the shy often are, and Mrs Clayburn decided that she did not much like him. But before she could convey this by the tone of her reply (and she was past mistress of the shades of disapproval) she heard Agnes speaking – yes, Agnes, the same, the usual Agnes, standing behind the doctor, neat and stern-looking as ever. 'Mrs Clayburn must have got up and walked about in the night instead of ringing for me, as she'd ought to,' Agnes intervened severely.

This was too much! In spite of the pain, which was now exquisite, Mrs Clayburn laughed. 'Ringing for you? How could I, with the electricity cut off?'

'The electricity cut off?' Agnes's surprise was masterly. 'Why, when was it cut off?' She pressed her finger on the bell beside the bed, and the call tinkled through the quiet room. 'I tried that bell before I left you last night, madam, because if there'd been anything wrong with it I'd have come and slept in the dressing-room sooner than leave you here alone.'

Mrs Clayburn lay speechless, staring up at her. 'Last night? But last night I was all alone in the house.'

Agnes's firm features did not alter. She folded her hands resignedly across her trim apron. 'Perhaps the pain's made you a little confused, madam.' She looked at the doctor, who nodded.

'The pain in your foot must have been pretty bad,' he said.

'It was,' Mrs Clayburn replied. 'But it was nothing to the horror of being left alone in this empty house since the day before yesterday, with the heat and the electricity cut off, and the telephone not working.'

The doctor was looking at her in evident wonder. Agnes's sallow face flushed slightly, but only as if in indignation at an unjust charge. 'But, madam, I made up your fire with my own hands last night – and look, it's smoldering still. I was getting ready to start it again just now, when the doctor came.'

'That's so. She was down on her knees before it,' the doctor corroborated.

Again Mrs Clayburn laughed. Ingeniously as the tissue of lies was being woven about her, she felt she could still break through it. 'I made up the fire myself yesterday – there was no one else to do it,' she said, addressing the doctor, but keeping her eyes on her maid. 'I got up twice to put on more coal, because the house was like a sepulcher. The central heating must have been out since Saturday afternoon.'

At this incredible statement Agnes's face expressed only a polite distress; but the new doctor was evidently embarrassed at being drawn into an unintelligible controversy with which he had no time to deal. He said he had brought the X-ray photographer with him, but that the ankle was too much swollen to be photographed at present. He asked Mrs Clayburn to excuse his haste, as he had all Dr Selgrove's patients to visit besides his own, and promised to come back that evening to decide whether she could be X-rayed then, and whether, as he evidently feared, the ankle would have to be put in plaster. Then, handing his prescriptions to Agnes, he departed.

Mrs Clayburn spent a feverish and suffering day. She did not feel well enough to carry on the discussion with Agnes; she did not ask to see the other servants. She grew drowsy, and understood that her mind was confused with fever. Agnes and the housemaid waited on her as attentively as usual, and by the time the doctor returned in the evening her temperature had fallen; but she decided not to speak of what was on her mind until Dr Selgrove reappeared. He was to be back the following evening; and the new doctor preferred to wait for him before deciding to put the ankle in plaster – though he feared this was now inevitable.

5

That afternoon Mrs Clayburn had me summoned by telephone, and I arrived at Whitegates the following day. My cousin, who looked pale and nervous, merely pointed to her foot, which had been put in plaster, and thanked me for coming to keep her company. She explained that Dr Selgrove had been taken suddenly ill in Baltimore, and would not be back for several days, but that the young man who replaced him seemed fairly competent. She made no allusion to the strange incidents I have set down, but I felt at once that she had received a shock which her accident, however painful, could not explain.

Finally, one evening, she told me the story of her strange weekend, as it had presented itself to her unusually clear and accurate mind, and as I have recorded it above. She did not tell me this till several weeks after my arrival; but she was still upstairs at the time, and obliged to divide her days between her bed and a lounge. During those endless intervening weeks, she told me, she had thought the whole matter over: and though the events of the mysterious thirty-six hours were still vivid to her, they had already lost something of their haunting terror, and she had finally decided not to reopen the question with Agnes, or to touch on it in speaking to the other servants. Dr Selgrove's illness had been not only serious but prolonged. He had not yet returned, and it was reported that as soon as he was well enough he would go on a West Indian cruise, and not resume his practice at Norrington till the spring. Dr Selgrove, as my cousin was perfectly aware, was the only person who could prove that thirty-six hours had elapsed between his visit and that of his successor; and the latter, a shy young man, burdened by the heavy additional practice suddenly thrown on his shoulders, told me (when I risked a little private talk with him) that in the haste of Dr Selgrove's departure the only instructions he had given about Mrs Clayburn were summed up in the brief memorandum: 'Broken ankle. Have X-rayed.'

Knowing my cousin's authoritative character, I was surprised at her decision not to speak to the servants of what had happened; but on thinking it over I concluded that she was right. They were all exactly as they had been before that unexplained episode: efficient, devoted, respectful and respectable. She was dependent on them and felt at home with them, and she evidently preferred to put the whole matter out of her mind, as far as she could. She was absolutely certain that something strange had happened in her house, and I was more than ever convinced that she had received a shock which the accident of a broken ankle was not sufficient to account for; but in the end I agreed that nothing was to be gained by cross-questioning the servants or the new doctor.

I was at Whitegates off and on that winter and during the following summer, and when I went home to New York for good early in October I left my cousin in her old health and spirits. Dr Selgrove had been ordered to Switzerland for the summer, and this further postponement of his return to his practice seemed to have put the happenings of the strange weekend out of her mind. Her life was going on as peacefully and normally as usual, and I left her without anxiety, and indeed without a thought of the mystery, which was now nearly a year old.

I was living then in a small flat in New York by myself, and I had hardly settled into it when, very late one evening – on the last day of October – I heard my bell ring. As it was my maid's evening out, and I was alone, I went to the door myself, and on the threshold, to my amazement, I saw Sara Clayburn. She was wrapped in a fur cloak, with a hat drawn down over her forehead, and a face so pale and haggard that I saw something dreadful must have happened to her. 'Sara,' I gasped, not knowing what I was saying, 'where in the world have you come from at this hour?'

'From Whitegates. I missed the last train and came by car.' She came in and sat down on the bench near the door. I saw that she could hardly stand, and sat down beside her, putting my arm about her. 'For heaven's sake, tell me what's happened.'

She looked at me without seeming to see me. 'I telephoned to Nixon's and hired a car. It took me five hours and a quarter to get here.' She looked about her. 'Can you take me in for the night? I've left my luggage downstairs.'

'For as many nights as you like. But you look so ill—'

She shook her head. 'No; I'm not ill. I'm only frightened – deathly frightened,' she repeated in a whisper.

Her voice was so strange, and the hands I was pressing between mine were so cold, that I drew her to her feet and led her straight to my little guest room. My flat was in an old-fashioned building, not many stories high, and I was on more human terms with the staff than is possible in one of the modern Babels. I telephoned down to have my cousin's bags brought up, and meanwhile I filled a hot water bottle, warmed the bed, and got her into it as quickly as I could. I had never seen her as unquestioning and submissive, and that alarmed me even more than her pallor. She was not the woman to let herself be undressed and put to bed like a baby; but she submitted without a word, as though aware that she had reached the end of her tether.

'It's good to be here,' she said in a quieter tone, as I tucked her up and smoothed the pillows. 'Don't leave me yet, will you – not just yet.'

'I'm not going to leave you for more than a minute – just to get you a cup of tea,' I reassured her; and she lay still. I left the door open, so that she could hear me stirring about in the little pantry across the passage, and when I brought her the tea she swallowed in gratefully, and a little color came into her face. I sat with her in silence for some time; but at last she began: 'You see it's exactly a year—'

I should have preferred to have her put off till the next morning whatever she had to tell me; but I saw from her burning eyes that she was determined to rid her mind of what was burdening it, and that until she had done so it would be useless to proffer the sleeping draft I had ready.

'A year since what?' I asked stupidly, not yet associating her precipitate arrival with the mysterious occurrences of the previous year at Whitegates.

She looked at me in surprise. 'A year since I met that woman. Don't you remember – the strange woman who was coming up the drive the afternoon when I broke my ankle? I didn't think of it at the time, but it was on All Souls' eve that I met her.'

Yes, I said, I remembered that it was.

'Well – and this is All Souls' eve, isn't it? I'm not as good as you are on Church dates, but I thought it was.'

'Yes. This is All Souls' eve.'

'I thought so. . . . Well, this afternoon I went out for my usual walk. I'd been writing letters, and paying bills, and didn't start till late; not till it was nearly dusk. But it was a lovely clear evening. And as I got near the gate, there was the woman coming in – the same woman . . . going toward the house. . . .'

I pressed my cousin's hand, which was hot and feverish now. 'If it was dusk, could you be perfectly sure it was the same woman?' I asked.

'Oh, perfectly sure, the evening was so clear. I knew her and she knew me; and I could see she was angry at meeting me. I stopped her and asked: "Where are you going?" just as I had asked her last year. And she said, in the same queer half-foreign voice: "Only to see one of the girls," as she had before. Then I felt angry all of a sudden, and I said: "You shan't set foot in my house again. Do you hear me? I order you to leave." And she laughed; yes, she laughed – very low, but distinctly. By that time it had got quite dark, as if a sudden storm was sweeping up over the sky, so that though she was so near me I could hardly see her. We were standing by the clump of hemlocks at the turn of the drive, and as I went up to her, furious at her impertinence, she passed behind the hemlocks, and when I followed her she wasn't there. . . . No; I swear to you she wasn't there. . . . And in the darkness I hurried back to the house, afraid that she would slip by me and get there first. And the queer thing was that as I reached the door the black cloud vanished, and there was the transparent twilight again. In the house everything seemed as usual, and the servants were busy about their work; but I couldn't get it out of my head that the woman, under the shadow of that cloud, had somehow got there before me.' She paused for breath, and began again. 'In the hall I stopped at the telephone and rang up Nixon, and told him to send me a car at once to go to New York, with a man he knew to drive me. And Nixon came with the car himself. . . .'

Her head sank back on the pillow and she looked at me like a frightened child. 'It was good of Nixon,' she said.

'Yes; it was very good of him. But when they saw you leaving – the servants, I mean. . . .'

'Yes. Well, when I got upstairs to my room I rang for Agnes. She came, looking just as cool and quiet as usual. And when I told her I was starting for New York in half an hour – I said it was on account of a sudden business call – well, then her presence of mind failed her for the first time. She forgot to look surprised, she even forgot to make an objection – and you know what an objector Agnes is. And as I watched her I could see a little secret spark of relief in her eyes, though she was so on her guard. And she just said: "Very well, madam," and asked me what I wanted to take with me. Just as if I were in the habit of dashing off to New York after dark on an autumn night to meet a business engagement! No, she made a mistake not to show any surprise – and not even to ask me why I didn't take my own car. And her losing her head in that way frightened me more than anything else. For I saw she was so thankful I was going that she hardly dared speak, for fear she should betray herself, or I should change my mind.'

After that Mrs Clayburn lay a long while silent, breathing less unrestfully; and at last she closed her eyes, as though she felt more at ease now that she had spoken, and wanted to sleep. As I got up quietly to leave her, she turned her head a little and murmured: 'I shall never go back to Whitegates again.' Then she shut her eyes and I saw that she was falling asleep.

I have set down above, I hope without omitting anything essential, the record of my cousin's strange experience as she told it to me. Of what happened at Whitegates that is all I can personally vouch for. The rest – and of course there is a rest – is pure conjecture; and I give it only as such.

My cousin's maid, Agnes, was from the isle of Skye, and the Hebrides, as everyone knows, are full of the supernatural – whether in the shape of ghostly presences, or the almost ghostlier sense of unseen watchers peopling the long nights of those stormy solitudes. My cousin, at any rate, always regarded Agnes as the – perhaps unconscious, at any rate irresponsible – channel through which communications from the other side of the veil reached the submissive household at Whitegates. Though Agnes had been with Mrs Clayburn for a long time without any peculiar incident revealing this affinity with the unknown forces, the power to communicate with them may all the while have been latent in the woman, only awaiting a kindred touch; and that touch may have been given by the unknown visitor whom my cousin, two years in succession, had met coming up the drive at Whitegates on the eve of All Souls'. Certainly the date bears out my hypothesis; for I suppose that, even in this unimaginative age, a few people still remember that All Souls' eve is the night when the dead can walk – and when, by the same token, other spirits, piteous or malevolent, are also freed from the restrictions which secure the earth to the living on the other days of the year.

If the recurrence of this date is more than a coincidence – and for my part I think it is – then I take it that the strange woman who twice came up the drive at Whitegates on All Souls' eve was either a 'fetch,' or else, more probably, and more alarmingly, a living woman inhabited by a witch. The history of witchcraft, as is well known, abounds in such cases, and such a messenger might well have been delegated by the powers who rule in these matters to summon Agnes and her fellow servants to a midnight 'Coven' in some neighboring solitude. To learn what happens at Covens, and the reason of the irresistible fascination they exercise over the timorous and superstitious, one need only address oneself to the immense body of literature dealing with these mysterious rites. Anyone who has once felt the faintest curiosity to assist at a Coven apparently soon finds the curiosity increase to desire, the desire to an uncontrollable longing, which, when the opportunity presents itself, breaks down all inhibitions; for those who have once taken part in a Coven will move heaven and earth to take part again.

Such is my – conjectural – explanation of the strange happenings at Whitegates. My cousin always said she could not believe that incidents which might fit into the desolate landscape of the Hebrides could occur in the cheerful and populous Connecticut Valley; but if she did not believe, she at least feared – such moral paradoxes are not uncommon – and though she insisted that there must be some natural explanation of the mystery, she never returned to investigate it.

'No, no,' she said with a little shiver, whenever I touched on the subject of her going back to Whitegates, 'I don't want ever to risk seeing that woman again. . . .' And she never went back.